Green Political Theory

Green Political Theory

Robert E. Goodin

Polity Press

First published in 1992 by Polity Press in association with Blackwell Publishers

Editorial office:
Polity Press
65 Bridge Street
Cambridge CB2 1UR, UK

Marketing and production:
Blackwell Publishers
108 Cowley Road
Oxford OX4 1JF, UK

238 Main Street, Suite 501
Cambridge, MA 02142, USA

ISBN 0 7456 1026 9
ISBN 0 7456 1027 7 (pbk)

A CIP catalogue record for this book is available from the British Library.

Library of Congress Cataloging in Publication data
Goodin, Robert E.
    Green political theory / Robert E. Goodin.
        p.   cm.
    Includes bibliographical references (p.) and index.
    ISBN 0-7456-1026-9 (hb). — ISBN 0-7456-1027-7 (pb)
    1. Green movement.   I. Title.
JA75.8.G66   1992   91-45859
324.1′8—dc20   CIP

Typeset in 10 on 12pt Times by Hope Services (Abingdon) Ltd
Printed in Great Britain by T.J. Press Ltd (Padstow)

This book is printed on acid-free paper.

Contents

Preface

This book provides a critical reconstruction of green political theory and defends it in that form. Hopefully my analysis sticks closely enough to the core concerns of actual green parties and of self-styled green activists to warrant the label 'green'. Explicating their self-conceptions is not, however, my principal aim.

This book is not intended, exclusively or even primarily, as an exercise in political hermeneutics or philosophical anthropology. My aim is not simply to set out, fully and faithfully, what self-styled greens happen for better or worse to believe. Considering the diversity of positions, both across countries and even among activists within any one country, that project would quickly degenerate into taxonomic tedium even if it did not prove altogether impossible.

The best I have been able to do – and, for the purposes of a theoretical book like this, the most I need to do – is to operate with a stylized account of a composite green political programme. The details of that rendering are relegated to an appendix. That has been done, in part, on the grounds that it can safely be skipped by readers already familiar with the broad outlines of green politics. But it has also been done on the grounds that that material will both age most quickly and matter least to the overall argument of the book. The politics of the German Greens (Die Grünen) have, for better or (probably) worse, moved well beyond their 1983 manifesto which I still regard as canonical for the green movement worldwide. But no matter: I am not writing current affairs or political history but, rather, political theory; I am interested not in what greens happen to say (still less in what they happen to say *today*) but rather in what they have to say, given their core values.

Thus, my aim in this book not merely, or even mainly, to describe what positions greens actually do take. My aim is instead to show what positions greens *should* take, given their core concerns – whether or not they actually do so. That is the sense in which my work is intentionally revisionist. It is designed as a guide *for* greens, at least as much as it is a guide *to* them. I hope to show greens how to cast their position in the strongest possible form, even if that means shifting some of their ordinary emphases and perhaps even abandoning (or, anyway, separating out) certain other views that they might happen also to cherish.

This amounts, politically, to an attempt to rescue greens from themselves. I try to carve out and bolster what I find strong in their public-policy positions, while insulating those policy proposals from other more personal-lifestyle aspects of green theory that I – and, more to the point politically, many among the electorate at large – find less persuasive.

Many greens see style as central. Greens of this stripe aspire above all else to be colourful – often quite literally. Their MPs wear bright clothes rather than dreary business suits to the openings of parliament. They take pride in being part of a 'multicoloured list' or a 'Rainbow Coalition'. They call upon us to help 'turn our grey earth green', in the concluding words to the European Greens' 1989 manifesto. The preferred party political contrast, from this perspective, is between parties that are 'green' (bright, lively) and ones that are 'grey' (dull, drab, flat, boring).

The risk with this style of greenery is that the medium will swamp the message, that style will supplant substance. My thesis is that there is a compelling case for taking seriously green public policy demands, whatever one might think of greens' modes of self-presentation. Mine is thus a limited defence of green politics – of its substance if not its stylistic affectations.

As a marker of the limits to my defence of green politics, I deliberately adopt a different way of characterizing the standard party political contrast. For me, the interesting contrast is not between parties which are 'green' and ones which are 'grey'. It is, instead, between ones which are 'green' and ones which are 'brown'. The problem with non-green parties is not so much that they are boringly grey as it is that they are committed to outmoded industrial technologies (brown rust) and consequent environmental despoilation (brown leaves and lakes).

The strategy I adopt is designed to win support for green positions, even at the inevitable risk of losing me friends among greens themselves. A great many of them are, after all, committed to the style as well as the substance of their distinctive political mode; green lifestyles and green political styles matter as much to many of them as green public policies.

Such greens ought not be unduly disappointed, though. My thesis is that green proposals for public policies form a tight, unified package that is compelling in its own right. My main purpose is to mount a positive argument for the policies constituting that package. Other aspects of green theory – recommendations for personal practices or political procedures – just do not form part of that package. The most I really want to say to fellow greens who part company with me on those matters is just that those are separate issues, which must be argued separately.

Although written all in one sitting – and a relatively brief one, as these things go – this book has in reality been long in the making. My first systematic introduction to these topics came as an Indiana University undergraduate in Lynton Keith Caldwell's cellar; there, he kindly coached me for interviews at the State Department and the United Nations, as part of a research project on US preparations for the seminal 1972 Stockholm Conference on the Human Environment which eventuated in the UN Environmental Programme. Over the next few years Brian Barry tried, with characteristic prescience but only partial success, to persuade me to devote my doctoral thesis to these topics. In the event the present book has taken some twenty years to appear, but in it evidence of those early influences nonetheless remains strong.

It was Albert Weale who put me up to writing the present text, and I am grateful for his continuing advice and encouragement as it progressed. The project has been powerfully shaped by various discussions – with John Dryzek, Jon Elster, Sheldon Leader, Philip Pettit and Richard Sylvan in its early stages and with John Passmore in its later stages – and by detailed written comments from John Braithwaite, Andy Dobson, Claus Offe and Onora O'Neill.

Its core argument has also been honed on various seminar audiences along the way. At the Economics, Justice and Society Program of the University of California, Davis, I am particularly grateful for the comments of Dick Arneson, David Copp, Mike Glennon, Jean Hampton and John Roemer; at the Conference on Socio-economics in Washington, DC, for those of Tom Donaldson, Bill Galston and Mark Sagoff; at the Australian Academy of the Humanities in Melbourne, for those of Tony Coady, John Mulvaney, John Passmore and Peter Singer; at the Australian Defence Force Academy, for those of Chandran Kukathas, David West and Paul Keal; at the University of Melbourne, for those of Verity Burgmann, Mark Considine, Les Holmes, Bruce Heady and Pete Shearman; and at the Colchester Joint Sessions of the European Consortium for Political Research, for those of Wouter

Achterberg, Ted Benton, Alan Carter, Andy Dobson, Judy Evans, Paul Lucardie and Michael Saward.

Various previous articles and conference papers have also been groping towards these conclusions. None of them is literally reproduced here, but many of their central ideas reappear. I ought therefore to record my debt to those who have, over the years, offered me advice on these problems in general and on those other papers in particular. Although there are too many to name, or even now to recall properly, they would certainly include, in addition to those already mentioned: Lincoln Allison, Alan Bellett, David Bennett, Jay Bernstein, Chris Bertram, David Braddon-Mitchell, Geoff Brennan, Tom Campell, Frank Castles, Peggy Clark, James Crawford, Robert Elliot, Debbie Fitzmaurice, Peter Frank, David Gauthier, Russell Hardin, Barry Hindess, Lisa Hooper, Dominic Hyde, Frank Jackson, Jeff Land, Michael Lipsky, Don Mannison, David Miller, Bill Mitchell, Mancur Olson, John Orbell, Elim Papadakis, David Pearce, Andy Reeve, Jack Smart, Peter Self, Cass Sunstein, Michael Taylor, Janna Thompson, Pat Troy, Robert van der Veen, Philippe Van Parijs, Peter Wagner, Ken Walker, Hugh Ward and Oran Young.

With help such as that, I wonder to what extent we really are the sole authors of our own books any more. Still, academic courtesy requires me to stipulate that the standard disclaimer applies. I trust that I can, without discourtesy, pay a fulsome tribute to the marvellous working environment of the Australian National University's Research School of Social Sciences and to the extended community of social and political theorists now centred there. Sad though I was in many respects to leave the once-mighty Essex Department of Government, I can truly say it is a better place to which I have gone.

1
What's New?

1 The Issues

Concern with the natural environment is nothing new. Fears of resource depletion, voiced most powerfully in recent times by the Club of Rome's 1972 *The Limits to Growth*, are in many ways little more than 'Malthus with a computer', as one of that report's early and best critics observed.[1] Like his modern imitators, the Reverend Thomas Malthus had at the end of the eighteenth century expressed fears that population demands would outstrip the earth's resources, his particular concern being its food-producing capacities.[2] Stanley Jevons, at the end of the nineteenth century, had voiced parallel fears that we would soon run out of coal.[3] And President Truman, like many political leaders laid seige to before him, agonized over the adequacy of America's 'strategic stockpiles' of crucial natural resources at the outset of the Cold War.[4]

Or again, we worry today about the unhealthy effects of polluting the air, water and oceans. But in many ways those just echo much older concerns. Anticipating the Garden City movement by fully two and a half centuries, John Evelyn's 1661 tract *Fumifugium* (subtitled *The Inconveniencie of the Aer and Smoak of London Dissipated*) 'humbly proposed . . . to his Sacred Majestie [Charles II] and to the Parliament now assembled' that sweet-smelling trees be planted around the city to freshen its air.[5] Longstanding suspicions about the role of air and water

---

[1] Meadows et al. 1972; Freeman 1973. See similarly the US Council on Environmental Quality's report, *Global 2000* (US CEQ 1980; 1981), and the reaction to it (Simon 1981; Simon and Kahn 1984).
[2] Malthus 1798.
[3] Jevons 1906.
[4] Paley 1952.
[5] Evelyn 1661.

quality in promoting the health of the general population were confirmed with early nineteenth-century discoveries of the particular mechanisms by which plagues of typhoid and cholera are spread.[6] And when in the early 1950s London's smoke-laden fogs were finally firmly proven to be 'killers', the government promptly required householders to burn only 'smokeless' coal in their grates.[7]

Or yet again, we worry today about despoiling areas of great natural beauty. But many people have long felt a special affinity with and responsibility for nature.[8] Earlier manifestations of this sort of attitude can, for example, be found in the work of the great romantic poets of Germany in the nineteenth century and before; in the work of the great landscape gardeners of England in the seventeenth and eighteenth centuries;[9] and in the writings of mid nineteenth-century American transcendentalists, Henry David Thoreau and Ralph Waldo Emerson.[10] And such examples are of course illustrative rather than exhaustive. Everywhere, this sort of 'respect for nature' has apparently long been with us.[11] Nor is this attitude prevalent only among artists, essayists and poets. At least since the turn of the century, it has manifested itself in public policy as well as in private attitudes, with certain areas being set aside as 'national parks' and suchlike.[12]

In all those ways, current concern with environmental issues might seem to be 'old wine in new bottles'. Still, something genuinely new does seem to have emerged in recent years.[13] Indeed, the face of the debate seems to have changed twice in as many decades. At the risk of imposing artificial periodizations up on a smoothly evolving process, we

[6] See e.g. Stewart and Jenkins 1867.

[7] Scarrow 1972. And not for the first time: Britons had been prohibited from burning sea coal, on account of the pollution it caused, from 1273 (McCormick 1989, p. 127; Paehlke 1989, p. 24).

[8] Passmore (1980) is of course the masterwork here. But see also Bramwell (1989), who fills in the foreground with detailed accounts of lesser figures in the German and English ecology movements from the 1880s forward.

[9] Thomas 1984.

[10] Nash 1973; Sagoff 1988, ch. 6.

[11] Everywhere, that is, once enough of the wilderness had been cleared for it to stop being threatening and start becoming inviting (Nash 1973, ch. 1).

[12] Beginning, in the US, with the 1864 Act of Congress transferring the Yosemite Valley to the State of California on condition it be held in perpetuity 'for public use, resort and recreation' (it formally became a National Park in 1890) and continuing with the 1872 Act establishing Yellowstone as the first formal National Park in the world (Nash 1970; McCormick 1989, pp. 11–12). In the UK, those were explicitly the aims not only of the National Trust founded at the turn of the century, but also of what is arguably the world's 'first private environmental group', the Commons, Open Spaces and Footpaths Preservation Society, founded in 1865 (McCormick 1989, pp. 5–6).

[13] For a more personal elaboration on these themes, see Goodin (1992a).

might say that recent years have seen the recognition of not one but two quite distinct 'environmental crises'.

Widespread appreciation of what might be called the 'first environmental crisis' might be dated only somewhat artificially, to the 1962 publication of Rachel Carson's enormously influential book, *Silent Spring*.[14] Her particular concern, of course, was with DDT and the way in which that and other pesticides impeded the reproductive cycle of bird life: hence the reference in her title to 'silence', the absence of bird song. But Carson was concerned, more generally, about the way in which the indiscriminate use of chemicals of all sorts might poison the environment for humans as well. These themes, and ones related to them, lay simmering for a few years. But by the early 1970s, they had well and truly seized the public imagination. The Cuyahoga River caught fire. Lake Erie was pronounced dead, killed by the indiscriminate dumping of industrial wastes. In the minds of many, that was merely a foretaste of things to come.[15]

While the concern in that first environmental crisis was with global collapse, the appropriate focus for social action and political pressure was nonetheless seen to be the individual state. Lake Erie was 'killed' by pollution almost wholly from Ohio industries, and could be (indeed, subsequently was) resuscitated almost exclusively through the efforts of people in one political jurisdiction. Population pressures were seen as crucial; but population was seen as being best controlled through small-scale policies, and indeed on a personal level as much as on a national one. The suggestion, recall, was principally that couples join the '2.1 club', confining themselves to reproducing themselves but no more.[16]

In that first environmental crisis, there were of course intimations of further, greater disasters to come, if the policies that environmentalists prescribed were not implemented.[17] But at least in the first instance, the policies were principally national rather than international in scope. Or, if international, that dimension just amounted to the replication of good

[14] Carson 1962. See Dunlap (1981) for the subsequent history of DDT and McCormick (1989, esp. ch. 3) for the consequences of that unfolding drama for the environmental movement more generally.

[15] The fate of Lake Erie, for example, formed a chapter in itself in Barry Commoner's influential tract, *The Closing Circle* (1971, pp. 94–111).

[16] Which, given that some would have no child or only one, in practice meant each couple having, on average, 2.1 children.

[17] There was even some anticipation in those years of the risks of global climate change; see Wilson (1970; 1971), Ward and Dubois (1972, pt 5) and the Stockholm Declaration (UN Conference on the Human Environment 1972, art. 1, sec. 7, pp. 1416–21).

national-level policy models in all other jurisdictions one by one.[18] It is good for the United States to stop polluting the Great Lakes; and it is better if Canada stops, too. There was urgency, no doubt. But there was also plenty that each of us – as individuals, small groups or single nations – could usefully do, while waiting for the others to come around.

But all that has now changed once again.[19] The issues presently at the forefront of our attention, in the midst of what might be called the 'second environmental crisis', are more genuinely global in scope. Primary among them are the twin threats of changing the global climate and destroying the ozone layer protecting the earth's plants and people from the sun's ultraviolet rays.[20] When the issue was just ordinary air pollution of the traditional sort, dirty air could effectively be cleaned simply through local regulations such as London's requirement for households to burn smokeless coal in fireplaces and industrial users to install scrubbers in smokestacks. But no such purely local remedies will reliably suffice to patch the hole in the ozone layer.

True enough, the industrialized countries of the First World contribute disproportionately to the problem. The United States produces something like 28 per cent of all the world's ozone-destroying CFC-11 and CFC-12, and West Europe another 30 per cent.[21] But it would be wrong to infer from that fact that if America – or indeed all the member countries of the OECD – singlehandedly banned the use of aerosols, it would in and of itself solve the problem of ozone depletion.

Presumably our goal is genuine stabilization of the ozone layer, rather than merely slowing its rate of depletion. And presumably we want to be reasonably certain of accomplishing that goal. But if so, then we cannot – within the limits of present knowledge – be sufficiently sure of achieving that goal, even through dramatic reductions in emissions by such major producers as the OECD. Initiatives by single countries or small groups of countries can serve as useful starts and important precedents, but they cannot in and of themselves be expected to solve the problem. Unless their lead is followed by others, we cannot be at all sure of stopping the damage.

---

[18] The best single statement of the international dimension, as it appeared in the 'first environmental crisis', is the Stockholm Declaration as annotated by Sohn (1973).

[19] For illustrative comparisons, contrast Caplan (1990) with Falk (1971), Commoner (1971) with Commoner (1990), or Caldwell (1990) with Caldwell (1971).

[20] For scientific background see US National Research Council (NRC) (1989), Schneider (1989) and Smith and Tirpak (1989). In a more popular vein, see McKibben (1988) and Boyle and Ardill (1989).

[21] Wirth 1989, p. 7.

These new environmental concerns, unlike the core concerns of the environmental crisis, are truly global. These problems are shared, internationally, in a stronger sense. They are not just problems for each nation, taken one by one. They simply could not be resolved by isolated actions of individual nations. The whole world, or some very large proportion of it, must be involved in the solution. That shift from issues which, while recurring the world over, can be resolved on a country-by-country basis to ones which require concerted action by all the nations of the world is what, to my mind, marks the shift from the first environmental crisis to the second. That is the sense in which present environmental concern, and the sorts of social and political theories spawned by it, seem to me genuinely new.[22]

That, anyway, is what I think has given rise to the recent upsurge in support for green causes and green political movements worldwide: in local politics, in national politics and in elections to supranational bodies like the European parliament. It is the need to take a genuinely 'global perspective', as green politics would apparently promise, to which voters seem to be responding.

Whether or not the greens themselves are fully up to this task is, perhaps, another question. Committed as they are to a programme of radical decentralization – 'thinking globally' but 'acting locally' – greens at one and the same time especially require but also singularly lack a theory of how the necessary coordination is to be achieved among all those autonomous smaller units. Absent such coordination, there seems to be a real risk that they might fail to achieve the results that they desire globally.

All this will be discussed more fully in chapter 4, section 4 below. There I suggest that we can, and probably should, accept green policy prescriptions without necessarily adopting green ideas about how to reform political structures and processes. As I conclude (chapter 5, section 2), electing a significant minority of greens to national or supranational legislatures – rather than giving greens their heads, and letting them reorganize those larger political entities out of existence altogether – might actually be just about optimal. That might enable us to secure what is best in the green programme while avoiding what is worst in it.

[22] And it was spawned a whole new sort of international politico-legal response, represented by the Vienna Convention (Convention for the Protection of the Ozone Layer 1985) and the Montreal Protocol (Protocol on Substances that Deplete the Ozone Layer 1987). I shall return to discuss these again briefly in closing (chapter 5, section 2); for a fuller discussion and an attempt to set those developments in a larger theoretical perspective, see Goodin (1990a).

All those are larger issues for later discussion. My aim in these introductory remarks is merely to emphasize the new, genuinely global orientation. It is what seems to mark the distinctively new class of environmental issues, and what has in turn given rise to the recent upsurge in green politics.

2   The Arguments

With these changes in the nature of the issues have come changes in the nature of the arguments offered for environmentalist measures. The older, and often more theologically tinged versions tended to appeal to notions of humanity's 'stewardship' of nature. Nature's being God's creation, it is not for us to destroy it; it having been bequeathed to us and our posterity jointly, it is for us to use but not to abuse it. Present people were, on these older theological models, little more than custodians or trustees for future generations – and, indeed, for all the other orders of creation. Human beings, as the crowning glory of God's creation, have a peculiar obligation to protect other realms of God's creation that would otherwise stand exposed and vulnerable.[23]

Lingering traces of such sentiments can of course be found in attitudes towards nature down to our own day.[24] But by the mid-nineteenth century, newer more explicitly utilitarian attitudes had gained the ascendancy. Cast in those terms – as the case increasingly had to be, if it was to prove politically persuasive – the most telling arguments were about the ways in which environmental protection was required in order to further human interests. Allowing indiscriminate dumping of industrial effluents into the air or water poisoned people and diminished profits overall (although not of course the polluter's own, at least not for a while). Allowing uncontrolled exploitation of common property resources led to the overuse and ultimately to the utter exhaustion of essential resources. Varied though the details of these arguments might be, their essence always remained the same: inadequate protection of the human environment seriously compromised human interests.[25]

Remedies, too, varied in their detail but not in their basic ethos.

[23] Passmore 1980. For a non-theological development of that latter theme, see Goodin (1985c, pp. 179–86).
[24] In modern restatements these traditional Christian themes are typically given a slightly new twist, be it derived from Eastern mysticism (Spretnak 1986; Capra 1982) or communitarian Catholicism (Daly and Cobb 1989).
[25] Certainly that is true of all the arguments surveyed in Goodin (1976, ch. 14).

Pollution was conceptualized as a divergence between private and social cost;[26] resource depletion was conceptualized as the result of overexploitation of common property resources.[27] Both represented failures of ordinary markets to force people to internalize fully the costs of their choices. The problem, on this utilitarian analysis, was essentially one of market failure. The remedy, in essence, was to correct that market failure.

Some thought that market mechanisms could be suitably adjusted – through privatization, pollution (or, more recently, carbon) taxes, marketable permits to pollute, and suchlike – to cope with the problem.[28] Others thought that the problem would ultimately require non-market controls, typically in the form of tough regulatory regimes of some sort or another.[29] Still others thought that the only thing that would suffice would be full-blooded public ownership, removing as it does the profit motive and with it the temptation to pass private costs of production off on to the public.[30] Diverse though those various remedies may be, all are responses to a problem conceptualized in basically the same terms – ones of making environmental choices better serve human interests.

This strand of argument, like the earlier one, has certainly not disappeared from contemporary environmental debates. A recent self-styled *Blueprint for a Green Economy* works in precisely these terms, urging rigorous application of the principle of 'polluter pays'. Effluent charges, conceptualized more as 'taxes' than 'fines', are recommended in good utilitarian, welfare-economic fashion as the mechanisms of choice for promoting efficient resource utilization and maximal satisfaction of human desires.[31]

[26] Pigou 1932, bk 2, ch. 9.
[27] Garrett Hardin's (1968) image of the 'tragedy of the commons' is echoed in economics literature on property rights (Gordon 1954; Coase 1960; Demsetz 1967).
[28] Kneese, Ayres and D'Arge 1970; Freeman, Haveman and Kneese 1973; Kneese and Schultze 1975; Weimer 1990; Grubb 1990; Epstein and Gupta 1990.
[29] Cf. Lave 1981.
[30] Dryzek (1987, p. 80, n15) recalls in this connection that 'large tracts of forest in the USA and UK are publicly owned,' remarking that 'under a system of communal property, ownership is vested in the community of resource users, who henceforth make decisions about access to the resource on a collective basis.' Zile (1982) provides an account of how such a system might be generalized in a thoroughly command economy, as the Soviet Union then was. The environmental consequences of public ownership in Eastern Europe does not serve as a happy precedent though (Goldman 1972; Ophuls 1977, pp. 203–6; Dryzek 1987, ch. 8).
[31] Pearce, Markandya and Barbier 1989; see similarly *Blueprint 2* (Pearce 1991). Indeed, the first demand in the section of the 1983 *Programme of the German Green Party* devoted to 'Environmental protection' is 'the immediate application of the

While both those older strands remain, there is an important new overlay on them in contemporary environmental debates. Arguments have come increasingly to be cast in terms of the interests of nature itself, rather than in terms of God's or humanity's interests in nature. It is easier to capture the spirit of these new arguments than it is to refine their details. We may well wonder whether self-styled 'animal liberationists' are literally proposing to give animals *rights* in any technical sense.[32] We may well wonder whether the suggestion to 'give trees standing' is just a delightful pun or whether the proposal is, literally, to give oaks (or their human mouthpieces) the legal capacity to bring anyone injuring arboreal interests before the bar of justice.[33] We may well wonder whether self-styled 'deep ecologists' really mean it, or whether it is just a rhetorical ploy, when they say that it is no more than blind prejudice on our part ('specieism', akin to 'racism' or 'sexism') to refuse to regard the interests of natural objects as wholly on a par with those of humans.[34] Still, there is no denying just how influential those models, even in their most exaggerated forms, have been on contemporary green thinking.[35]

Without getting bogged down in details, let us simply note for now the new argumentative style that those propositions represent. However exactly we cast the argument, it is clear that nature is now taken to have an independent role in the creation of value. The value of nature is no longer regarded as wholly reducible to its value to God or to humanity. And it is this insight that drives, most powerfully, the current wave of environmental concern.

Environmentalist tracts of the 1970s can be characterized as 'eco-doom' tracts. The doom in question is, almost invariably, doom for humanity.[36] Concern for the environment as such – for its doom – took

---

principle that the causer of pollution must pay its costs' (Die Grünen 1983, sec. iv.1, p. 30).

[32] Singer 1976.

[33] Stone 1972.

[34] Routley and Routley 1979; 1980; Naess 1973; 1984; 1989. Nash (1989, pp. 5–7), taking all this really rather literally, represents concern with all living things as the ultimate stage in the expanding scope of moral concerns that started with the shift from a focus on self and immediate family to local and national community; and, perhaps even more tendentiously, he represents recognition of rights of animals (in the Endangered Species Act) as the culmination of the process that started with the recognition of the rights of man in the Magna Carta and carried on through the recognition of rights of women, religious minorities and blacks (the Civil Rights Acts, etc.).

[35] Spretnak and Capra 1986, ch. 2; Sylvan 1985; Luke 1988.

[36] In the justly famous 'Blueprint for survival' printed in an early issue of the

decidedly second place. Environmentalist tracts today are different. Although they are far from sanguine on the subject, the future of humanity no longer seems to be the major issue. In a nice turnabout on the older emphases, there is a certain air of satisfaction evident in the writings of Gaia theorists when they say that Nature will survive just fine – it is merely the survival of humanity that is in doubt.[37]

3 The Organizations

Just as green issues have long been with us in one way or another, so too, organizationally, have green political groupings long been with us in one way or another. People have been organizing themselves into pressure groups devoted to lobbying legislators for better protection of the natural environment for a century or more. In America, the Sierra Club was founded in 1892, with the explicit aim of 'enlisting the support of the people and the government in preserving the forests and other features of the Sierra Nevada Mountains'.[38] In Britain, the Commons, Open Spaces and Footpaths Preservation Society was founded in 1865, the National Trust in 1893, and the Council for the Protection of Rural England in 1926, all with the avowedly political aims that their various titles suggest.[39] And of course those groups are just the most famous. Various other groups focused on public policies to secure the protection of animals (the various national organizations for the protection of birds and for the prevention of cruelty to animals), of fresh-water fishing (the Izaak Walton League), of the rights of hikers (the Ramblers Association) and so on.[40]

The point about all these older organizations, though, is that they all had – to greater or lesser extents – a narrowly single-issue style. In that, they were very much on a par with other single-issue lobbies, such as veterans' organizations, the Women's Electoral League, and so on. Each was advocating a cause that was undoubtedly important. Perhaps in the view of many of its members it was overridingly so. However much importance adherents attached to their own particular cause, though, each group would in all honesty have had to concede that its

---

Ecologist, for example, the 'survival' in question was first and foremost that of humankind (Goldsmith et al. 1972).

[37] Lovelock 1987; 1989; Sale 1985, chs 1–3, 12.
[38] Sierra Club, *Articles of Association*, quoted in Nash (1973, pp. 132–3).
[39] McCormick 1989, pp. 5–6; Shoard 1987, pp. 109–10.
[40] McCormick 1989, p. 15, provides a useful table listing many of them.

concern formed only a very small part of the larger political agenda. None could seriously maintain that its interest group offered anything approaching a comprehensive political programme, addressing each and every issue of broader social importance.

That is as true of environmentalist groups as of other single-issue groups. Furthermore, it is as true of the more highly politicized groups founded in the heyday of the 'first environmental crisis' of the early 1970s as of their older counterparts. The Friends of the Earth, for example, was formed in 1969 explicitly to do political work that the Sierra Club was unwilling or unable to undertake; and the still more political group Greenpeace arose shortly thereafter. Both campaigned hard for various politically highly charged environmental causes: against nuclear energy, private automobiles, acid rain, whaling, nuclear weapons testing, and suchlike. But both were still properly regarded, by themselves as well as by others, as being essentially 'single-issue interest groups'. Their job was to lobby governments for environmental protection, and that alone.

With the formation in recent years of self-consciously green parties in various countries of the world, that has notably changed.[41] Anti-abortionists, feminists and even blacks have run party lists of their own only very occasionally – and then only in very special political circumstances, when they could credibly claim that theirs was the overwhelmingly dominant issue then on their society's political agenda. Greens, in contrast, now enter the electoral lists year in and year out, on an utterly regular basis. That in and of itself makes contemporary greens different, both from other 'single-issue' groups and even from their own most highly politicized precursors.

Furthermore, they offer a fully fledged political agenda. The 1983 election manifesto of the German Greens (Die Grünen) contains, predictably enough, a long section devoted to discussing 'Environment and nature'. But alongside that there are also long sections discussing problems of 'Economy and work', of 'Foreign policy and peace policy' and 'Individual and society' (including issues of law, health, education, women, children and the aged). The English translation runs to over fifty pages.[42] That is not as long as some or as comprehensive as other

[41] I shall speak, colloquially, of 'parties' though greens themselves often prefer to avoid the term, styling themselves instead 'movements' or some such. Often it is a distinction without a difference, with green movements politicking in ways indistinguishable from political parties of an ordinary sort. Often such activity is accompanied by (and sometimes it is supplanted altogether by) extraparliamentary action – some aimed at political goals, some not – of a sort that is rarely if ever associated with political parties of a more ordinary sort.

[42] Die Grünen 1983.

parties' manifestos, perhaps. But it is certainly a substantial enough programme to qualify Die Grünen as more than a single-issue party. And other green parties seem to be equally ambitious in this regard.[43]

Of course it is wrong to set too much store by formal pronouncements and institutional structures. Modern political science has taught us that much, at least. It is perfectly possible for manifestos to be mere window dressing. Just because a group organizes a formal political party that purports to take a stand on a wide range of issues does not necessarily mean that it attaches equal importance to, or even that it genuinely cares about all those issues mentioned.[44] Still, such formalisms as party lists and election manifestos can sometimes serve as good guides to what actually is going on. Judging from them, something in the environmental movement has indeed changed with the advent of green parties worldwide.

Formerly, green activists would have been located organizationally in one of two places. Either they were found in special interest groups trying to influence the policies of political parties from the outside; or else they constituted 'factions' or 'sections' within older, more established political parties striving to get particular planks included within those parties' programmes.[45] Now, clearly, greens think that theirs is a sufficiently comprehensive programme of social reform that they can credibly mount a party and a programme all their own.

What makes these new green parties all the more striking, of course, is their electoral success. With the March 1983 breakthrough of Die Grünen into the West German Bundestag, a self-styled 'green' political grouping had for the first time won enough votes to secure substantial parliamentary representation.[46] The numbers might still have been relatively meagre: Die Grünen's 5.6 per cent of the vote translated into a mere twenty-seven parliamentary seats. But the impact on political perceptions was resounding.[47]

From that moment onwards, the green movement seized the political imagination of friend and foe alike. Older, more established parties

[43] See the appendix below for details.

[44] In 1968, for example, many suspected with much cause that whatever else George Wallace's platform might have said, all that really mattered to him and his supporters was the question of race.

[45] Naess, in a 1976 book only belatedly translated into English and only lightly revised in the process, thinks they still should (1989, pp. 154–5).

[46] As distinct from the sort of token representation greens secured in, e.g., Belgium in 1981 election (McCormick 1989, p. 140; Spretnak and Capra 1986, p. 172; Kolinsky 1984; Hülsberg (1985).

[47] Certainly the scene was compelling as theatre, with informally and colourfully clad greens wedged between rows of sombrely clad members of the more established parties (Spretnak and Capra 1986, p. 5).

across Europe, America and Australasia have been desperately striving to put on new, greener faces. They have been busily revamping their electoral manifestos, creating new ministerial portfolios, and generally doing their best to appropriate these new issues as their own.

Clearly, though, those manoeuvres amount to little more than face-lifts, the political equivalents of cosmetic surgery. For all the lip service presently being paid to green causes, virtually none of the established parties is treating the green movement as more than a passing political fancy. Naturally, mainstream parties are only too happy to embrace some of the greens' more popular proposals – reforestation, pollution abatement, and suchlike – in the cynical hopes of stealing the greens' political thunder. But they also feel perfectly free to pick and choose items willy-nilly off the green agenda, merrily incorporating some of its more congenial components within their own programmes while casually discarding all its more radical proposals.[48]

That they should do so comes as no surprise. Such is the standard way of political compromise, in general. Such is the standard way for mainstream parties to try to marginalize single-issue political movements, in particular. And so far as the more established parties can apparently see, that is all that is really involved in the green movement. Virtually none of them seem to regard it as presenting any deeper challenge.

In politics-as-usual, there is always 'room for . . . "earlier-or-later" or "more-or-less" positions between contrasting claims. . . . In principle, there is always a "middle-range solution". . . . Yes-or-no questions which cannot be settled by a compromise are rare occurrences and, when they do arise, they can still be handled through traditional log-rolling, i.e., a yes to one question will assure a similar concession from the opponent on some other question.'[49]

The peculiarity of green parties is that their demands prove so utterly impervious to those ordinary political solvents. 'These groups', Offe remarks, 'cannot be bought off by offering them benefits and concessions in other, less important realms of political action. Traditional patterns of cooptation and patronage simply fail to work.' As Offe goes on to say, 'It is not very helpful to get aggravated over the stubbornness and ideological obstinacy of these political actors. The causes for their lack

[48] The German Greens, particularly incensed by the practice, have even coined a term for the phenomenon: *Themenklau* (Papadakis 1989). Petra Kelly (1989, p. 26), for example, complains that 'other parties have literally copied parts of our programme. But they don't implement them. They only do it cosmetically. . . . What's sad is that, when the Greens act as pioneers and initiate such things, everyone soon forgets that it was us who started it.'

[49] Offe 1983, p. 49.

of tolerance and willingness to compromise is neither individual nor institutional, but rather themes and problems which are, by their very nature, ill suited to compromise. They have to be either ignored or taken seriously.'[50]

Green parties present their agenda as a peculiarly all-or-nothing package. Furthermore, they do so genuinely as a matter of high principle. Other parties might adopt a similar stance tactically, as an audacious (albeit perhaps a high-risk) way of trying to force more concessions from prospective coalition partners. At the end of the day, though, those other parties would always be prepared to take something rather than nothing of what they want. For greens, in contrast, there are reasons of principle rather than mere calculations of political advantage lying behind their all-or-nothing stance. If in the end they are prepared to settle for something rather than nothing (and I argue below that they should be), they would do so with far more genuine regret and far less self-congratulation than would other parties adopting a similar stance out of purely tactical considerations.

4 The Thesis

That the greens do indeed pose a fundamental challenge to the existing sociopolitical order is, in one sense, plain for all to see. Politically, the greens are obviously making some awfully radical demands. They call, predictably enough, for drastic measures to curtail pollution of the air, waterways and oceans, to control disposal of hazardous wastes, to protect the ozone layer, and to conserve forests, landscapes, natural resources and ancient monuments. Beyond all that, though, they would also have us: take steps to protect animals, both individually and especially as species; wind down modern technology generally, and nuclear electricity generating plants particularly; disarm militarily, disposing straightaway of our entire nuclear and chemical/biological weapons arsenals; and change our lifestyles quite generally, especially as regards attitudes toward women, children, elders and 'marginalized groups' in society, such as homosexuals, immigrants and gipsies.[51] Accepting all those demands would clearly commit us, both domestically

[50] Ibid., pp. 49–50. As Habermas (1981, p. 33) puts it, 'the[se] new conflicts are not sparked by *problems of distribution*, but concern the *grammar of forms of life*.' Cf. Papadakis (1988), who is more sceptical of what he calls the German Greens' 'self-limiting radicalism'.

[51] This list is based on Die Grünen (1983). See further the appendix below.

and internationally, to a very basic reorientation of crucial components of the present political, economic and social orders.[52]

What is less obvious and requires rather more argument is the further proposition that the greens' demands really do – as greens themselves say they do – have to be taken on something like an all-or-nothing basis. Showing that that is true is the major burden of the central sections of this book.[53] Once established, that proposition logically militates against picking and choosing items off the green political agenda – breaking apart the package, buying some parts of it without buying all the rest as well. Showing the fallacies that are involved in such magpie-like borrowing from the greens is the political punchline of this book as a whole.[54]

What, at root, makes the green political agenda form a peculiarly tight package is the fact that all the elements within it are informed by a single moral vision.[55] Specifically, all are arguably manifestations of one and the same 'green theory of value'. What makes the green agenda form something very much akin to an all-or-nothing political package is the simple incoherence of accepting the validity of that particular theory of value for some purposes but not for others. A theory of the Good holds good regardless of context: goodness does not flicker on and off like some faulty light switch.

That is not to say that we must always accept green conclusions everywhere if we ever accept them anywhere. Of course we do not. That issue will be discussed more fully in chapter 3 below. For now, suffice it to say that, purely as a matter of logic, it is illegitimate for us utterly to disregard for some purposes considerations which we take to be utterly compelling in others. As I shall argue in my conclusions, that logic might come to have real political consequences for any mainstream political parties that try to defy it.

It is my larger thesis in this book that green political theory is actually

---

[52] Although their full implementation can come only through collectively enforced political decisions, there is much that individuals can do in the meanwhile – in their roles both as consumers and producers – to further these policy goals. When proprietors of major mining corporations or large agricultural holdings adopt environmentally·responsible practices in their own operations, that seems more a case of the incomplete implementation of a public policy than of a green personal lifestyle on the part of private green consumers.

[53] Chapters 2 and 3 below.

[54] I see this principally as a moral problem facing mainstream parties trying to capture the green position, rather than as an objection to greens compromising their own programme by joining in coalitions with other parties. I shall discuss this further in chapter 3, section 6 below.

[55] In this, their programme really is radically different from those of other more established parties, for reasons discussed in chapter 3, section 1 below.

comprised of two quite separate principal components. Typically conjoined with these two elements is yet a third – personal lifestyle recommendations, of an essentially non-political sort – which is actually separate, yet again, from either of the two more specifically political strands in green thought.

These strands in green thought are separate, in the sense that the arguments used to support any one of them do not necessarily commit us to any of the others. All the strands might – or might not – ultimately prove justifiable. My point is just that, by and large, each of them will have to be justified separately, rather than any one piggybacking on the justification given for any one of the others.

At the core of green political theory's public-policy stance is a 'green theory of value'.[56] It is that theory of value that provides the unified moral vision running through all the central substantive planks in the green political programme; it is by virtue of that unified moral vision that the green agenda can legitimately be thought to form something akin to an all-or-nothing package; it is the inconsistency of endorsing that theory of value for some purposes but not for others to which it is equally applicable that allows greens properly to complain, in a way that would not be appropriate for an ordinary single-issue group, when mainstream parties borrow piecemeal from the green agenda. All of that follows from the green theory of value, and from that alone.

The second strand of green political theory is a 'green theory of agency'.[57] Whereas the first strand tells us what things are of value and why, the second strand advises on how to go about pursuing those values. Such a theory is action guiding in both a negative and a positive direction: it tells us what not to do in pursuit of the Good, as well as what we must (or may) do in pursuit of it. Such a theory is also agent creating as well as being agent instructing: as well as telling natural individuals what they should and should not do, directly, it also tells them what sort of collective organizations they should create and what they should and should not do indirectly through the agency of such artificial entities.

Such a theory of agency is pitched at the level of principle rather than of mere pragmatics, to be sure. Of course, greens have to take due account of pragmatics and tactics, too. But that is not all that is at work in their theory of agency. They also have certain principled views as to which sorts of political agency are to be preferred to which others. They are decidedly of the view that decentralized, egalitarian political mechanisms are to be preferred to centralized, hierarchical ones. For

[56] To be elaborated in chapter 2 below.
[57] Discussed in chapter 4 below.

them, it is a matter of principle and not mere pragmatics that we should 'think globally, act locally'. For them, nonviolence is a matter of principle, not merely a useful tactic.

What the relationship is that is supposed to exist between the green theory of value and this green theory of agency is unclear. Green writers rarely address the problem explicitly. Furthermore, through their silence, they are implicitly suggesting that there is no problem there to be addressed at all. The implication seems to be that all the strands of green political theory hang together, both at root deriving somehow from the one and the same normative premise.

I think that implicit claim is untrue – or anyway, unproven.[58] Basically, greens could derive their theory of agency from their theory of value only by asserting that one mode of human organization was uniquely natural. But that would amount to privileging as uniquely 'natural' one particular phase of human history, such as hunter-gatherer society, for example. Such judgements seem arbitrary and insupportable.

In the end, I think we have to say that the green theory of agency is a separate component of green political theory. It exists in addition to, and substantially independently of the green theory of value. Furthermore, it ought to be seen as subsidiary to the green theory of value.[59] The green theory of agency is a theory about how best to pursue the Good and the valuable, according to a distinctively green analysis of what is good and valuable. Some theories of agency might elevate right action, regardless of consequences, to an art form in and of itself. Green theory is not among them. It aims first and foremost at producing good green consequences.

Those two more political strands of green theorizing are of course set in the context of a larger body of green thought on the place of humanity in the world more generally. But just as it is a mistake to suppose that both strands of green political theory necessarily go together, merely because self-styled greens happen to espouse them both, so too is it even more of a mistake to suppose that all other elements of the larger green social theory necessarily have to go together, merely because many greens happen to espouse them all with the same breath.

Green theory, like all social theories, has its core and its periphery. Green theorists, like all theorists, take some positions because they have to – because they are committed by the basic logic of their deepest principles to those propositions. Like all social commentators, though, they also find themselves taking stands on various issues of the day in a way not at all dictated by the logic of their deeper principles. There is no

[58] For reasons given at the outset of chapter 4 below.
[59] As I shall argue in discussing priorities in chapter 4, section 1 below.

reason why they should not speak their minds in this way. But in interpreting green theory, as with any other social theory, it is important to separate these more ephemeral remarks from the core concerns of the theory.

Thus for example Hobbes scholars, applying the principle of charity to try to derive the strongest possible version of Hobbes's theory, characteristically distinguish between 'what Hobbes (*actually*) said' and 'what Hobbes *should* have said' or 'what (given the fundamental logic of his theory) Hobbes *had* to say'. If we are trying to be charitable and construct the strongest version of his theory, rather than knocking down straw men, we cannot hold Hobbes to every silly thing he ever happened to say. We cannot dismiss his political theory automatically, just because in his extended writings on geometry Hobbes persistently claimed to be able to 'square a circle'. We must be prepared to turn a blind eye to some of his crazier views which, while indisputably representing what he thought, were accidentally what he thought rather than being necessarily connected in any logical way to his larger world-view.

The same is true in reading green social theory. We should turn a blind eye to some of the crazier views (views about personal life-styles, transformations of consciousness, New Age cosmology, and so on) that greens happen sometimes to espouse.[60] If those views are not connected to the deeper logic underlying the distinctively green political theory – here understood as the conjunction of the green theory of value and, secondarily, the green theory of agency – then we should not hold it against green political theory that some (perhaps many, perhaps most) greens happen to hold such views.

I refer to such views as 'green heresies'.[61] The phrase may be tendentious. Practical political activists among the greens may complain that it costs them invaluable allies. In a particularly astute essay on 'Green strategy', Sara Parkin writes:

> I like to think of the green movement as having four divisions: (1) people who provide practical examples of how a green lifestyle might work, including organic farmers, people developing alternative technologies, and so on; (2) single-issue pressure groups; (3) people who work by example or propaganda in the existing establishment – traditional political

[60] Others, of course, would put those propositions at the core of green thinking and treat the more political – and, indeed, more environmentalist – aspects as peripheral. Note that it is essentially a transformed state of consciousness to which Reich (1970) alludes in *The Greening of America*, which to my mind dates the book really rather badly.

[61] In chapter 2, section 7 below.

[62] Parkin 1988, p. 168.

parties, churches, trade unions, universities, and so on . . .; (4) the
distinctively green political parties.[62]

She regards this heterogeneity as strategically advantageous, observing
that 'the pressure for change is greater if it comes from several
directions and, importantly, each division appeals to a different sort of
recruit.' In any case,

> there is no way in which one division of the green movement can carry out
> the whole range of offensive actions that will be required to survive in
> hostile enemy territory, never mind win . . . any significant skirmish. The
> green movement will succeed only if the specialist divisions share out the
> jobs according to the abilities of their foot-soldiers and the sort of territory
> over which they operate best.[63]

Parkin has a point. No doubt offending advocates of green lifestyles
would carry short-term political costs for the movement. I can only say,
in reply, that incurring those costs is almost certainly a necessary
condition for any larger, longer-term political success. If green causes
are to acquire political converts in anything like the numbers required to
make a real difference, it is important that people realize that they need
not be bean-eating homoeopaths constantly chanting mantras to be well
and truly green, in the public policy terms that matter most to the fate of
the earth. So showing that questions of green lifestyle can be separated
from those of green politics, as I shall be doing here, is important not
only theoretically but ultimately also practically as well.

In short, I concur in Tim O'Riordan's diagnosis of the current malaise
of the greens. Observing that 'in the December 1990 German elections,
the old green party failed to capture the necessary five per cent of the
vote for direct representation in parliament,' he offers the following
speculations as to the possible sources of their failure:

> Part of the problem is that environmentally more sophisticated voters are
> actually reading the green manifestos and do not like what they see. Part
> is due to the continuing inability of green parties to organize as a credible
> and coherent political force with clear policies and articulate leadership.
> Part, too, is a function of the 'capturing' of green issues by mainstream
> parties – all of whom take what they want, and ignore or misinterpret
> what is ideologically uncomfortable.[64]

Leaders must be found where they can. But here I hope to do at least
something to tidy up the green manifesto, making it easier for voters to
swallow, and harder for other parties to steal piecemeal.

---

[63] Ibid., p. 176.
[64] O'Riordan 1991, pp. 181–2.

2

A Green Theory of Value

1 The Good and the Valuable

Let us begin by reflecting upon the nature of a 'theory of value' more generally. A theory of value is, quite simply, a theory of the Good. Much is asked of such a theory. Ideally, it should tell us both *what* is to be valued and *why*. We expect any truly comprehensive theory of the Good to tell us not only which things are good and which are not; we expect it also to tell us for what reasons, or in respect of what attributes, those things are supposed to be considered good.

It is important to recognize, right from the start, that not all theories of the Good – try as they might – necessarily succeed in providing theories that are altogether complete in such ways. That incompleteness, in turn, gives rise to possibilities (which advocates of each of the theories involved might, and usually will, find highly embarrassing) for legitimately mixing and matching ostensively incompatible theories. I shall say more about those possibilities later. For now, though, let us confine ourselves to the pure cases.

It is also important to recognize, from the outset, that a theory of the Good is not necessarily all there is to moral evaluation. Philosophers standardly say that morality is a theory both of the Right and of the Good.[1] Different philosophers differ in the emphasis that they accord to each of those components and, indeed, some attempt to subsume one wholly within the other. Thus from a certain ('deontological') perspective we can exhaustively analyse the Good in terms of the Right: on this analysis, good states of affairs are just those which are produced when all moral agents perform right actions. Similarly, from the opposite ('consequentialistic') perspective we can exhaustively analyse the Right

[1] Ross 1930; Brandt 1979.

in terms of the Good: right actions are just those actions which would produce maximally good consequences. In what follows, I want so far as possible to avoid taking sides on those larger issues.

Still, it must be admitted that what I shall be investigating is indisputably a theory of the Good. So even if I were to demonstrate conclusively that the particular theory of the Good that I shall be discussing is the very best available, the moral significance of that conclusion inevitably remains somewhat uncertain. After all, how important a component of overall morality that theory of the Good will turn out to be depends on how important one supposes considerations of the Good ought to be, relative to considerations of the Right, in the final moral mix.

Nothing I shall say here will address the concerns of those who would accord literally *no* independent role at all to considerations of the Good in their moral reckoning. But that fact hardly needs to worry us unduly, since virtually no one is prepared to embrace quite such an extravagant position, anyway. Hardly anyone would really want to assert that any action is right or wrong literally '*whatever* the consequences'.[2] Virtually everyone concedes a place in moral evaluation to considerations of the Good and to the calculations of consequences that derive from them. And of course, in so far as deontologists are prepared to concede even in that very limited way a moral role to the assessment of consequences, a theory of the Good is to that extent morally relevant even within their ethical outlook.

What I shall really be discussing is, as I have said, a theory of the Good. But rather than phrasing my arguments in those terms, I shall henceforth talk instead in terms of a 'theory of value'. I do not intend anything subtle or sneaky by that shift in terminology. On the contrary, I take those terms to be absolutely equivalent, or nearly enough so for present purposes. Where the one talks about what is good and why, the other talks about what is valuable and why. It is a distinction without a difference, so far as we are here concerned.

Or, I should say, the difference is a purely practical one. Economists simply seem to feel more comfortable with – and hence more threatened by – arguments couched in terms of a theory of value than a theory of the Good. And, of course, connecting with the discourse of economists is crucial in environmental contexts. After all, it is economists who are, intellectually, the most direct targets of 'green' political movements, certainly on this narrower point and arguably more broadly as well.[3]

[2] As Bernard Williams – himself no friend of consequentialism – is the first to admit (1973, p. 90).
[3] See e.g. Naess 1989, ch. 5.

The dominance of a particular and peculiarly economic theory of value is, green theorists would say, what leads us to overvalue material prosperity and to undervalue all that is sacrificed in pursuit of it.[4]

That economic theory of value does, of course, have deeper philosophical underpinnings. Indeed, in many respects its underlying theory of the Good amounts to little more than a stripped-down form of Bentham's hedonic calculus. Much can be said against that deeper philosophical theory. But so much already has been said against it that those who still do not see the problems with crude Benthamite utilitarianism probably never will. It would almost certainly prove pointless to try yet again to join issue with economists on that deeper philosophical plane.

From a pragmatic point of view, surely it would be more fruitful to try to meet the dominant practitioners of the pernicious art on their own chosen ground. If talking about a theory of value rather than a theory of the Good helps us join issue with them more directly, little is lost and much gained by translating our arguments into those terms.

Of course economists are notoriously reluctant to join issue with philosophers, or anyone else, on these or any other issues. They jealously guard their exclusive sphere of special expertise. They staunchly deny the relevance of contributions from anyone outside that narrow faith to any of the questions that centrally concern them. Thus, for the same reason that economists refuse to talk in more philosophical terms of a theory of the Good, they will also inevitably resist philosophers' attempts to meet them on their own ground.

The excuse that they are most likely to offer is that the philosophical challenge blurs a distinction, crucial in their self-conception, between 'positive' and 'normative' theories of value. The economic theory of value, they will assert, is no more than a predictive device in positive economics. Its function is merely to allow us to explain and predict the rate at which various things will exchange for one another.[5] The philosopher's theory of value, in contrast, is normative. It purports to tell us values, not just prices. It tells us how much things are really worth, not merely how much they actually cost.

If any such sharp distinction between positive and normative theories of value could be sustained, and if economists were systematically operating within the former just as philosophers surely are within the

---

[4] The importance of engaging with economists in this way is quite sufficient to justify focusing here, within ethics, strictly on consequentialistic theories of the good – to the exclusion of non-consequentialistic theories of the good, much less other more realist, relativist or deontological accounts of the nature of moral reasoning.

[5] Robbins 1932.

latter, then economists would be right to resist philosophers' intrusions into their domain. Translating philosophical points about the Good into the language of value would amount to little more than a pun. The 'value' in question would still be the wrong sort of value – normative rather than positive – to engage with the arguments of economists.

As it happens, though, none of that is true. Whether the distinction between positive and normative theories of value ever could be sustained is a larger issue, and one into which we need not venture here. Suffice it to say, for present purposes, that in practice it is not sustained in the ordinary discourse of economists. They simply do not stick nearly as faithfully as they would have us believe to a purely positive theory of value in their discussions. For all their positivistic pretensions, economists' choice of normatively loaded terminology gives their game away. A theory of value, for economists as much as for philosophers, is what is *and ought to be* of value. That is certainly true in the various economic theories of value I shall be discussing in the next section of this chapter.[6]

All of that is merely to say that it is doubly propitious to couch the ethical arguments of the greens in terms of a green theory of value. Not only does that formulation best capture the core concerns of greens themselves, as I shall argue in chapter 3 below. It also enables green theories to engage directly, in ways that cannot decently be evaded, with the arguments of economists that have been responsible for so much of the environmental despoilation that greens bemoan.

2   A Taxonomy of Theories of Value

Approaching the problem of the Good from this vaguely economistic angle, there are essentially three distinct bases on which we might ground a theory of value – consumer satisfaction, labour inputs or natural resource inputs.[7] These options correspond to a 'capitalist' theory of value, a 'Marxist' theory of value and a 'green' theory of value, respectively.

[6] In their candid moments, neoclassical economists, for example, clearly regard consumer satisfaction both as the analytical source of market prices and as the moral justification for allocating resources through the mechanism of markets that rely upon such price signals; see e.g. Knight (1922, p. 454; 1935a, p. 19), Friedman and Friedman (1980) and Brittan (1988, pp. 35–148). Similarly, both John Locke and, in his moralizing moments, Karl Marx regarded labour not only as the source of value but also as the source of moral entitlements to material resources; see e.g. Reeve (1986) and Cohen, Nagel and Scanlon (1980).
[7] On these topics, see quite generally Knight (1935b).

Those latter labels are adopted purely for expository convenience, and I should warn at the outset that they may be misleading. Naming as they do three historically warring camps, such labels may make those options seem more mutually exclusive than they actually are. Here, as with the clash between theories of the Right and of the Good, there is no particular reason to suppose that we must inevitably favour any one option absolutely to the exclusion of others. In the end, we may want to – in the end, we may have to – concoct some mixed theory of value drawing on all of these theories, and perhaps more besides.[8] Even if we do end up mixing and matching the theories, though, it is nonetheless important to see clearly from the start the character of the three distinct components that are being intermixed.

First, then, we have the 'capitalist' – or, if you prefer, 'neoclassical welfare economic' – theory of value. This is essentially a *consumer* based theory. It traces the value of things to values which people derive in the course of partaking of them.

There are myriad variations on that basic theme. Some crudely link value to subjective mental states, like happiness. (That is the Benthamite version, of course.) Others link it, less crudely, to satisfaction of subjectively felt desires, where there is no assumption that want satisfaction equates necessarily to 'happiness'. (You can take satisfaction in having discharged well a nasty duty.) Others link it, less crudely still, to the capacity of something to satisfy desires that are or will be or otherwise would be subjectively felt. (Eating before you feel hungry preemptively satisfies your desires.)[9]

There are important differences between all these alternative ways of filling out the basic logic of that consumer-based theory of value, of course. Much philosophical ink has been spilt debating their relative merits. Happily, though, we can afford to skirt those issues here, since our present concern is simply with the common theoretical core that all of those variations share. At root, all are essentially *consumer* based theories of value. That category forms our first broad class of value theories.

[8] Indeed, as Claus Offe has pointed out to me, each of us probably subscribes to each theory of value in one or another of the various social roles that we all occupy. As consumers striving to maximize satisfaction, we subscribe to the 'capitalist' theory of value: as producers, we subscribe to the 'labour' theory of value; as creatures situated in and capable of responding emotionally and aesthetically to the natural world, we subscribe to the 'green' theory of value.

[9] Knight's (1935b) essay on 'Value and price' is a good guide to how economists traditionally have – and have not – addressed these issues. For recent philosophical accounts, see Brandt (1979) and Griffin (1986, esp. pt 1).

Second is the 'Marxist' – or, if you prefer, 'Ricardian' – theory of value. This is a *producer* based theory. It traces the value of things to values that people impart to them in the course of producing those things.

In principle, these values might derive from any number of different attributes of producers or productive activities. In practice, though, this sort of theory almost always amounts to a labour theory of value. Certainly that is its most familiar form, both in its Marxian and in its more general Ricardian-cum-Lockean forms.

Here again, there are endless variations on the theme. The basic idea is that the value of an object corresponds to the amount of labour time invested in producing it. But more subtle versions of the theory might differentiate between skilled and unskilled labour time, between the amount of time actually spent producing a thing and that which is 'socially necessary' to produce it, and so on.[10] Again, though, the many and subtle variations should not blind us to what all of them have in common: these theories are all, at root, *producer* based theories of value.

Third and nowadays less familiar is the class of value theories that I associate with the 'green' theory of value. This is a *natural resource* based theory of value. This links the value of things to some naturally occurring properties of the objects themselves.

I use the phrase 'natural resource' purely in deference to the standard economistic way of partitioning inputs into the production process. The literal-minded will find it misleading, though. For literally, of course, calling something a 'resource' implies that it is 'instrumentally useful for producing human satisfaction' – which would reduce this third theory of value back to the first, straightaway. Obviously, that is not what is here intended. A more awkward but technically more correct way of describing this third theory is to say it is a 'natural attribute based' (or, at the risk of question begging, 'nature based') theory of value. I shall avoid that awkwardness by sticking to the 'natural resource based' terminology. But remember that it is only an imprecise shorthand.

Here, as before, there are countless variations on the basic theme, depending on what exactly it is about naturally occurring properties of objects that is said to give them value. Some theories point, disingenuously I believe, to objective attributes of objects – the 'hardness' of diamonds, and suchlike – in this regard.[11] Another variation on these broad

[10] Vianello 1987. See also Elster's (1985, pp. 127–41) discussion of 'The labour theory of value'.

[11] The reason for regarding such arguments as disingenuous is just that, as a long string of economists dating back beyond Adam Smith rightly complain, references to

themes, one which is perhaps historically the most famous, is the physiocrats' claim that land alone has the capacity for producing value.[12]

The 'green' answer that I shall be sketching below constitutes yet another way of filling out that same basic formula.[13] I happen to think it is the most satisfactory way of filling out a natural resource based theory of value at this point. But I should emphasize at the outset that it is only one way among many possible ways of explicating what it is about naturally occurring properties that makes them so valuable.

In any case, it ought to be tolerably clear by now how a theory of value that is natural resource based, the green theory of value being an instance, is to be distinguished from the other two general sorts of value theory already discussed. It differs from a producer based theory of value in so far as it insists that those value-imparting properties are natural, rather than being somehow artefacts of human activities.[14] And it differs from a consumer based theory of value in so far as it insists that those value-imparting qualities somehow inhere in the objects themselves, rather than in any mental states (actual or hypothetical, now or later) of those who partake of those objects.

Of course, hard-line proponents of each sort of value theory will naturally try either to discount or to reduce the others to their own. Thus, for example, Marxists would emphasize in reply to greens that natural resources are of no use to anyone until they have been shaped by human hands to human purposes: in the classically Lockean version of this tale, even acorns must be picked up off the ground before they can be eaten. And neoclassical welfare economists would emphasize, in reply to both Marxists and greens, that while they may well be right about *why* people value objects, what it *is* for a thing to have value is intimately connected with the consumption act: at the end of the day, there can be no value without valuers; and in Adam Smith's memorable example, if someone is dying of thirst, diamonds are not nearly as valuable to that person as is water, whatever the productive histories, intrinsic properties or objective scarcities of the two commodities.

considerations like 'hardness' are implicit appeals to the human purposes for which hard objects might be handy. And when the implicit is made explicit in such theories, this theory of value ceases to be natural resource based at all. Instead, it becomes consumer based: naturally occurring properties are then valuable really only in relation to, and indeed by virtue of, human purposes.

[12] Weulersse 1935.

[13] That the green theory of value is a subspecies of this class is, I think, moderately uncontentious. See e.g. Georgescu-Roegen (1971, ch. 10) and Schumacher (1973, ch. 1).

[14] Hence the green position on the appropriate bases of taxation: 'taxes . . . on labour should be reduced in favour of a system of environmental taxes on goods and resources that are scarce . . .' (European Greens 1989, sec. 1).

Such refutations and reductions may work well or badly. Or, more likely, they may force us to tell a rather more nuanced story about value, distinguishing *inter alia* between what it means for something to have value, where that value comes from, how it is realized, and so on. By seeing all these competing theories of value as answers to slightly different questions about value, we might be able to concoct a composite theory that combines the strengths of all.[15] I do not want – or need – to contend that the particular theory of value I am investigating here is correct utterly to the exclusion of all others. I shall merely be insisting that it has a legitimate place, alongside others perhaps, in any larger mixed theory of value.

3   History and Process as Sources of Value

Taxonomies are not arguments. The taxonomy just produced is even less of one than most. It has merely served to situate the green theory of value in relation to other, more familiar ones. The green theory of value is a particular instantiation of the 'natural resource based theory of value'. The distinctive feature characterizing such theories in general is that they trace the value of a thing to some attribute of the natural resources comprising it, rather than to any facts about the people who have produced or will consume it.

Nothing I have said so far, however, specifies what exactly it is about natural resources that makes them valuable. The different answers they provide to that question serve to distinguish all the various 'natural resource based' theories of value from one another. There are many ways of filling out the more general 'natural resource based' theory of value, at that point. The green theory of value offers one solution, but it is only one among many.

According to the distinctively green variant, what it is that makes natural resources valuable is their very naturalness. That is to say, what imparts value to them is not any physical attributes or properties that they might display. Rather, it is the history and process of their creation.

---

[15] Or we might not. In particular, the Marxist and green theories of value might at first seem particularly hard to reconcile, in so far as the one says that things have value by virtue of having been shaped by nature and the other by virtue of having been moulded by the labour of humanity. Alongside this economic theory, which does seem hard to reconcile with green values, Marx also of course ran a 'materialist' theory of history. That may (Benton 1989) – or may not (Schmidt 1971, esp. chs 2 and 6) – be much more congenial to a green theory of value.

What is crucial in making things valuable, on the green theory of value, is the fact that they have a history of having been created by natural processes rather than by artificial human ones.[16]

By focusing in this way on the history and process of its creation as the special feature of a naturally occurring property that imparts value, the green theory of value shows itself to be an instantiation of yet another pair of other more general theories of value – a *process* based theory of value, on the one hand, and a *history* based theory of value, on the other.[17] Before going on to say what is so valuable about a thing's having the *particular* sort of history that the green theory favours, I should first say something to ease disquiet about those larger classes of value theory.

This task is made harder through the association, in recent social philosophy, of such theories with the 'historical entitlement' theory of distributive justice advanced by Robert Nozick.[18] For Nozick, a distribution is just so long as everything within it was originally acquired justly by its first owner and was subsequently transferred justly from each owner to the next, all the way down the line.

That is, at least potentially, a deeply conservative theory of justice.[19] Many take strong exception to it. Those who do often let their repugnance for Nozick's conclusions spill over to his methodology as well. But of course that is a mistake. While Nozick's theory of justice certainly is one example of a process based, history based ethical theory, his is hardly the only way of fleshing out such a theory. Those who are appalled by the use to which Nozick puts such methods ought not

---

[16] 'Rather than' rather overstates the contrast, in ways explained in discussing 'humanity as part of nature' in section 5 below. Nor do I mean to suggest by this that human creations in general have no value, or even that humanly produced replicas of natural products are without value. The green position is merely that those replicas have *necessarily less* value than the ones arising out of natural processes. For a homely example recall that while natural pearls are considerably more valuable than cultured ones the latter are not without value. Or, in the example from aesthetics elaborated below, a perfect replica of the *Pietà*, though less valuable than the original of that work, may well be more valuable than an original work by a less talented sculptor.

[17] Although logically distinct, I shall here conflate these two types of value theory – as they inevitably are conflated, wherever (as in the green theory of value, as well as in the other examples I shall discuss below) what matters about an object's history is the fact that certain processes figure in it.

[18] Nozick 1974, esp. ch. 7.

[19] 'At least potentially', because of course it is a fair bet that no one can claim an absolutely clean title of this demanding sort to any piece of property you care to name. So, in practice, everything comes to turn on how far followers of Nozick want to carry the rectification of past wrongs and to what extent they want simply to 'grandfather' past wrongs.

necessarily be put off from that larger class of value theories in consequence.

In light of those potentially off-putting associations, then, it is particularly important to recall some of the other more positive associations which such value theories also enjoy. In many of those other connections, it seems perfectly familiar, natural and plausible to suppose that process based and history based considerations are indeed crucial in fixing the value of things. Recognizing that fact will usefully clear the ground for my own green theory of value.

Consider, first, the rule of process based considerations in imparting legitimacy to the outcomes of political deliberations. Decisions largely devoid of substantive merits are reckoned nonetheless worthy of respect just so long as they have arisen through the workings of democratic processes. In a democracy, it is the history of the process by which a decision has been reached that serves to confer legitimacy on any given action of a regime. Similarly, administrative actions are typically deemed socially acceptable, to a surprisingly large extent regardless of their substantive merits, just so long as the canons of 'due process' have been respected in reaching them. There, too, it is the history of the process by which the decision has been reached that serves to confer legitimacy on the actions of administrative agencies.[20]

Some might query whether this is an apt example for present purposes. 'Conferring legitimacy' (which is what having the right process-based history seems to do) is, they may say, importantly different from 'imparting value' (which is what the green theory of value requires). Far from valuing those outcomes more highly on account of their histories, what we are actually doing when accepting those outcomes as 'legitimate' might be no more than merely saying that we are prepared to accept even less valuable outcomes, just so long as they have the right histories. Or so our doubters might suppose.

But why should we be willing to accept less valuable outcomes, just because they have the right histories? Only, presumably, because we attach some independent *value* to the process of the creation of those outcomes. If so, then what is really going on is just this: outcomes which are less valuable to us, in purely substantive terms, nonetheless turn out to be more valuable to us overall once the extra value derived from the process of their creation has been added in. In other words, then, it is not just legitimacy but also (and more importantly, for present purposes) *value* that, at the end of the day, familiar political theories of

---

[20] That proposition, commonplace among political theorists, turns out to be equally common among ordinary citizens as well; for empirical evidence, see Tyler (1990).

democracy and due process must be asserting attaches to outcomes by virtue of the history surrounding the process of their creation.[21]

For another very different example, consider next the problem, from the realm of aesthetics. What value ought we attach to fakes, forgeries, replicas, reproductions and restorations? The answer is easy, the explanation less so. We standardly suppose that such things are less valuable – not just contingently but *necessarily* less valuable – than the original which they replicate. But why?

Surely that is not just a matter of copies necessarily being, to some greater or lesser extent, bad copies. For we can imagine (even if we can never make[22]) an absolutely perfect copy, one that reproduces all observable features of the original absolutely perfectly. Surely, though, most of us would still suppose that a perfect replica of the *Pietà* was less valuable than the masterpiece that sits in St Peter's.[23]

Supposing that it really is a perfect replica, though, there can be none of the standard aesthetic grounds for that judgement. *Ex hypothesi*, all of its observable features – colour, texture, line, shape, etc. – are identical to those of the original. So if the replica is less valuable, that can only be so on account of its history. The grounds for devaluing replicas, fakes and forgeries have to do, once again, with the history of the process by which they were created.[24]

The particularly potent value-imparting feature of the Vatican *Pietà* which no other *Pietà* can replicate is the fact that it was created by the hand of Michelangelo. Similarly, the *Mona Lisa* has the peculiar value it does because of the history of who painted it. Were it to turn out that the copy hanging in the Louvre is a Napoleonic-era forgery, the image would remain the same but the significance of the painting would

----

[21] And thus democratic or administrative due process is a matter, not just for a theory of the Right, but also ultimately for a theory of the Good.

[22] Received wisdom has it that 'even the most . . . perfect imitator . . . has his own distinctive inflection. . . . Every forgery will . . . show symptoms of the style of the epoch which produced it' (Kurz 1967, p. 317).

[23] Most of us modern Westerners', at least. 'Fakes an imitations are as interesting as originals' within a culture – as Arata Isozaki depicts Japanese culture as being – in which 'the concept of "high art never really took shape in Japan" and everything instead turns on how well the 'forms' and 'conventions' are respected (Hilton 1991).

[24] The argument in the text in couched in terms of the visual rather than the performing arts, but *mutatis mutandis* the same can be said there as well. Of course, in works written to be performed the objection is not to the faithful rendition of the text or the score: it is a virtue, not a defect, in a performance that it reproduces exactly the author's words or the composer's notes. The equivalent in that realm of our objections to reproductions or restorations in the realm of visual arts would be a work (or a pastiche) 'in the manner of' Shakespeare or of Mozart.

nonetheless have altered. It would have lost the value it once had for us as a manifestation of Leonardo's genius.[25]

In aesthetics as well as in politics, then, history and process impart value. An original was created by the master's hand – and necessarily so, for that is what it means for it to be an 'original'. The fake, forgery or replica was not – and necessarily so, for that is what it means for it to be a 'fake', 'forgery' or 'replica'. And it is necessarily having that history that, in turn, makes the one sort of object necessarily more valuable than the other.[26]

4   Naturalness as a Source of Value

All of that is merely by way of working up some intuitions for the plausibility – and, more especially, of undermining intuitions about the implausibility of attaching value to a thing by virtue of the history of the process by which it has come about. Hopefully, the upshot of the previous discussion will have been to show that, Nozick notwithstanding, there is nothing outrageous about that as a general value stance.

That said, however, the question remains why we should attach special value to the *particular* sort of history which greens identify as a source of value. What is so especially valuable about something having come about through natural rather than through artificial human processes? In the words of one memorable title, 'What's wrong with plastic trees?'[27]

We might make a start on this question by assimilating it to the

---

[25] This theme is effectively elaborated by Sagoff (1976; 1978). See also Radford (1978) and, more especially, the papers collected in Dutton (1983). 'For us' signals that my argument from aesthetics works within a purely subjectivist framework, rather than (necessarily) appealing to any 'realist' metaphysic to explain the value attaching to originals or organic wholes. The next section of this chapter similarly traces the value of setting our lives in a larger context beyond ourselves to the satisfaction of our subjective desires in that regard, rather than to anything objectively valuable in that.) In the aesthetic case just as in the environmental one, I do not deny that that stronger 'realist' argument might also be true; I merely do not rely upon its being true.
[26] The same is transparently true of historical landmarks, of course. Independence Hall is especially valuable because of the history of what happened there. Had it a different history – had the US Constitution been drafted and signed elsewhere – that particular building would lose its significance and its peculiar value to us. See, more generally, Golding and Golding (1979) and Jamieson (1984).
[27] Kriger 1973.

problem of fakes and forgeries.[28] The title just mentioned refers to events that are real, not merely feared or fantasized. When the city fathers discovered that real trees could no longer survive the polluted air surrounding the Los Angeles freeways, they tried planting plastic ones there instead. When they found that those plastic trees kept being chopped down, they professed genuine surprise. If so, I suspect that they were just about the only ones to be surprised.[29]

Most of us, confronting schemes involving the destruction of some especially unique bit of the natural landscape, would leap almost automatically to protest at its loss. But perhaps we are too quick to protest. Not so long ago, the Queensland government was proposing to allow the mining of sand on Fraser Island – the only purely sand island on the Great Barrier Reef. When the scheme met with fierce protests, the Deputy Prime Minister of Australia of the time ventured the opinion that such mining could be resumed just as soon as 'the community becomes more informed and more enlightened as to what reclamation work is being carried out by mining companies'. The same is often said by, or anyway on behalf of, a frequent despoiler of the American landscape, the US Army Corps of Engineers.[30]

Now, we might doubt those claims on any of several grounds. When confronting a particularly notorious mining company or the Army Corps of Engineers making such claims, we might well doubt their sincerity, or their capacity, or their willingness. But let us set all those doubts to one side.

Let us imagine, purely for the sake of argument, a best-case scenario. Let us suppose – *per impossibile*, perhaps – that the developers in question offer an iron-clad, legally binding promise to recreate that landscape just as it was, once they have finished. Let us suppose that they provide detailed plans for how they would go about doing so. Let

[28] The analogy is strongest if we adopt a religious attitude towards nature, so in both cases we accord particular value to the unspoilt original (environment; work of art) as a manifestation of our respect for its creator. That line has obvious appeal for a 'social ecologist' for whom the value of untouched nature is always necessarily derivative, in some way or another, from the values and interests of people (be they consumers or producers, present or future generations). But, as I shall argue below, we can derive value from certain attributes of a natural *process* of creation without talking about a Creator.

[29] For interestingly varied reasons, legal philosophers who subsequently joined the debate inspired by Kriger's (1973) article were not (Tribe 1974; 1975; Sagoff 1974).

[30] Similarly, the US Army Corps of Engineers – a frequent despoiler of the American environment – regularly asserts its capacity to restore whatever its activities might have damaged. For an excellent discussion both of those cases and of the larger issues they raise, see Elliot (1982).

us suppose that we find those plans absolutely convincing. In short, let us suppose that we have no doubt that the landscape will indeed look just the same after they have finished as it did before they began.

Still, I think, we are inclined to object to the proposal.[31] Even if we are convinced that the landscape will look the same, still it will not really *be* the same. Previously it has been the work of nature; afterwards, it will have become the work of humanity. However talented as restorationists the developers' landscape architects might be, the one thing that they cannot possibly replicate is history. They might be able to restore something perfectly in every other respect, but the very act of restoration itself necessarily alters irrevocably a thing's history.

Just as a talented forger might replicate the *Mona Lisa* perfectly, so too might landscape architects replicate nature perfectly. But just as the one amounts to 'faking' a painting, so too does the other amount to 'faking' nature.[32] Fakes might look the same as the originals but they cannot possibly be the same, for they have different histories and different origins. And in so far as the historical origins of the original are what matter to us, neither can those fakes possibly have the same value for us.

The point of producing fakes, in general, is presumably always to substitute (and, indeed, to attempt to pass off) something less valuable for something more valuable. But whereas in the case of the faked *Mona Lisa* the fake might exist without the original being extinguished, in the case of the faked landscape here in view the fake – the restored landscape – would be in place of the original. It is not just a matter of creating in the world something extra, with less (but nonetheless real) value. It is there a matter of extinguishing something more valuable and replacing it with something less valuable. To adapt the examples from aesthetics discussed earlier, it is as if we were to make a cast of the *Pietà* through some process which would destroy the original. Even if we could, using that cast, produce a perfect replica of the *Pietà* – even if we could produce such replicas in virtually unlimited quantities – I take it that few would be tempted by the prospect.

---

[31] As indeed we would object even if the visual aspect of the landscape were never changed in the first place. Consider, in this connection, objections to the 1981 proposal to lease a National Trust property at Bradenham in Buckinghamshire to NATO for use as a bunker. The bunker would have been below ground, so (damage done by construction apart) the purely visual aspects of the site would have remained unchanged. Even granting that, though, protestors complained that their appreciation of the site would be lessened by the knowledge that there was a bunker beneath the ground. I am grateful to Albert Weale for this example.

[32] Elliot 1982.

Putting the point in terms of 'fakery' rather begs the question, of course. By pretending to be something that they are not, fakes necessarily concede their own inferiority. The things which they pretend to be must be somehow superior to that which they actually are, or else there simply would be no point in the pretence.

But it is not just the element of fraud that makes fakes, forgeries and counterfeits less valuable. The same is true (to a lesser but nonetheless significant extent) with restorations, reproductions and replicas, where the element of fraud is absent. It is the very act of copying something else which, in the end, crucially concedes the superiority of that which is copied. What is the point of copying, if you could have done better all by yourself, starting from scratch?

The developers in our hypothetical example can thus ill afford to accept 'faking nature' as a description of what they propose doing. That much was probably obvious from the start. The more surprising implication of those observations just offered is that it is not merely the pejorative description which the developers must shun. If they are to avoid conceding the necessary inferiority of the landscape which they will leave, as compared to that which they had found, they must not even try to recreate the original. They must instead assert that they will create something different from and better than – or, anyway, not comparable to – the natural landscape which their handiwork will replace.

Landscape architects themselves may well suffer just such hubris. They may well regard that claim, however immodest, as being nonetheless perfectly true. Still, few firms proposing to despoil the natural environment would be willing to take any such stance publicly. That does not necessarily mean that they think that it is untrue, of course. They might merely regard it as impolitic. But even for such a claim to be impolitic, it is necessarily the case that it must be seen as untrue – indeed, untrue to the point of outrage – in the eyes of the public at large.

Why should that be so? There are many possible reasons, of very different characters. In practice, such attitudes may reflect no more than well-founded scepticism about the strictly limited capacities of restorationists. We may suppose that the technology is simply not (or, anyway, not yet) up to the task. That is undoubtedly true at present. As long as it remains so, that is a sufficiently compelling consideration in and of itself: there is hardly any pragmatic need to search for further arguments against any proposal involving destroying-then-recreating nature.

If that were all that was involved in objections to those proposals, though, then objections to restoring nature would be merely contingent

A Green Theory of Value

rather than analytically necessary ones – as the parenthetical 'anyway, not yet' in the earlier formulation was meant to emphasize. Suppose technology someday makes sufficient strides to enable it, finally, to replicate nature perfectly.[33] Once a perfect replica really can be produced, we would have no basis for continuing to object – on these grounds, at least – to a strategy of destroying-then-recreating nature.

For larger philosophical purposes, then, we need to probe further. In the world as we know it, it may well be enough to say that the restorers just are not good enough. But for deeper theoretical purposes, we must try – however hard it may be – to contemplate a world where the restorer's art really has been mastered to perfection. Would we still have any objections, even if restorers could guarantee with complete certainty to restore the natural world to precisely its original state, after developers had despoiled it? And if so, how might we ground such objections?

For a clue, let us return to the problem of the value of the fake *Mona Lisa* as compared to that of the original. Intuitively, we want to say that the original is necessarily more valuable because of who painted it – Leonardo rather than some second-rate imitator. But if the agent responsible for the fake were so talented as to be able to reproduce the image *perfectly*, then she must be awfully good indeed. As sports commentators might say, 'on the day' she was every bit as good as Leonardo himself. And if it is talent – as represented in the capacity to paint a picture like *Mona Lisa* – that makes us value paintings created by Leonardo, why not value equally paintings done by others who were, at least on the day the painting was done, every bit as good as Leonardo himself? After all, the painter of the perfect copy painted a *Mona Lisa*, too.

In the case of the fake *Mona Lisa*, the reason for rejecting that line of thought is clear enough, I suppose. The reason we value Leonardo's works especially highly has to do not only with their own merits, taken individually, but also with who their creator was and with *all else* that he did. We value the *Mona Lisa* in part as a beautiful painting, in its own right. But we also value it, in part, as a 'manifestation of Leonardo's genius', as I said in introducing this example.

It might at first seem odd to suggest that, had Leonardo accomplished less, we would value the *Mona Lisa* less: after all, it would retain all its ethereal beauty, even as a one-off. In other ways, however, this theory is far from counterintuitive. We undoubtedly do tend to value lesser works from the hand of Leonardo more than on their purely aesthetic

---

[33] And we have no reason, on this argument, to suppose that it cannot.

merits we ought to do, just because they are from his hand.[34] By the same token, we seem not to value paintings of considerable merit from those who produced only one such masterpiece in their lives as much as we do similar works from those who have produced a substantial corpus of such works – and, once again, this sort of analysis seems to help explain why.

Transpose that argument, now, from the realm of art into the realm of the natural environment. The analogy would suggest that one reason we might not be satisfied with restorers' recreation of nature is that they could only do it on a one-off basis. They might be able to reproduce any *particular* element in the natural world – just as the artistic forger might fortuitously manage to reproduce any particular image. But they would not be able to recreate nature as a whole, across the board, any more than the cleverest forger could manage to reproduce perfectly all of Leonardo's many works. And in so far as their talents are limited in this way, they deserve less respect than does the master craftsman whose talents are not similarly circumscribed.

This sort of argument carries us a considerable distance. But the philosopher's philosopher might insist – rightly, alas – that it still constitutes a merely contingent objection to a strategy of destroying-then-recreating nature. For it is a purely contingent matter that our capacity to create a perfect replica of nature as a whole is limited in this way. Although that is undeniably true, I am not at all sure that we need to be particularly embarrassed by that fact. After all, though a mere contingency, that contingency is virtually certain to be true for as long as any present policy-maker cares to contemplate. Still, for those who demand cast-iron arguments to show that nature's products are *necessarily* superior to humanity's, this argument will not (quite) suffice.

Much the same objection proves even more telling against another initially plausible analysis of this problem. Another reason for valuing Leonardo's original works more highly than the talented copyist's perfect reproductions has to do with their very *originality*. This analysis, too, would have us accord Leonardo's *Mona Lisa* extra value on account of who Leonardo was – but on this approach not merely, or even mainly, on account of what Leonardo actually did so much as on account of what all else he *might* have done. Even if the copyist can reproduce perfectly each work that Leonardo actually executed,

---

[34] Dutton, in his editorial preface to *The Forger's Art* (1983, p. ix), reflects upon the all-too-standard case of 'a musicologist who would wax ecstatic over some trifling bit of Mozart's juvenilia ("adumbrations of the great *G Minor Symphony*") treats with barely disguised contempt a really outstanding and inventive quartet by the generally second-rate Luigi Cherubini.'

copyists by their nature require an original from which to copy. They may be able to paint a perfect *Mona Lisa* once they have seen Leonardo's, but they could never have come up with the image themselves in the first place. That, on one plausible account, is why the copyists' work must necessarily be disvalued compared to that of the original artists whose work they copy.[35]

Something very much like that might be said about the special value of naturally occurring properties. Much of the sense of wonder that people feel in confronting the natural world has to do with the endless variation and rich complexity that they find within it. And if that is any large part of what we value about natural, then simply being able to restore or recreate or replicate nature perfectly is not good enough. In supplanting nature, we have not just taken away what was actually there; we will also have taken away what all else might have been or might yet be there.

However plausible that may be as an argument in the aesthetics, it probably has to be regarded as fatally flawed in its environmental application. There, it is not just the philosopher's philosopher who would rightly worry about the possibility that artificial processes might be able someday to mimic natural ones perfectly.[36] As regards living organisms, at least, it seems that modern technology is – alas – every bit as capable of generating genetic variation, by inducing mutations, as is any naturally occurring process. Furthermore, through the further perfecting of recombinant DNA technology we might even be able to meet or beat nature's capacity for 'creativity'. None of this is necessarily meant as praise for those modern technologies, mind you. But praise or criticism, those observations nonetheless undermine any analysis that traces the peculiar value of nature to its unique variability or creativity.[37]

[35] Thus, Kurz (1967, p. 319) says, 'The reasoning "if my work is mistaken for a Rembrandt, I am as good as Rembrandt" is illogical because it confuses original creation with imitation . . .' Of course, masters can serve as copyists, too. 'A copy of a Lastman by Rembrandt may well be better' – more valuable – 'than the original', Goodman (1968, ch. 3; 1983, p. 100) says. But if so, it can only be because it is a poor copy (different from but better than the original) or, if a perfect copy, because it is set in the context of a better painter's corpus (Rembrandt's, rather than Lastman's). In any case, as Rembrandt paintings go, it would definitely count among his lesser works, precisely because it embodied less of his own originality.
[36] Landscapes might still be a slightly different matter: even master landscape gardeners such as Capability Brown still had to work form naturalistic models; and it is hard to imagine any of them conceiving a design for something like the Grand Canyon or Yosemite, *ex ante* of anyone having described those canyons to them.
[37] Notice, however, that that is once again an argument not so much for *recreating* nature as for being as *creative* as nature, perhaps in some other direction altogether.

There is a parallel problem with various other ways of characterizing what is valuable about nature in terms of 'diversity', 'complexity' or 'fecundity'. Certainly those are attributes of natural creation, and certainly they are valued ones. But of course genetic engineering can (in principle, and probably even in practice) generate just as much diversity, complexity and fecundity – yet it would not be the same. It is not diversity, complexity or fecundity *as such*, that we value. It is instead the diversity, complexity and fecundity of natural processes and their products. The value of such attributes derives from the fact that they result from natural processes, rather than the other way around. Pointing to such attributes cannot, then, explain why we value the natural processes that manifest them.

To explain that, we are, I think, driven to an argument along the following lines. (1) People want to see some sense and pattern to their lives. (2) That requires, in turn, that their lives be set in some larger context. (3) The products of natural processes, untouched as they are by human hands, provides precisely that desired context.[38] In what follows, I shall discuss each of these propositions in turn.

The first step in that argument is a familiar philosophical theme growing out of recent critiques of utilitarianism. In the now-familiar objection, utilitarianism as sometimes construed would seem to recommend that people be constantly investing the next ounce of their energies wherever it would do the most good for humanity at the margin. People following that advice would be spending twelve minutes raising money for starving Eritreans, two-and-a-half minutes feeding their own children, ten seconds signing a petition for world disarmament, eighteen minutes sweeping the floors of the local charity hospital, and so on. Such a life might be utility maximizing for the world at large. But from the inside, such a life would seem deeply unsatisfying. It would lack unity, coherence, purpose.[39] How telling that proposition is as a critique of utilitarianism is unclear.[40] But the truth of that basic

Supposing it is its creativity that we value about nature, the implication is that if modern technology is to aspire to similar value as nature then it must not merely mimic nature but transcend it. On its face, that seems to be an argument for running roughshod over nature's creation. But, equally (in my view, preferably), it might be regarded as a *reductio ad absurdum* of that analysis of what it is that we value about nature.

[38] 'Untouched by human hands' is only a first approximation to the value at work here: for a more refined statement, see the discussion of 'humanity as part of nature' in the next section.

[39] Williams 1973; 1981. See also Wollheim (1984) and Nozick (1981, esp. pp. 403–5).

[40] The utilitarian reply – trivial, but decisive – surely is simply to say that, assuming the psychological fact of the matter is as the critics claim, then utilitarian calculations should simply be revised accordingly.

proposition seems indisputable. What makes people's lives seem valuable to those who are living them is the unity and coherence of the projects comprising them.

The Green theory of value next adds a second thought closely related to that first one. Just as people want to see some unity and coherence among the various plans and projects that comprise their lives, so too do they want to see those plans and projects set in some larger context outside their own lives.[41] That is not necessarily to say that they want to 'change the world' or even necessarily that they want to 'make their mark on the world'. It is just to say that, whatever the source of people's undeniable desire to see some coherence within their lives, the same thing would naturally lead them to want to see some continuity between their inner worlds and the external world. Whatever makes people strive for harmony within their own lives would also lead them to strive to lead their lives in harmony with the external world.[42]

The third and final step in the argument is just to say that natural processes provide just such a larger context. The products of a purely natural process are ones that are, by definition, not the product of deliberate human design.[43] Things that are natural in that sense therefore provide a context of something outside of ourselves – a larger context within which we can set our own life plans and projects.[44]

The idea that what is especially valuable about the products of natural processes is that they are products of something larger than ourselves is, of course, a familiar enough theme throughout history. Its most powerful restatement among recent green writers comes in Bill McKibben's *The End of Nature*. 'We have deprived nature of its

[41] A contingent preference along these lines would suffice for my purposes, just as long as that contingency was sufficiently common and the resulting preferences socially standard ones. A bolder version of this thesis might hold that people do not just happen to want to set their lives in some larger context but, rather, are morally obliged to do so. The sort of 'humility' thus involved might be deemed a precondition for other human moral excellences – most especially, of to a capacity to appreciate the Good, as opposed merely to one's own good (Hill 1983; Elliot 1989). Passmore's (1980, pp. 28–42) denigration of environmental 'vandalism' suggests something of the same line of reasoning.

[42] Regan (1986, pp. 199–202) develops G. E. Moore's theses about 'organic unity' in an ecological context. Nozick (1981) develops similar themes in more theological directions.

[43] That definition is defended, with slight qualifications, in section 5 below.

[44] There is an intermediate case consisting of those states of affairs which are the accidental, unintended consequences of intentional human actions which are directed at other ends. For those seeking to set their lives in the context of something outside of themselves, that intermediate case is of intermediate value: less good (because less 'outside of themselves') than nature, but better (because more 'outside of themselves') than states which are the products of deliberate human design.

independence, and that is fatal to its meaning,' McKibben writes. 'Nature's independence *is* its meaning; without it there is nothing but us.' Consequently, 'We can no longer imagine that we are part of something larger than ourselves – that is what all this boils down to.'[45]

One particularly striking illustration of this theme is humanly engineered changes to the global climate. 'The greenhouse effect is', for McKibben, 'a more apt name than those who coined it imagined. . . . We have built a greenhouse, a *human creation*, where once there bloomed a sweet and wild garden.'[46] McKibben continues,

> By changing the weather, we make every spot on earth man-made and artificial. . . . A child born now will never know a natural summer, a natural autumn, winter, or spring. Summer is going extinct, replaced by something else that will be called 'summer'. This new summer will retain some of its relative characteristics – it will be hotter than the rest of the year, for instance, and the time of year when crops grow – but it will not be summer, just as even the best prosthesis is not a leg.[47]

In short, not even the weather can any longer be seen as a manifestation of some forces that are larger than ourselves.

When I join writers like McKibben in saying that we value the products of natural processes precisely because they are the products of something larger than ourselves, I trust that no questions are being begged by the word 'larger'. That is the standard way of putting the point, to be sure. But for my purposes, it would do equally well to say that the processes in question are things 'outside' of ourselves.[48] The point is merely that such natural processes, and our relation to them, serve to fix our place in the external world. They help to 'locate the self', in a deep psychological sense that matters enormously to people.[49]

To say they 'give meaning to our lives' would be to skate dangerously near thin theological ice. Some green writers, of course, have no hesitation in casting their case in explicitly spiritual terms.[50] But that

---

[45] McKibben 1989, pp. 58, 83.

[46] Ibid., p. 91.

[47] Ibid., p. 59.

[48] Or, more precisely still, those processes are things 'outside of just ourselves' – for as I go on to say in section 5 below, people are part of nature, too.

[49] Manion 1991.

[50] Many, for example, would reflect upon notions of 'stewardship' found both in the Judeo-Christian tradition (Passmore 1980, pp. 28–42) and among more explicitly green contemporaries (Leopold 1949; Spretnak 1986; McKibben 1989, pp. 70–80). For 'deep ecologists', expressions like the 'unity and diversity of life', 'oneness' and 'wholeness' often evoke more Buddhist or Hindu echos (Naess 1989, ch. 7; Sylvan 1985; Capra 1982). For historical background see Thomas (1984) and Nash (1973); for evidence of the sociological significance of the spiritualism embodied in environmentalist appeals, see Cotgrove (1976).

makes green arguments dependent upon, and (since arguments are only as strong as their weakest links) no stronger than, the arguments such writers might offer for those larger theological propositions. Those are notoriously contentious matters, on which opinion is deeply divided and knock-down arguments apparently impossible. Linking the green case to spiritual values in this way thus seems to borrow an awful lot of trouble – and unnecessarily so, as it happens.

For my part, therefore, I would wish to remain as agnostic as possible as regards any possible metaphysical load that such arguments might be asked to bear. There may or may not be any 'meaning' or 'purpose' underlying the larger natural order. There might not even be very much orderliness to the natural order. As John Stuart Mill inveighs, 'Even the lover of "order" which is thought to be a following of the ways of Nature, is in fact a contradiction of them. All which people are accustomed to deprecate as "disorder" and its consequences, is precisely a counterpart of Nature's ways. Anarchy and the Reign of Terror are overmatched in injustice, ruin, and death, by a hurricane and a pestilence.'[51] Be all that as it may, it is nonetheless undeniably true that there are forces in nature operating independently of us – and, increasingly, in spite of us. And whether people regard them as friend or foe or as being oblivious to their fate, it is nonetheless undeniably true that they derive deep satisfaction from seeing their lives as being set in some such larger contexts, however meaningless or disorderly they might be.

How all of this would impinge upon arguments for respecting nature should be clear enough. Suppose that what people value about nature's creation is that it was produced by processes larger than (or merely outside of) humanity. Then an object loses that value-imparting property once it has been restored, replicated or recreated through human interventions.[52]

[51] Mill 1874/1969, p. 386; in the more famous passage along the same lines, Mill (p. 385) writes, 'In sober truth, nearly all the things which men are hanged or imprisoned for doing to one another, are nature's every day performances. Killing, the most criminal act recognized by human laws, Nature does once to every being that lives; and in a large proportion of cases, after protracted tortures such as only the greatest monsters whom we read of ever purposely inflicted on their living fellow-creatures.'

[52] Cynics might say that we could equally fix our place in the external world by adopting, as our life's project, the destroying or taming of things outside of and larger than ourselves. This theme is not unfamiliar: frontiersmen talk in these terms of 'taming the wilderness', Marxian economists of productive labour infusing value into intrinsically worthless raw materials. But in so far as the satisfaction in view is derived from the fact that you bring under your control what was originally outside of yourself, then to that extent this project is self-defeating. The more you succeed in

Restoration may still be preferable to the alternatives. Restoring as best we can a once 'wild and scenic river' to its former glory may well be better than devising a new and wholly artificial watercourse; reclaiming waste land to create a New Forest, rather like the old that used to be there, might be better (especially after several decades of letting nature take its course) than planting a wholly artificial ornamental garden on the site. Letting clear-cut lands regenerate vegetation might be better than letting cattle or sheep continue grazing them to the ground. Given the degraded state of various environments which have been bequeathed to us, 'environmental restoration' absorbs much of the energy of the environmental movement as a whole.[53]

Nonetheless, a restored bit of nature is necessarily not as valuable as something similar that has been 'untouched by human hands'. Even if we simply stand back and 'let nature take its course' once again, and even if after several decades most of what we see is the handiwork of nature rather than of humanity, there will almost inevitably still be human residues in the final product. Even if we subsequently 'let nature take its course', *which* course it has taken will typically have been dictated by that human intervention in the causal history. To the extent that that is true, even things that are largely the product of natural regeneration are still to some (perhaps significant) degree the product of human handiwork. And they are, on the green theory of value, that much less valuable for their being so.

5 Humanity and Nature

Two related sorts of objections can easily be anticipated to the general line of argument that I have here been developing. Because they are so easily to be anticipated, and so substantively important, it is worth

bringing everything under your control, the less there is of a world that is outside of and larger than yourself in which you can set your life's work.

[53] A special issue of the *Whole Earth Review*, for example, was recently dedicated to this topic (Nilsen 1990). But this is a longstanding emphasis even within the most respectable sections of the movement. Famous as author of *A Sand County Almanac* (1949), Aldo Leopold himself served as the first director of the University of Wisconsin Arboretum, 1,280 acres of wetlands, forests and prairies 'reconstruct[ed as] . . . a sample of original Wisconsin – a sample of what [it] . . . looked like when our ancestors arrived here during the 1840s'; and through a committee chaired by his son, it became the goal of the national park system as a whole that parks be 'maintained, or where necessary recreated, as nearly as possible in the condition that prevailed when the area was first visited by the white man' (Chase 1987, pp. 37, 40).

sketching in advance my general response to each. And, as it happens, this turns out to be more than a purely negative exercise of parrying attacks. Responding to these challenges actually gives me an opportunity to develop my own positive analysis of green value theory in some practically important directions.

Both of the objections I have in view here pertain to the question of the place of humanity in nature. The second objection, which I shall address shortly, queries the artificiality of any separation between humanity and nature. People are part of nature, too, it insists – and, I think, rightly so. I think I can concede that point and still sustain all the arguments that I really want to be making here. Before addressing that issue, however, let us consider an even more predictable complaint from self-styled 'deep ecologists'.

Values and Valuers

The most stinging form that that objection might take would be to assert that, on the account of it just given, the green theory of value would reduce right back to the neoclassical welfare economic one. That complaint is all the more stinging for its being partially true. Both the neoclassical welfare economic theory and the green theory of value as I have presented it link the value of nature to the satisfaction that consumers derive from it, in one way or another.

But when I say that people derive deep satisfaction from seeing their lives being set in some larger context, 'deep' satisfaction ought not to be read simply as 'great' satisfaction. The point of calling it deep is that all other sorts of satisfaction are somehow parasitic upon this sort, in turn. People must be able to see some sense and pattern in their own lives if they are to be able to see sense or value in any other more specific project they might pursue as part of their larger life plans. And that in turn presupposes that their lives form part of something outside of themselves, individually or collectively.

Even if my version of the green theory of value does not reduce back to the neoclassical welfare economic one, though, it still seems to come down decisively on the 'shallow' side of the 'deep ecology' debate. The question at the centre of that dispute, recall, is whether natural objects have value in and of themselves or whether they have value only in relation to people and their purposes.[54]

The green theory of value, on my analysis of it, would seem to deny the former and affirm the latter. It traces the value of nature to its value

[54] See e.g. Naess 1973; 1984; 1989, esp. ch. 1 and 7; Sylvan 1985; Devall and Sessions 1985.

to human beings and the place it occupies in their lives. That conclusion runs contrary to the self-conception of most greens – certainly, at least, to the self-conceptions of the most vociferous and dedicated among them, who most assuredly see themselves as deep ecologists.[55]

Let us not allow the terms of this debate to polarize too strongly too quickly, though. Most of all, let us not allow the debate to be decided by cheap rhetorical tricks. Surely, we might naively assume, anyone who genuinely cares about the environment should be a deep ecologist. Surely 'shallow' ecologists are simply lacking in moral fibre; they are just insufficiently committed to the cause. Surely that follows straightforwardly, just from the meaning of the terms 'shallow' and 'deep' respectively. Or at least so greens suppose, I suspect, in signing so unanimously and so firmly on to the principles of deep ecology.

But if that is all there is to the argument, then it is an argument that works just through a 'persuasive definitions' alone. Were the description of each respective position actually warranted, then the conclusion that true greens should shun shallow ecology would indeed follow straightforwardly. After all, who would embrace a shallow view of any subject which one genuinely cares about, when a deeper view is available?[56]

The question, though, is whether or not the description really is warranted. Implicit in the shallow/deep dichotomy is, in effect, an assertion that the deeper view of the matter contains all the truths of the shallower view, plus some additional ones as well. The truth of the matter is, of course, otherwise. The shallow view is in no sense a proper subset of the deep one. Rather, the two are simply *different* views. Which is the right view is, therefore, a genuinely open question. And I see no reason, in principle, why greens themselves – once they have overcome the prejudicially loaded language involved in the deep ecology debate – should not be prepared to consider shallower versions of the deep ecology creed.

That last phrase has been cast in comparative terms quite deliberately. In assessing these issues, it is important to realize that there are a great many gradations of shallowness and depth, here as elsewhere. The deepest ecology, perhaps, would be one claiming that things have value quite independently of the existence of any conscious valuers. Thus, the deepest ecologists would say, it would be wrong for the 'last person' left

---

[55] See e.g. Spretnak and Capra 1986, ch. 2; Sylvan 1985; Naess 1989; Luke 1988; Stone 1987. For an indication of how widespread this view is, see Davis's (1989) *Ecophilosophy: A Field Guide to the Literature*.

[56] As Brian Barry (1989, p. 303) complained of a similar rhetorical trick in Steven Lukes's 'three-dimensional analysis of power': who would want a one- or two-dimensional analysis of anything when a three-dimensional analysis was on offer?

on earth to push the nuclear button to destroy all non-human creation as that person was about to expire.[57] Conversely, the shallowest ecologist – an economist, perhaps – would say that things can have value only in relation to human uses, and things should be saved (if at all) only for possible subsequent human use. In between those extremes are a variety of intermediate positions.

The green theory of value that I have been advancing here is one such halfway house. It does indeed entail the proposition that things can only have value *in relation to* us'. But that is very different from the proposition, favoured by the shallowest ecologist-cum-economist, that things can 'only have value *to* us' or '*for* us'.[58] Saying that things can have value only in relation to us is very different from saying that the value of nature reduces to purely human interests.[59]

The proposition I am advancing asserts merely that: (1) values presuppose valuers, that valuing presupposes consciousness; and, perhaps slightly more tendentiously, (2) human beings are the only beings on earth with a 'sufficiently sophisticated consciousness' for this purpose.[60] That being so, it is necessarily the case that 'human beings figure essentially' in deriving value from nature. But to say that the

[57] Routley and Routley 1980, pp. 121–2; Attfield (1983, p. 155) adapts the story to involve merely the destruction of the 'last surviving elm tree', which he thinks 'most people' still think 'would be wrong'. This is not necessarily to say that the non-human world has 'objective value independent of human consciousness'. The appeal could be to transworld evaluation, with the presence of human consciousness in some other world, W2, forming the basis for the value judgement that it would be wrong for the last person to destroy world W1 as that person departed from it. But what of the *last* last person? Would it be all right for *that* person to destroy the world as that person expired, on the grounds that once that person is gone there is no other human consciousness present in any other then-existing world to impart value to what would be left behind? Presumably those who think it wrong for the last person in the original argument to destroy the world would be equally opposed to the last last person doing so, which (unless they want to run a broadly discredited line about posthumous valuation, cf. Feinberg 1974/1980, pp. 173–6) means that they really are committed to a strong thesis about nature's having objective value independently of human consciousness.

[58] Regan 1986, p. 203.

[59] That is to say, our ethics and our theories of value can be 'human centred' without being 'human instrumental', to employ the useful terms suggested in Dobson (1990, pp. 63–72). Cf. Routley and Routley 1979.

[60] There is an interesting analogy here to contemporary philosophical treatments of 'secondary qualities', like colour for example. There is a longstanding dispute between Realists who say redness is an objective property of things (reflecting light of so many Angstrom units, or whatever) and Idealists who suppose that redness is a purely subjective property in the eye of the perceiver. The halfway house currently much in fashion is to say that secondary qualities like colour are instead 'relational', intimately involving both objective attributes and subjective dispositions.

Good of nature can only be realized through interactions with human consciousness is not to say that nature is 'good' merely because it is, in some crassly material way or even in some deeply spiritual way either, 'good for' the human beings involved.[61]

So much for distinguishing my view from that of the shallowest ecologist. Now let me say something less purely defensively and more positively to suggest how my view might be regarded as at least moderately deep. In contrast to the claims of the most shallow ecologists, it is not my view that values are all in people's heads. The existence of people, as valuers, may be crucial in imparting value. But some feature of nature, existing independently of human beings, is crucial in this process, also. Just as you cannot reduce the value of nature wholly to natural values (as the deepest ecologists might attempt), neither can you reduce the value of nature wholly to human values (as the shallowest ecologists would wish). There are two independent factors at work here.

On my analysis, natural objects have certain value-imparting characteristics. They actually create value when – *only* when – in the presence of (human) consciousness. But those characteristics of nature that, on my analysis, are crucial in imparting value is the characteristic of something 'being part of something larger than/outside of ourselves'. That characteristic, by definition, must necessarily be separate from and independent of humanity. Hence, those value-imparting properties (if not the values themselves) exist independently of humanity. And that, I submit, is sufficient to qualify mine as at least a 'moderately deep ecology'.

Humanity as Part of Nature

So much for the first easily foreseen objection to my analysis of the green theory of value. Let us now consider a second objection, still very much a variation on the general theme of the place of humanity in nature.

One way of describing the green theory of value I have been advancing is to say – as I have myself been saying, as a convenient kind of shorthand – that it attaches special value to those parts of natural creation that have been untouched by human hands. But 'human hands', it might reasonably be objected, are part of the natural order too. When someone insists that some bit of the landscape should be untouched by human hands, that is not to insist that nature be kept

[61] Regan 1986, p. 203. Perhaps Rolston (1981; 1985; 1988) is trying to get at something similar.

separate from something unnatural. Rather, it is to insist that one part of nature be kept separate from another.

The problem, notice, is not the relatively trivial definitional one. It is not that we cannot make meaningful distinctions between these two different aspects of nature. We might easily enough distinguish a sense of the term 'nature' according to which it would refer 'only to what takes place without the agency, or without the voluntary and intentional agency, of man'.[62]

The challenge is not to draw some such distinction between the results of human and of non-human (stipulatively 'natural') processes. The challenge is instead to justify attaching any moral importance to the distinction, thus drawn. According to the green theory it is the naturalness of the process that imparts value. But if so, then why is the sort of voluntary, intentional agency associated with *human* nature any less natural – or hence any less valuable – than other aspects of the natural order?

Only those with a very strong sense of humanity's very special place in the order of creation could fail to feel the force of this objection. Yet the objection, if allowed free rein, would threaten to license wanton human destruction of (other parts of) the natural environment, on the grounds that anything that humans do is natural, too. If as Mill says, 'human nature cannot help conforming to Nature', then it follows that 'everything we do is part of nature . . . in that primary sense', as one contemporary philosopher has inferred.[63] The upshot would be to license wanton human destruction of (other parts of) the natural environment, on the grounds that anything that humans do is natural, too. That, clearly, cannot be right. Clearly, I think, we ought be seeking some middle ground in this dispute.

One form this middle ground might take is to say that if we respect and value the products of natural creation, then we ought take steps to protect that natural creation from destruction – even by natural forces. We should, on that account, dam the Colorado River above the Grand Canyon so that it does not undo through future flooding all the wonderful work that it has done through past erosion; or we should artificially reinforce the lip of Niagara Falls so that the Niagara River

---

[62] Following Mill 1874/1969, p. 375. See similarly Passmore (1975) and Frankel (1976).
[63] Mill 1874/1969, p. 380; Sober 1986, p. 180 (the passage appears in italics in the original). For an evocative albeit unphilosophical retort, see McKibben (1989, pp. 64–8).

does not eat away at the perfect horseshoe falls that its cascading water has created through past erosion.[64]

That line is not altogether appealing, though. For one thing, it attaches evaluative significance to a distinction between creation and destruction in a way which seems wholly unwarranted, even within its own theoretical terms.[65] On the green theory of value, what imparts value to an outcome is just the naturalness of the historical process through which it has come about. On that account, two outcomes that have come about through equally natural processes ought be equally valuable. There seems no room in that model for distinguishing further between outcomes that are constructive or destructive, between ones that result in some object's existing that did not before or ones that result in some object's disappearing or disintegrating or increasing in entropy.

In an unjustifiably neglected essay on 'Nature', John Stuart Mill poses the problem for us in an unusually stark form. Either humans are part of nature, too – in which case the results of human interventions are as natural as the state of things before humans intervened – or else whatever humans do to nature necessarily counts (from the human perspective at least) as an improvement on nature. Mill's own words are worth quoting at length on this point:

> If the natural course of things were perfectly right and satisfactory, to act at all [to improve upon nature] would be gratuitous meddling. . . . If the artificial is not better than the natural, to what end are all the acts of life? To dig, to plough, to build, to wear clothes, are direct infringements of the injunction to follow nature. . . .[But] everybody professes to admire many great triumphs of Art over Nature: the junction by bridges of shores which Nature has made separate, the draining of Nature's marshes, the excavation of her wells, the dragging to light of what she has buried at immense depths in the earth; the turning away of her thunderbolts by lightening rods, of her inundations by embankments, of her ocean by breakwaters. But to commend these and similar feats, is to acknowledge that the ways of Nature are to be conquered, not obeyed. . . . All praise of Civilization, or Art, or Contrivance, is so much dispraise of Nature; an

---

[64] Indeed, if human creation is natural too, then on this account stopping humans from destroying ancient monuments and historical landmarks that past humans have created is just part and parcel of preventing naturally created values from being naturally destroyed.

[65] Notice that the self-defeatingness objection, canvassed in note 52 above, does not generalize as an objection to all destruction. The point there was merely that humanity is destroying its own source of satisfaction, in so far as satisfaction is derived from destroying things only if they have been created by non-human forces. If instead humanity could derive similar satisfaction from destruction *per se* (of human as of non-human creation, equally) then we really would have the basis for a perpetual-motion satisfaction machine.

admission of imperfection, which it is man's business, and merit, to be
always – endeavouring to correct or mitigate.[66]

Now, I suspect that the automatic first response, of greens or anyone
else, to Mill's dilemma would be to deny its second premise. There is no
reason to believe that every human intervention improves the world.
Nor is there is any compelling reason – in logic, still less in recent
experience – to suppose even that all human interventions taken
together make for a better world than would have existed absent such
interventions. Nor can we even be confident that any given intervention
will have had consequences that are on balance beneficial when all is
said and done, in light of the various knock-on effects that any action
will inevitably have into the distant future.

Thus, we can easily enough avoid being impaled on the horns of Mill's
dilemma by pointing out that there is a third possibility which Mill
himself has missed. That amounts to admitting that human interventions
are not natural – but then going on to point out that, contrary to Mill's
supposition, being non-natural does not necessarily ensure that they will
constitute improvements upon nature, either.

That argument is true and important. And it is, in itself, more than
enough to defuse Mill's dilemma. But there is another way of evading
Mill's dilemma that is even more in keeping with the green theory of
value that I have been developing here. Whereas the reply just given
basically queries the second of Mill's premises, this alternative reply
queries the first.

Greens might say that, yes, humans are part of nature. But greens
might go on to say, not everything that human beings do – not all forms
of human society, not all forms of human activity – are *equally* natural.
Some may be more natural than others. And if so, then some forms of
human society and human activity would actually be more valuable than
others, purely on the basis of a green theory of value that assigns more
value to the natural over the artificial.

That is the version of the argument which I want to explore here at
greater length. It is important to recognize that humanity is part of
nature and that human interventions are natural, too. But surely it is
wrong to leap from that to treating all human interventions as if they
were equally natural. We want to make – and, if I am right about it, the
green theory of value allows us to make – some important distinctions
between different modes of human intervention.

As a start, let us consider the case of the English hedgerows. Groups
like the Council for the Protection of Rural England are much exercised

[66] Mill 1874/1969, pp. 380–1.

to prevent hedgerows from being ploughed under in order to merge small fields and make them more amenable to modern, mechanized farming methods. But those hedgerows, like many of the other aspects of the natural environment that conservationists most cherish, are not in fact purely the work of (non-human) natural forces.

We might, of course, value hedgerows for a variety of instrumental reasons. They provide habitats for a considerable amount of wildlife that would otherwise be disappear, and so on. Conservationists would of course make much of those instrumental arguments in framing their case for hedgerow preservation. But over and above those instrumental reasons for preserving hedgerows, they want to claim that we would be destroying something intrinsically valuable about the English countryside by eradicating all the hedgerows.

The thing to notice, in the context of the present argument, is that that 'intrinsically valuable' aspect of the countryside is in no sense a natural part of the countryside. Hedgerows are human artefacts – not just in the weaker sense of being residual by-products of the places where humans choose to plough and where they do not, but also in the stronger sense of being quite deliberate, intentional human creations. Hedgerows and the peculiar habitats associated with them simply did not exist before human cultivation. They were created, intentionally, as part of a deliberate policy of clearing the primordial forests and of carving up and fencing off the commons. So what conservationists today are wanting to preserve as part of the quintessentially English environment is not the product of nature but rather the product of past phases of English society.

The same can obviously be said in trumps for other aspects of English villages – ancient churches, old houses and suchlike – that such conservationist groups would also want to preserve. They would less often phrase those claims in terms of protecting the environment, perhaps.[67] But the arguments given for preservation of the surrounding hedgerows are obviously of a cloth with the arguments given for preservation of the village green and surrounding structures.

Ancient monuments of that sort can obviously qualify for protection on account of their *historical* value. They might qualify for protection on account of their *ethnographic* value, as representative of dead or dying cultures. The question before us is to what extent they can qualify for protection on account of value derived from their being part of *nature*, somehow construed.

---

[67] Though the phrase 'built environment' is indeed in common currency, among these groups just as much as among centre-city architects.

These things were all shaped by human hands rather than natural forces, to be sure. So they do not, on the face of things, qualify for the strong sort of special status, described by the green theory of value above. People cannot set their lives in the context of something larger than themselves if that context is merely one which they have themselves created.

That argument might move a little too fast, though, in sliding between individual and group levels of analysis. If the issue is merely one of setting your own life in the context of something larger than yourself, then setting it in the context of any history larger than your own personal history can qualify.[68] The history of your group – race, club, nation, species – could count as that. Hence, things that have value on account of their (purely human) history might well derive value from a source *akin* to, if not strictly identical to, that imparting value to naturally occurring objects in the non-human world.

There is, then, a case to be made for the conservation of things in general on account of their history, whether human or natural. That provides an argument which is both intellectually important and politically powerful for the preservation of ancient monuments and historical landmarks.[69] I do not want to say anything here to undermine that case. Rather, I want to supplement it with yet another.[70]

The distinction that will prove crucial for this further argument is between forms of human society in which people live broadly in harmony with nature and ones which attempt to impose upon and tyrannize over nature. An example of the former is the small-scale, close-to-the-land culture of the medieval English cultivator, as represented by the traditional English village, its church, houses and hedgerows.[71] An example of the latter is Los Angeles: a megalopolis of several million so inappropriately sited on a semi-arid plain that it can provide its citizens with adequate water only by piping it in from hundreds of

---

[68] Or, indeed, just setting your own life in the context of that of your group as a whole – its plans and projects every bit as much as its history – could serve the same purpose. To some extent, the case for environmental protection is itself justified in just such terms, as in Sagoff's (1988, ch. 6) discussion of 'Nature and the national ideal'.

[69] Golding and Golding 1979.

[70] Which I think will generally, if not invariably, tend towards the same practical conclusions. Not invariably, though, because many of the ancient monuments in question might be regarded as every bit as much triumphs of the human will over natural barriers as is the city of Los Angeles.

[71] All is relative here, however, Compared to the original inhabitants of New England, colonial settlers attempting to reproduce English village life are the tyrants who are guilty of bending nature to their will (Merchant 1989).

miles away.[72] Or, if that contrast is too stark to grasp firmly, consider the contrast between the English landscape garden and French formal gardens of the same period: although both were intentional human creations, one attempted to harmonize with nature while the other superimposed its own order upon it.[73]

Green commentators are certainly sensitive to such distinctions. 'An ecological policy', according to the 1983 manifesto of the German Greens, 'means understanding ourselves and our environment as part of nature', which would lead, in turn, to 'an all-encompassing rejection of an economy of exploitation and the uncontrolled pillage of natural resources and raw materials, as well as refraining from destructive intervention in the circuits of the natural ecosystem'.[74] Similarly, 'ecological wisdom' according to the North American greens' *Ten Key Values* amounts to appreciating 'that we are *part* of nature, not on top of it'.[75]

The temptation at this point is of course to say that one mode of life is more 'natural' than the other, and on the green theory more valuable in consequence. In attempting to give the flavour of this response to Mill's challenge, I have (as a kind of shorthand, once again) been speaking this way myself. But, in the end, I think a slightly more nuanced response really is going to be required.

Certainly English village life requires less – though, in the end, nonetheless considerable – human intervention into various natural processes in order to sustain it. But if humanity is to be regarded as part of nature, then there can be no grounds for disparaging as 'artificial' the interventions required to sustain civilization (if it can be called that) in Los Angeles. Human interventions are required, to be sure: the natural rainfall and river flow and water table are not adequate to meet the demands of the population now resident there. But, on this analysis, there is nothing artificial about human interventions. They are part of nature, too.

What we can still say, I think, is this. People who live more in harmony with nature – in traditional English villages, rather than postmodern Los Angeles – are living more in a context that is outside of themselves, individually or even collectively. Even those who merely

[72] Reisner 1986. Lest this be thought a peculiarly American – or peculiarly capitalist – form of megalomania, reflect upon the reports that Soviet planning agencies were at least seriously contemplating building a string of nuclear power plants with the explicit purpose of reversing the direction of flow of various north-flowing rivers to make them water the dry regions of the south (Zile 1982, pp. 206–7).

[73] Mukerji 1990.

[74] Die Grünen 1986, sec. 1, p. 7. See further Spretnak and Capra 1986, p. 33.

[75] Green CoC 1986, item 1.

visit those places from time to time are reminded, by the existence of such places, of that larger context in which they might see (if not live) their own lives. Places and peoples embodying such down-to-earth lifestyles are well worth preserving and conserving (or indeed creating or recreating, if they have been lost) as a means of providing everyone, whether directly party to them or not, of this larger perspective on their own lives.

All that can be claimed without claiming that St Mary Mead is more 'natural' than Los Angeles or hedgerows are more natural than freeways.[76] What is at issue is not the naturalness of its creation, since humanity is part of nature, and its creations are therefore natural too. What is at issue instead, on this account, is the modesty of its creation. It is not that, in the one, nature is 'in better balance'.[77] It is rather that, in the one case, humanity does not ride roughshod over other parts of nature. And that allows humanity to derive satisfaction from reflection upon its larger setting, in a way that it cannot where that larger setting is more exclusively of its own creation.

Saying that the small-scale English village is 'more in harmony with nature' is simply to say that it represents a form of life that is better, from the green perspective, than does a postmodern megalopolis. But 'better' is, of course, very different from 'best'. If our choice is between St Mary Mead or Los Angeles, then the former is clearly the option to be preferred. And that is, indeed, the form in which the choice is typically presented to us. But it should go without saying that there is nothing in this argument to suggest that, if faced with a choice between preserving pristine nature and grubbing it out to build even the most harmonious small-scale village development, we should of course prefer the former to the latter option in *that* pair.

Even with those caveats in place, environmentalists might still be hesitant to retreat quite so far as this. One particularly striking example recalls the great debate in Australia in the early 1980s over the

[76] John Passmore has suggested to me that the one is 'natural' in a way the other is not because in the one case the things being artificially introduced are themselves living natural objects (trees, shrubs and so on). But the materials out of which a freeway is constructed are, or at least originally were, natural objects too. Nor can the fact that the one involves living organisms in a way the other does not make all the difference, since a living ecosystem of sorts grows up on the verges of the freeway just as in the interstices of the hedgerow. The difference really does, I think, have to be cast in terms of 'forms of society' as a whole. It is (oddly enough, perhaps) at that macrosociological level that we can best talk about living in harmony with nature.

[77] It may well be more 'natural' for nature to be perpetually out of balance, displaying wild cycles with great regularity.

Tasmanian proposal to dam the Franklin River below the Gordon.[78] Environmentalists cherished that part of the Tasmanian rain forest as genuine wilderness – a primordial part of the Australian landscape untouched by human hands. The then-new Hawke government was sympathetic to their cause, but damming rivers was under the constitution strictly a matter for the states. If the Commonwealth wanted to save the rain forest, it would have to find some grounds for claiming jurisdiction in the matter. The most promising turned out to be to appeal to international treaty obligations; the best way to do that turned out to be to get the area listed as a World Heritage site; and that turned out to depend, in large part, upon evidence of early human habitation on the site.

When anthropologists supplied just such evidence, though, their findings were greeted with considerable ambivalence among environmentalists. At one and the same time, environmentalists recognized the pragmatic importance of demonstrating human habitation on the site, but they also deeply wished that that was not so. There was a side of environmentalists that said that, in so far as the site is not really pristine nature after all, it is to that extent not so very much worth preserving after all. And I suspect that there is a similar side to almost every environmentalist. Most, I suspect, would be tempted to equate 'unspoilt nature' with 'that part of nature that is *literally* untouched by human hands'.

One moral of the Franklin-below-Gordon story would be to say that insisting upon that would be to set the standard too high. There is virtually nowhere of which we can say that with confidence. The more important moral of the story, deriving from my larger theoretical argument, is that that is not an unacceptably bitter moral for environmentalists to swallow. For them to insist upon nature's being 'literally untouched by human hands' would be to set the standard unnecessarily high. If what we value about nature is that it allows us to see our own lives in some larger context, then we need not demand that that nature be *literally* untouched by human hands. We need demand merely that it have been touched only *lightly* – or if you prefer, *lovingly* – by them.

Some cultures, including earlier periods of our own cultures, have managed to live in harmony with nature rather than trying to dominate nature and bend and subordinate it to their will. Those cultures still shaped nature, in various ways, through their interactions with it. But they do so respectfully, and in a way that allowed nature to retain some

[78] This is a tale told me by the distinguished Australian prehistorian, John Mulvaney. It is retold in Griffiths (1991) and Mulvaney (1991).

real independence from humanity. And that, in turn, allows nature to retain its valued role for us.

This conclusion is particularly important in a setting – like Australia, or even Arizona – where so much of the case for environmental preservation is couched in terms of respect for the attitudes towards the land of the aboriginal inhabitants and their contemporary heirs. There is not an inch of the continent that is without meaning to the original Australians – not an inch that has not been incorporated into their legends, and perhaps not an inch that has not been touched by their hands at some point over the course of their long habitation.[79] That fact would come as desperately bad news to environmental purists who infer that there is not an inch of the continent that is pristine nature untouched by human hands. But recalling the attitude that the original inhabitants, both in Australia and the Americas, took towards the land that they knew so well, there is no need to see it as having been somehow contaminated by their touch in the way that it might have been by the the hand of more domineering subsequent settlers.

6   Green Corollaries

I should admit straightaway that the green theory of value described above is my own invention. Anyway, it is *largely* my own invention. Some writers, describing and defending green positions, do sometimes talk in similar – sometimes very similar – ways. Others, however, cast the green case in what would seem to be very different terms indeed. They put what would appear to be very different values at centre stage. They apparently want to relegate what I regard as central to what would seem to be, at most, bit roles.

Now, I cast the green case in the terms I do because I believe – and think I can show, in chapters 3 and 4 below – that that is the strongest way to make the case. A green political programme cast in those terms is the logically most compelling; and (as I shall argue in chapter 5, section 1 below) being logically compelling in these ways might just, for once, translate into its being politically compelling, too. Thus, in so far as my analysis of the core of green political theory is genuinely revisionary, so be it. If what I am proposing is a radical revision rather than a mere restatement of green values, then it is a revision that it would be politically prudent for greens to adopt forthwith.

---

[79] As Jones (1991) suggests may well be the case.

Having made that plain, though, I now want to go on to show that a great many of the most familiar ways of putting the green case can in fact be accommodated to my own way of talking. The green theory of value I have elaborated above is, in fact, capable of subsuming many of the more standard green themes. Or, where it does not actually subsume them, it isolates the most defensible – and the most distinctively green – core of those more familiar propositions.

Postmaterialism

One way of characterizing green politics is to say that they, like the 'new social movements' more generally, are a manifestation of 'postmaterial values'. That characterization comes most commonly from survey-driven social psychologists, anxious to find developmental sequences in political attitudes akin to the various other 'stages of development' that are their stock in trade.[80] But the 'postmaterialist' characterization of green politics has a certain ethical resonance as well, especially for those of a vaguely Stoic bent who suppose that there is something innately virtuous in the renunciation of unnecessary material comforts.[81]

Impressive statistics can be offered in support of the more sociological side of this claim. It really does seem to be a whole set of social attitudes that hang together in people's heads and that comes to the fore only after their more material needs have been tolerably well satisfied.[82] Perceived scarcity and limits to growth may well be what occasioned green political movements.[83] But paradoxically, those perceptions seem sociologically most common – or anyway, motivationally most compelling – among those who enjoy comfortably high levels of consumption.[84] Such, anyway, is the sociology of the phenomenon of green politics.

Of course, factor analysis of public opinion surveys merely reveals patterns in people's attitudes. It does not explain them (except in so far

[80] The phrase was coined by Inglehart (1977), following Maslow (1954).

[81] Thus, tellingly, prominent German social theorists as well as empirical sociologists, writing about the greens, invoke Inglehart's name and theories; see Habermas (1981, p. 33) and Offe (1985, pp. 832ff.)

[82] In Inglehart's (1977, p. 46) original ten-nation study of the US and Western Europe, 'postmaterialism' amounted to worrying about having more say in government and on the job, having freedom of speech and beautiful cities, for example, rather than fighting crime, inflation or foreign enemies. But political-sociological studies of 'environmentalism' in Britain have decisively tied concern with the natural environment into that attitudinal complex (Cotgrove 1976; 1982; Cotgrove and Duff 1980; cf. Lowe and Rüdig 1986).

[83] Note, for example, Ophuls's (1977) title, *Ecology and the Politics of Scarcity*.

[84] See Goodin (1976, pp. 168–71) for further discussion of the distributional aspects of environmental concern.

as an explanatory sketch is implicit in the very act of assigning a name to a cluster of attitudes). Still less does factor analysis purport to offer any moral justifications for the complex attitudes that it reveals.[85] For justifications, especially, we need to look to other disciplinary traditions.

Viewed from an ethical perspective, the answers to such queries are readily at hand, though. It is not at all hard to see why green politics should indeed be a 'postmaterial' phenomenon, given my account of its underlying ethical premises. Green political theory rests, I have argued, upon a particular theory of value. It tells what is valuable in life and what is not. It speaks to issues of the quality of our lives. It tells us how to lead the good life.

By its very nature, though, such a theory of value can come to the fore only after the prerequisites of life itself have been secured. Logically, living comes before living well. It makes little sense to worry about the quality of life before we are reasonably certain of life itself.

Thus, both sociologically and intellectually, it only stands to reason that green politics should emerge only after – and only among those for whom – the material conditions of life itself have been pretty well secured. Sociologically, they are the ones who can afford the luxury of worrying about the quality of life. They are the ones for whom quality of life is the next item on their agenda. Intellectually, the content of their concerns is properly described as 'postmaterial' since it reflects worries about the value and meaning of life rather than the material prerequisites of life itself.

Although green values can truly be described as 'postmaterial', so too can much else. 'Postmaterial' describes values in terms of what they are not. Any values that affect indifference to the more materialistic side of politics – issues of economic management and suchlike – would qualify as postmaterial. Green values as here characterized would qualify. But so too would various others.[86]

For that reason, it seems better to regard postmaterialism as a corollary of green political theory rather than the other way around. A green theory of value, through its emphasis on questions of value that can emerge only after questions of material existence have been pretty well settled, can explain why a different set of values should come to predominate at later stages of socioeconomic development. Being green

[85] Quite the contrary, social psychology tends to deal in terms of 'causes' rather than 'reasons' for people's behaviour. It rather suggests that people's adopting one set of values rather than another is something to be explained, sociologically, rather than justified, morally.

[86] Note the various not-particularly-green values at work in Bookchin's (1971) *Post-scarcity Anarchism*, for example.

explains, sociologically, why people are – and, ethically, why they should be – postmaterialists. Merely being postmaterialist in the sense of merely having the material prerequisites of life satisfied cannot in and of itself explain, either sociologically or still less morally, why people should adopt green values. There are many things they could start worrying about, once they no longer have to worry where their next meal is coming from. It takes something beyond mere postmaterialism – green value theory – to tell them that it should be green values, rather than macramé.

Irreplaceability

Many informed commentators would say that the greens owe their electoral success, in no small part, to the persuasiveness of a particular 'vision of political rationality' based on 'avoiding irreparable and irreversible catastrophes'.[87] The environmental ethic quite generally is commonly characterized as a rule requiring, first and foremost, the protection and preservation of irreplaceable assets.[88] Exhaustible natural resources, once used up, cannot be replaced.[89] From that fact it follows that we ought to be particularly careful in using up such resources. At the very least, we should husband them more carefully – use them up more slowly – than other resources that are renewable and constantly being replaced.[90] Some commentators (resource economists, most typically) recommend simply that we use up irreplaceable resources more slowly than replaceable ones.[91] Others (philosophers, most typically) insist that we do not destroy them at all, in so far as possible. Or, more modestly, they insist that there is always a presumption – a *prima facie* reason – for not destroying what is truly irreplaceable.[92]

[87] Offe 1983, p. 46.

[88] I have myself characterized it like this in a previous paper (Goodin 1983) on which much of the discussion of this section is based.

[89] At least they cannot be replaced by any human devices – and natural processes operating on geologic time scales are too slow to be of much help to us in the here and now.

[90] Or, more precisely, are being renewed more quickly – the pace at which the oxygen we use up is reproduced by photosynthesis is radically different from the pace at which nature is replacing the oil and natural gas we use up.

[91] Hotelling 1931; Dasgupta and Heal 1979; Fisher 1981, chs 2 and 3.

[92] Goodin 1983. But perhaps that is just a philosopher's way of putting the economist's (Arrow and Fisher 1974; Fisher 1981, ch. 5) point that destruction of assets truly irreplaceable always entails the loss of an 'option value' necessarily lodged in those assets.

The concept of irreplaceability that figures so crucially in these arguments is a tricky one, though.[93] Intuitively, to say that things are replaceable one by the other is to say that they are interchangeable. But that does not necessarily mean that they are absolutely identical in every respect. To say that one thing is an adequate (indeed, a 'perfect') replacement for another is merely to say that it can take the place and perform the function of the other, perfectly substituting for it for the purposes at hand.

Thus characterized, though, the notion of replaceability has a largely subjective component. It is not a purely objective matter of finding objects that are objectively identical in all (or even most) respects to one another. To be replaceable one for the other, things need not be identical in all (or indeed any) of their objective attributes; they need merely be able to perform the same function, however differently they may accomplish that. For what counts as an adequate replacement depends on the purposes for which we want them and the functions that we want them to perform. And that, of course, is essentially a question of our subjective preferences.

The practical consequences of this formulation of the notion of replaceability are considerable. Were replaceability to be characterized in strongly objective terms – were we to demand that two things had to be absolutely identical in every respect before the one could be a 'perfect replacement' for the other – then everything would be irreplaceable. Nothing is exactly like anything else in absolutely every respect. But if replaceability is characterized in basically subjective terms of one thing's serving the same purposes equally well, then many resources that we might intuitively regard as irreplaceable are not. So long as there are 'close substitutes' – good functional equivalents – then anything might be regarded as replaceable. Thus, both economists and philosophers can be found saying that oil is a replaceable resource, not in the sense that we can make more of it ourselves but rather in the sense that improved technology can enable future generations to do the same things (make the same products) with less oil.[94]

Not content with this perfectly proper watering down of the notion of replaceability, some economists would go further still. They insist that it is fetishistic for us to focus on particular goods or particular processes. To do so is to treat what is actually a mere means as if it were an end in

[93] The best single account is Martin (1979); see also Goodin (1983). Perhaps for that reason economists sometimes prefer to talk in the apparently more technically tractable terms of the 'irreversibility' of the processes by which such resources are exhausted; see Arrow and Fisher (1974).

[94] Krutilla 1967, pp. 777–8; Barry 1983.

itself. Our ultimate goal is, or ought to be, couched in terms of the impact of our policies on people's utility.[95] And what it would be for something to be a good substitute or a good replacement for something else is, in those terms, just a matter of its yielding the same utility to people. Replacing something you have destroyed is, in those terms, just a matter of substituting something of equivalent value – however different it might, in every other respect, be from that which you have destroyed. And, depending perhaps on just how 'value' is here construed, that might be very easy indeed.

On this weakest of all notions of replaceability, nothing is in principle irreplaceable. There is no longer any need to seek functional equivalents for what is being replaced. Everything substitutes for everything else under the influence of the universal solvent of utility. Everything trades for everything else under the common measuring rod of money. At a personal level, monetary damage awards compensate for, and in utility terms therefore replace, a widow's dead spouse – to 'make her whole' again, in the delightful phrase of tort law.[96] At a societal level, the extra GNP produced from cheap hydroelectricity is compensation for, and in utility terms therefore replaces, the glorious canyon that was flooded by the building of the dam.

If environmentalists are to resist those conclusions, and to rescue a notion of irreplaceability that has any practical bite to it, they must resist the suggestion that utility is some sort of universal solvent. They must deny the economist's proposition that two things that yield the same utility level – the same quantum of human satisfaction – can substitute perfectly well for one another, however different they may otherwise be.[97]

In making that case, they are aided by a central feature of the economist's own logic. Utility, remember, is purely subjective. It is for people themselves to say what makes them happy and how happy it makes them. By the same token, it is for people themselves to say whether in their own private utility functions they partition satisfactions according to their sources. It is for people themselves to say whether the satisfactions derived from cheap electricity are equivalent to the satisfactions derived from viewing the canyon that would have to be flooded to provide it. And, crucially, it is for people themselves to say whether the satisfaction gains in one column – though equally

---

[95] Or preference satisfaction or well-being or whatever formulation you prefer.

[96] For discussion of notions of compensability in tort law, see Goodin (1989).

[97] For further discussion of these issues see Goodin (1983; 1989), upon which the following comments are largely based.

'satisfying', in some sense – can really substitute for the satisfactions lost in the other.

That is essentially an empirical question, of course. As an empirical fact, it seems that most people do not regard all goods as interchangeable and substitutable for one another in the ways that that would suggest. Most people appreciate, as one economist wryly put it, that 'bread cannot save someone from dying of thirst' and 'living in a luxurious palace does not constitute a substitute for food.'[98]

Clearly, then, not everything is substitutable for everything else through the medium of utility. And a corollary of that fact is the further fact that some things are irreplaceable. A particularly effective way to bring this point home to economists is to remind them of the disparity between the 'ransom value' of things and their 'insurance value'. Take the case of family snapshots, or mastectomies. People typically go to a lot of trouble and expense to prevent losing their family mementos to fire or their breasts to the surgeon's knife. But the same people would typically spend far less insuring against those losses. The reason for the disparity has to do with the irreplaceability of the things. It is precisely because money cannot take the place, for them, of their breast or of lost pictures of their children that people do not bother insuring against those losses heavily, even though they would be willing to spend heavily to avoid those losses in the first place.[99]

As those examples suggest, though, there are many things that people might regard as irreplaceable and especially valuable on that account. Furthermore, the general tenor of this discussion – following economists' own – has been to suggest that whether or not something is irreplaceable is a matter of subjective taste. People might take this attitude towards any of the goods that they want, or towards none of them. According to economists, irreplaceability is purely an artefact of quirks of people's preferences.

The green theory of value I have sketched above has a particularly important role to play in both these respects. It explains why some things – and why products of natural processes, in particular – should be regarded as irreplaceable, in just such ways. It traces the peculiar value

---

[98] Georgescu-Roegen 1954, p. 516. See similarly Lancaster's (1967; 1971) 'new consumer theory', arguing that it is the underlying 'characteristics' of goods – what purposes they can serve – rather than goods themselves from which utility is derived and over which utility functions are defined. Sen (1977, p. 335) similarly inveighs against traditional utility theory's having 'too little structure'. Like Lancaster, Sen (1985) distinguishes between 'commodities' and the 'capabilities' that they bestow; and people's reluctance to trade those off for one another gives rise, in Sen's (1980–1) terms, to 'plural utilities'.

[99] Cook and Graham 1977; Zeckhauser 1975, p. 454.

of naturally occurring properties of things to the history of their creation by processes outside ourselves. And both of those valued components – both the thing's history and the process of its creation – are not reproducible by intentional human interventions.

History, by its nature, is necessarily irreproducible. Very talented hydraulic engineers might manage to rush water over another valley in just the right way to create another canyon looking ever so much like the Grand Canyon that was carved by the Colorado. But even if it is identical in every outward respect, that canyon will have the wrong history for us to value it as we do the Grand Canyon, as something created by forces outside of our control. The very intentionality of the human intervention makes the process – and hence the history – wrong in that regard.

All of that is merely to say that humanity cannot create new things to substitute for bits of nature that have been destroyed. It does not deny that there might be some already existing bits of nature that can substitute for one another, when any one of them has been destroyed.

That, I submit, is why the protection of endangered species is so much more important to greens than the protection of particular specimens. For purposes of setting our lives in some larger context, what is crucial is, I would suggest, that there be some blue whales, not that there be any particular number of them. Any one blue whale can, for that purpose, substitute for any other – or any number of others – that have been lost through whaling. It is only when so many whales have been killed that the species as a whole is threatened that we fear something truly irreplaceable is about to be lost.[100]

The advantage of seeing environmentalist concerns about irreplaceability in this way – in the context of a larger green theory of value – is precisely to help us make sense of such attitudes. The green theory of value helps us explain why people should regard nature as irreplaceable. It helps us explain why they should value the respect in which nature is irreplaceable. And it helps us explain why not all elements of the natural order need be so regarded. Merely treating irreplaceability as a primitive value in an environmental ethic would leave all those things woefully unanalysed.

---

[100] I discuss these issues further in chapter 3, section 2, and in section 2 of the appendix below.

Sustainability

The green case is also couched increasingly commonly in terms of the sustainability of ecologically sound strategies and, conversely, the unsustainability of unsound ones.[101] It is in our collective self-interest to manifest 'biocentric wisdom' and show 'respect for self-regulating natural systems', if we do not wish to 'destroy the stability of the ecosystem' on which we ourselves depend.[102] And that, on these accounts, is what green politics is all about. 'The overriding, unifying principle', some would say, 'is that all human activities must be indefinitely sustainable.'[103]

One familiar gloss on those themes, redolent of the mid-1960s and early 1970s, evokes the image of the earth as a 'spaceship'.[104] The imagery, however quaint, is nonetheless apt. Spaceships are paradigmatically closed systems. Being closed systems, we can neither import additional resources into them nor expel unwanted wastes from them; and that, in turn, makes notions of 'materials balance' and 'stationary state' obviously crucial in governing such systems.[105] Denizens of 'spaceship earth' must, on the rhetoric that this imagery inspired, realize that there is 'only one earth', and they must adopt the sorts of steady-state policies that are sustainable over the long term accordingly.[106] From the first Earth Day to this day, 'sustainability' and 'steady-state economics' have continuously been the catchwords of green economic policy statements.[107]

[101] Many might be tempted to place at the core of green values the need for modes of existence (economic, social and political) that are sustainable in the face of natural limits to growth in material consumption. The best recent exposition of this line is to be found in Dobson (1990, esp. chs 1 and 3). However, those who would make sustainability a fundamental axiom rather than a mere corollary must explain – in a way that Dobson, for example, does not – why sustainability ought be valued (except, obviously, in the human-instrumental terms that greens so clearly want to eschew).

[102] As the goals are expressed by the Green Committees of Correspondence (1986, p. 230) in the US and by Die Grünen (1983, p. 7), respectively.

[103] *British Green Party Manifesto, 1987*, PB [Philosophical Basis] 303, quoted in Dobson (1990, p. 68).

[104] A less rhetorical, more scientifically sophisticated variation on these themes is Georgescu-Roegen's (1971; 1972) appeal to the Second Law of Thermodynamics, which was picked up again properly in environmentalist debates only with Amory Lovins's (1976; 1977) critique of nuclear energy in terms of 'Second Law efficiency'.

[105] Boulding 1966; 1973; Kneese, Ayres and D'Arge 1970.

[106] Boulding 1966; 1973; Ward 1966; 1979; Ward and Dubois 1972; Ophuls 1977, esp. ch. 8; Daly 1972; 1974a; 1974b; Daly and Cobb 1989.

[107] Thus, Jonathan Porritt (1984, p. 126) writes, 'Green economics is all about sustainability and social justice: finding and sustaining such means of creating wealth

This style of argument has recently been resurrected by the World Commission on Environment and Development, chaired by the sometime Norwegian Prime Minister, Gro Harlem Brundtland. That Commission coined the catchphrase 'sustainable development', with the aim of suggesting that environmentally responsible practices are actually in the interests of developing nations themselves – or at least of any of them that want to keep on developing.[108] Largely through the influence of that Commission, the phrase has spread among centre-left commentators and centre-right governments alike.[109]

Whether or not sustainability is an independent value is an open question, though. There is something to be said for stability in people's lives, in general, to be sure. It facilitates planning, both on their own part and on the part of those that rely on them. It allows them to see some order and coherence within their own lives, which is satisfying to themselves and useful to others. It enables them to make promises and commitments that others can count on being kept. In all of those ways, the sheer fact of stability in their lives is important to people.[110]

But none of that argues for stability over the very long time horizons that ecologists seem to have in view. The sorts of earnings stabilization schemes that operate in our social welfare policies seem to suggest that the crucial thing is to protect against very rapid changes in people's lives. After a year or at most two, we seem to expect people to adapt to their new circumstances, radically different though they may be.[111] If they want more – if they want sustainability over decades rather than days, over millennia rather than months – then environmentalists cannot simply appeal to the commonplace desires people have for stability in their own lives.

Neither do those familiar sorts of concerns for macro-stability in the overall course of a person's life lead to the environmentalist's concerns for the micro-stability of very particular patterns and processes. Those simply demanding stability in the overall course of their lives are usually willing to accept substitutes. They might be indifferent between getting to work by car or train or telephone. Environmentalists fixated on sustainability are less inclined to tolerate such trade-offs. They have no

as will allow us to meet the genuine needs of all people without damaging our fragile biosphere.' See similarly the UK Ecology (since renamed 'Green') Party's economic manifesto, *Working for a Future* (1980).

[108] World Commission on Environment and Development 1987, ch. 2.

[109] Redclift 1987; Australia, Department of Prime Minister and Cabinet 1990. Cf. World Bank 1984.

[110] Those themes are explored in relation to social security policy in Goodin (1990d).

[111] Goodin 1990d.

doubt that, through the interrelated connections that characterize the system as a whole, if any one factor is altered compensating variations in various other factors are bound to occur. But they are rather inclined to dread rather than welcome that fact.[112] While accepting that such processes can never be suppressed completely, the whole point of their trying to achieve sustainability, system balance and a homeostatic equilibrium is to suppress such alterations as much as they can. Again, if environmentalists want micro-stability whereas all that ordinary people actually seem to demand is macro-stability, then environmentalists must offer some further justifications beyond appeals to the commonplace that people desire stability in their lives.

Sometimes environmentalists try to appeal to brute facts to settle that matter. The ecological balance, they say, is enormously delicate. Even slight deviations – or, anyway, deviations of the not-so-slight sort that humanity is currently imposing – risk provoking intolerably large reactions that are unprecedented in human history and incompatible with continued life as we know it. The *Limits to Growth* literature of the 1970s took as its theme that we are standing on just such a precipice.[113] Those themes are echoed today in models of climate change or ozone depletion and, in a less modest fashion, in various forms of the Gaia hypothesis.[114]

Brute facts, if factually true, can sometimes settle arguments over principles. But, by their nature, these facts are such that we cannot afford to wait to see whether or not they turn out to be true. And in any case, if it can be shown that we should do the same things for reasons of principle and, perhaps, of brute fact as well then that constitutes a pretty clear case for supposing that we should do it *tout court*.

The principles to which environmentalists need to appeal to carry their case for sustainability, though strong, seem not to be independent principles. In so far as their argument for sustainability of particular processes is an argument for accepting no substitutes, their case for sustainability hinges on arguments concerning irreplaceability just discussed. In so far as their argument for sustainability is an argument for adopting longer time horizons, their case for sustainability hinges on the argument from futurity to be discussed below. And both of those other arguments, in turn, are best understood as mere corollaries of the green theory of value developed in earlier sections. Seen in that light,

---

[112] That is rather the implication of the Gaia hypothesis, for example: nature will survive all right; the only question is whether humanity will be able to tolerate the changes it makes in response to our interventions (Lovelock 1987; 1989).

[113] Forrester 1971; Meadows et al. 1972; Goldsmith et al. 1972; US CEQ 1980.

[114] Wilson 1971; US NRC 1989; Lovelock 1987; 1989.

the value of sustainability – far from constituting an independent moral basis for environmental ethics – would seem to constitute little more than a second-order derivative from the true basis.

Futurity

Another crucial component of the environmentalist ethic is concern for the further future. 'How can we induce people and institutions to think in terms of the long-range future, and not just in terms of their short-range selfish interest?' asks the umbrella group for American greens, who reckon that a 'future focus' ought to figure conspicuously among 'key green values'.[115] The 1983 Manifesto of the German Greens echos these themes:

> The pillage of nature brings about long-term damage, part of which can never be restored. This is accepted in the interest of short-term profit. The very basis of people's lives is endangered by nuclear installations, by air, water and soil pollution, by storage of dangerous waste products and by the squandering of raw materials. . . . We stand for an economic system geared to the vital needs of human beings and future generations, to the preservation of nature and a careful management of natural resources.[116]

This is no mere matter of worrying about one's own future or that of one's own immediate family. There are good grounds for that, too, environmentalists would argue. Pollution is imprudent. It amounts to fouling our own nests, and we or those whom we care about will (or may well) ultimately suffer in consequence.

Such concerns stretch only a little way into the future, however. They are consistent with activities that create environmental time bombs of colossal proportions, so long as they have moderately long fuses.[117] Full-blooded environmentalists would worry about those, too, however long their fuses. Greens are concerned with entire future generations, not just with their own progeny, and with distant generations, not just their own children and their children's children. Their concern, as they standardly say, is with the long-term future of life on earth.[118]

In this as in so many other matters, the environmentalist's principal opponent in policy debates is the economist. On the question of the

---

[115] Green Committees of Correspondence 1986, item 10.

[116] Die Grünen 1983, p. 9.

[117] As Barry (1977, p. 277), for example, rightly objects against Rawls's (1971, sec. 44) derivation of intergenerational justice.

[118] Thus, for example, Ophuls (1977, p. v) dedicates his *Ecology and the Politics of Scarcity* to 'the posterity that has never done anything for me'. See similarly Routley and Routley (1978) and Page (1977, chs 7–10).

proper treatment of the further future, the environmental ethic is counterpoised most directly to the standard economic practice of discounting the future.[119] Economists standardly advise us to weigh future pay-offs (costs or benefits) less heavily – indeed, disproportionately less heavily – the further in the future they come. Technically expressed, they discount future income streams according to a discount function that is exponential (that is, geometrical) in form.[120]

The consequence of that practice is obvious. Costs and benefits that are relatively near to hand weigh relatively heavily. The £1 million that will accrue next year has a present value of £952,400, assuming a (relatively modest) 5 per cent discount rate. But the further in the future a cost or benefit is, the disproportionately less heavily will it weigh with us now. Thus, for example, the present value of the same £1 million twenty years away is reckoned to be merely £376,000, and the same sum a century away appears in current accounts with a paltry present value of only £761.

(The cynical may say that sounds about right. Inured as we all are to the fact of inflation, we rightly regard large sums in the distant future as 'funny money'. But all these calculations – and all that follow later in this section – are expressed in terms of 'constant prices'. The effects of inflation have already been factored out. The suggestion is that, even after inflation has been taken into account, we should regard £1 million next century as equivalent to no more than £761 today.)

Discounting in that way is commended, virtually as a hallmark of rationality itself, in just about every economics text and development manual in print.[121] But is it so obviously rational to ignore almost completely what the consequences of our present actions will have beyond a few generations? That is not a long time, even in terms of human history much less in terms of geological time. On economistic calculations of present values, though, consequences that come in a century or two – however large or however certain they may be – are treated as being simply of no proper concern to us.

---

[119] There have always been some economists opposing those practices, of course (see e.g. Page 1977). With the 'second environmental crisis' and growing concerns about global warming or destruction of the ozone layer, more and more are coming around to such longer-term perspectives (D'Arge, Schultze and Brookshire 1982; Nordhaus 1982).

[120] Technically, the standard formula is $PV = X/(1+r)^t$, where PV is present value, X is the sum that will accrue in t years and r is the discount rate.

[121] For just two of the most influential example, see the OECD manual on *Project Appraisal and Planning for Developing Countries* (Little and Mirrlees 1974, secs 1.7 and 4.1) and the textbook for the required course on policy analysis at Harvard's Kennedy School of Government (Stokey and Zeckhauser 1978, ch. 10).

There are many ways to resist such conclusions, of course. Perhaps the most obvious strategy – and certainly the one most often employed by writers on ethics in general, and on environmental ethics in particular – is to shift the terms of discourse. Essentially, the aim is to concede the low ground of pragmatics to economists, while claiming for oneself the high moral ground.

Perhaps, this line goes, it is peculiarly efficient – peculiarly rational, even, in some narrowly economistic sense of that term – to discount the future as economists would recommend. Here as elsewhere, though, a trade-off must be made between equity and efficiency, between the maximization of total social utility and its just distribution. Hence, philosophers deploying this device would say, it may be economically efficient for us to shortchange the future; but it is nonetheless wrong for us to do so. It would amount to unjust treatment of future generations.

Of course, those taking this tack must then provide some theory of intergenerational justice strong enough to sustain such a claim. Many avenues have been explored but most, it is probably fair to say, are variations on one basic theme. Justice, it is standardly said, ought to be blind to facts about people that are truly arbitrary from a moral point of view. Among those arbitrary facts is the precise timing of one's birth. Indeed, the century of one's birth is as irrelevant from a moral point of view as the precise microsecond. Justice therefore requires that we weigh equally in our present decisions the interests of all generations, whenever they come in human history.[122]

If that sort of argument goes through, the upshot is that high morality requires that we not discount – or, as economists would put it, that we apply a 'zero discount rate' – whereas the low morality of economic rationality requires some positive rate of time discounting. How well the argument goes through, in the first place, depends on the relative weight of arguments for both moralities (high and low) on these questions.

Even if the philosophers' arguments go through, though, the form of their rejoinder has conceded some important ground to the economists. There is a trade-off to be made, they will have implicitly agreed. And that is in itself a costly concession. Maybe the moralistic arguments against discounting will prevail in nine cases out of ten, or ninety out of a hundred. But in casting their rejoinder as the other side of an important value trade-off, philosophers are conceding that there is always going to be something to be said for the economists' case. That

[122] Such arguments are of course inspired by, though typically go well beyond, Rawls (1971, sec. 44). See e.g. Barry (1977; 1978; 1983; Sikora and Barry (1978); Feinberg (1974); Page (1977, ch. 9); Partridge (1981); and MacLean and Brown (1983). For a rather different derivation, see Goodin (1985c, pp. 169–79).

being so, it will inevitably sometimes prevail – if only occasionally, and if only at the margins.[123]

Environmentalists would therefore be well advised to look for some better way of resisting the economists' devil-may-care conclusions about the further future. Ideally, they should try to meet the economists on their own ground, and to undermine their case for discounting from within. On inspection, it turns out that there is indeed some considerable scope for exposing obvious flaws in the justifications that economists themselves offer for discounting.

Those justifications are, of course, many and varied.[124] Some hardly count as justifications at all. Perhaps the most standard among them appeals to nothing more than people's blind prejudice in favour of the present over the future, in a way that many economists themselves cannot quite countenance.[125]

Other economistic arguments for discounting the further future turn on just plain sloppy thinking. They confuse the argument in favour of discounting for time *per se* – which is what they are seeking – with arguments in favour of discounting future pay-offs on account of things that merely correlate (and then only imperfectly) with the passage of

[123] If they have further consented to the economistic way of putting their point against discounting – as an argument for a 'zero discount rate' – then there will be yet more room for compromise between the contending principles, each of which has something to be said for it. If moral principle requires a zero discount rate and economic efficiency a 10 per cent discount rate, and economic efficiency is say one-tenth as important as moral principle in the case at hand, then the obvious compromise is to apply a discount rate one-tenth of the way between what moralists and economists recommend – that is, a 1 per cent discount rate.

[124] These arguments are elaborated in Goodin (1982a). See also Parfit (1983; 1984, pp. 480–7).

[125] This is what economists call 'pure time discounting'. Some economists would themselves reject discounting grounded in no more than this: Pigou (1932, pt 1, ch. 2, sec. 3) lambasts pure time discounting as a mere failure of the 'telescopic faculty', and Ramsey (1928, p. 543) says plainly that it 'is ethically indefensible and arises merely from the weakness of the imagination'. Others bemoan that as 'an authoritarian rejection of individual preferences', arguing that if individuals discount the future for no good reason in this way then so too should democratic governments committed to reflecting faithfully their preferences (Marglin 1962, p. 197; 1963, p. 97). What that argument overlooks is that the people themselves, who would now have us discount future pay-offs, would wish come the time the pay-off occurs that we had not done so; it is not a case of substituting planners' judgement for citizens' own, but rather a case of planners choosing which of citizens' conflicting judgements to track in their plans (Sen 1957; 1961, p. 482; Goodin 1982a, p. 55; 1982b, ch. 3). As Sen (1961, p. 482) astutely puts it, 'If the difference is only due to the distance in time, then the position is symmetrical. A future object looks less important now, and similarly, a present object will look less important in the future. . . . [T]here is no necessary reason why to-day's discount of to-morrow should be used, and not to-morrow's discount of today.'

time. Thus, it may well be true that the further we are looking into the future, the more uncertain we will be what the pay-offs actually will be and whether we will ourselves be around to experience them; or the later the pay-offs come the more resources we are likely to have to cushion us against, or at least to compensate us for, their evil effects. But all those things – increased uncertainty, technology, wealth – are only contingently connected with the passage of time. They therefore provide no reason for supposing that it will necessarily be proper to discount later pay-offs.

Furthermore, and in a way more importantly, none of these considerations – not even the first-mentioned brute psychological fact – provides any reason at all for the rapidly progressive form that the economist's geometric discount function ordinarily takes. There is no reason to suppose that uncertainty or technological progress or wealth or even people's psychological attachment to the future alters at some fixed rate of r per cent per year, compounding continually on into the further future. Yet, of course, if the rate varies then the case for compounding collapses and (depending on the details of the formula we use instead) the further future may well loom larger in our present calculations than the standard economic formula suggests.

Environmentalists can get a long way towards undermining disregard for the further future merely by attacking the bad arguments that economists themselves give for discounting. Economists do, however, have one good argument to justify discounting in that powerfully exponential form. And it is this argument that environmentalists, and friends of the further future in general, must be principally concerned to address.

This one good argument for exponential discounting of future costs and benefits treats discounting as a form of compound interest in reverse. A smaller sum now ought, on this argument, be seen as equivalent to – ought be deemed the 'present value' of – a larger sum later, simply because if you put that smaller sum into the bank earning compound interest now it will actually have grown into that larger sum by the later date. Thus, £761 now ought be seen as equivalent to – the present value of – £1 million next century, simply because £761 invested now at 5 per cent per year, compounded, will amount to £1 million in a hundred years' time.[126] So money, or anything that can be bought and sold for money, ought be discounted at a rate that is equal to the long-term interest rate.[127]

---

[126] Marglin 1967, pp. 59–61; Little and Mirrlees 1974, p. 11; Stokey and Zeckhauser 1978, ch. 10.

[127] Environmental costs and benefits are standardly treated in this way. Similarly,

That way of summarizing the conclusion, however, only serves to highlight what is most wrong with this argument. First, it requires us to guess what the interest rate really will be over the (possibly very) long term. Real interest rates have, in fact, been highly variable, so there is no good way of knowing what discount rate to use.[128] Second and more important is the fact that that argument for discounting applies, first and foremost, to money and things that can be bought and sold in exchange for money.

The argument for discounting the future value of things that can be bought and sold goes like this. We should be indifferent between being given £37,600 today or the guarantee of a £100,000 house in twenty years' time, because we can put that smaller sum on compound interest and (assuming a constant 5 per cent interest rate over the entire period[129]) have in hand at the end of twenty years £100,000 with which to buy that exact house. By the same token, we should be indifferent between being given a £37,600 house today or the guarantee of a £100,000 house in twenty years' time, because (ignoring transaction costs and making the same heroic assumptions about interest rates) we could sell the cheaper house today, put the money on compound interest in the bank, and buy the more expensive house later.

But obviously that argument only works for things, like houses, that really can be bought and sold. Consider, by way of contrast, the case of something that cannot: human lives. That is not to deny that lives have 'monetary equivalents'. Of course they do, in all sorts of ways. We might look at the sum for which people insure their lives, or at the compensation payments that courts order when someone has been killed. Suppose such measures suggest that the going rate for the life of someone like Mr Smith is £100,000.

Even if we can, in such ways, come up with a monetary equivalent of non-tradable commodities, it would be fallacious to use those sums in

the standard resource-economic advice is to exhaust exhaustible resources up to the point at which their increase in scarcity value equals the market interest rate. Hotelling 1931; Marglin 1962; Page 1977.

[128] In a way, it might not matter much. The nature of exponential decay functions of this sort is such that, just about whatever rate you use, costs and benefits in the distant future will virtually disappear from present calculations. But that is true only so long as you can be reasonably certain that on average interest rates will at least be positive over the relevant period. (Were they negative, then the present value of £1 tomorrow would be more – not less – than the value of £1 received today.) If the darker fears of the eco-doomsayers prove well founded, even that may well not be true. There are some circumstances under which we should contemplate a negative interest rate (Stokey and Zeckhauser 1978, p. 175).

[129] Or – what is more realistic in some ways, but less so in others – a constellation of varying interest rates over the period with the same practical consequences.

any scheme of discounting justified in the way sketched above.[130] Adapting the house example, devout discounters might reason as follows. Mr Smith should be indifferent between getting – £37,600 now or medical treatment to remove a latent tumour that will cause his certain death in twenty years' time; that would be equivalent to conferring on him a benefit worth £100,000 (what his life is worth) in twenty years, and £37,600 invested at 5 per cent compound interest will grow to £100,000 by the end of twenty years.

But what is not true in the case of the life, in a way that it is in the case of the house, is that invested proceeds of the smaller sum could later be used to buy the greater good. Mr Smith may have an extra £100,000 in the bank on the day he dies, thanks to the workings of compound interest. But he cannot use it to buy off the Grim Reaper, in a way that the person in the earlier example could use it to buy exactly the same house.

What makes discounting rationally mandatory, in the case of things like houses that genuinely can be bought and sold, is that money put on compound interest can buy exactly the same things later. Then it really would be irrational – it would be to distinguish between things that are indistinguishable – categorically to refuse the offer of a smaller sum now which will yield exactly the same goods later.

In the case of things that cannot be bought and sold, though, that is not what will happen. Money invested on compound interest will not buy us exactly the same thing later. It will buy us something that is 'equivalent' or 'as good', perhaps. But what it will buy us will undeniably be something that is different.

It follows from that fact alone that it is not necessarily irrational to reject discounting for non-tradable commodities. It is not irrational, at least, in the sense that it does not amount to drawing distinctions between things that are literally indistinguishable. Clearly, in the case of things that cannot be bought and sold, we will be getting things that are different – albeit 'equivalent' – if we discount than if we do not.

That is to say that discounting is not necessarily rational, in such cases. That is not to say, though, that discounting is necessarily not rational. Everything depends, in these cases, on just how close is the 'equivalence' between what we would be getting and what we would be

---

[130] It is no mere 'straw man' that is here being attacked. Notice, for example, health economists writing, 'The reason for discounting future life years is precisely that they are being valued relative to dollars, and since a dollar in the future is discounted relative to a present dollar, so must a life year in the future be discounted relative to a present dollar' (Weinstein and Stason 1977, p. 720).

losing if we discounted the present value of future losses of non-tradable commodities.[131]

At this point, then, the case against economistic discounting of the further future links up with previous discussions of irreplaceability. The losses that, on the argument just sketched, we may rightly refuse to discount are losses of things for which there are no good substitutes or equivalents. If something is replaceable, or if there are good substitutes for it, then there is no reason in principle not to discount the prospect of its future loss. It is only the irreplaceable whose future is potentially immune to the solvent of compound interest calculations.[132]

A theory of irreplaceability is therefore what is needed to resist the economists' strongest argument for discounting the future. And a theory of irreplaceability is precisely what the green theory of value, sketched above, has provided. It is a partial theory, in the sense that there may be other things (like human lives, or anyway the lives of particular human individuals) that are also irreplaceable.[133] But the green theory of value gives us grounds for supposing that at least some things produced by natural forces are irreplaceable, precisely because they have a history of having been produced by those natural forces. The things might be replicated artifically. But history cannot be so replicated.

Depending on exactly what it is about natural creation we value, some limited discounting might still be justifiable on compound-interest-in-reverse style arguments. Suppose that our reason for valuing natural creation is, as I have suggested, that we want to see our lives as being set in some larger context. Suppose that what we value about nature is therefore its general order. That is to say, suppose our concern is with natural types rather than with mere tokens. We do not much care about the deaths of individual animals. We do care powerfully about the loss of whole species.

Then we might be prepared to tolerate a certain limited discounting of future streams of resources. In this discounting, we would be limited to trading like for like – whales for whales, baboons for baboons. So long

[131] In the case of £100,000 for Mr Smith's life, it is essentially a question of whether he would be willing to commit suicide for that sum.

[132] That point is sometimes phrased, somewhat misleadingly, in terms of 'sustainability' – i.e. the sustainability of the particular resource flows which we regard as irreplaceable and non-substitutable. That is, I think, the sense in which Achterberg (1991), for example, sees a broadly overlapping consensus organized around ensuring the sustainability of the Dutch environment for future generations.

[133] And for analogous reasons: the reason that still-fertile parents, distraught at the loss of a child, suppose that they cannot just have another to take that child's place is that the new child will have a different personality shaped by a different history than the first.

as what we care about is types rather than tokens – the natural order, rather than the particular animals – we should regard them as good substitutes for one another. And so long as those populations have the characteristics of an interest-bearing resource, growing with time if not destroyed now (as biological populations obviously do), then the compound-interest-in-reverse case for discounting applies. We should care less about saving a single baboon in the future than in the present simply because, if the one in the present lives and mates, then it will produce many more in the future.

This sort of argument, notice, applies only to particular sorts of environmental assets. It applies only to those akin to interest-bearing resources. It discounts each resource according to a different rate, depending on the growth rate of that resource itself. And since no resource (no biological population, even) continues growing at exponential rates indefinitely into the future, neither can our discounting of such resources. The structure – the formula – as well as the rate at which we discount these sorts of resources must match the pattern of growth in those resources themselves. Hence, discounting justified in these resource-specific ways cannot display the marked unconcern for the further future that geometric discounting implies.

If our concern is for the general shape of the natural order, a second consequence for resource futures follows. Suppose our basic aim is, in so far as possible, to 'leave no footprints'. Suppose that we are therefore trying to preserve distinct natural types into the indefinite future, not worrying too much about the fate of particular tokens of those types (individual animals, as distinct from whole species). Then we may cream off only as much of the resource flow as is consistent with leaving enough to reproduce at least as much in the future.[134] In biological terms, we should take only as much as is consistent with leaving a breeding population. In economic terms, we should be striving to 'maximize sustainable yield'.[135]

Liberation

Green rhetoric is replete with the language of 'liberation'. It arises most commonly in connection with those famous forms of hyphenated environmentalism – 'eco-socialism' and 'eco-feminism' – both of which

---

[134] 'May', notice – not 'should'. This argument permits discounting, of this distinctly limited sort. It does not require it – or, indeed, provide any positive justification at all for it.
[135] Williams 1978.

equate the liberation of nature from domination by humans with the liberation of oppressed humans from domination by others.[136] But greens also talk of 'animal liberation' and, internationally, of the 'liberation' of oppressed peoples of the Third World (especially from the environmental degradation forced on them by overconsumption in developed countries). Some greens even talk of the 'liberation of nature' as such.[137]

Such rhetoric contains the recognizable echos of countercultural and New Left politics of the 1960s and early 1970s which played such a major role in spawning the current green movements.[138] It is understandable that contemporary greens should want to recall their roots in these ways. The rhetorical device serves, in that way, a perfectly proper sociological function. And provided that is the only purpose it is meant to serve, then there is nothing wrong with that way of formulating the problem.

The question before us here is merely whether that is indeed the only purpose being served. Is there, over and above its rhetorical-cum-sociological/genealogical aim, any genuinely argumentative purpose served by casting the green case in terms of 'liberation'? Is the green case better put – more aptly characterized, more powerfully advanced – by being seen as an argument for liberation of some sort, rather than by being couched in terms of the green theory of value sketched above? I think not, and I shall proceed to show why.

The notion of 'liberation' at work here is (at least) two-sided. On the one side, it is the opposite of 'domination'.[139] Liberation in this sense is

[136] For example, Val Plumwood (1986, p. 120) defines eco-feminism as 'a body of literature whose theme is the link between the domination of women and the domination of nature'. The same might equally well be said, *mutatis mutandis*, of eco-socialism (Hayward 1990). For a good overview of how both fit into the larger green theory, see Fox (1989), Dobson (1990, ch. 5) and Salleh (1991).

[137] Though the phrase figures more frequently as chapter headings than as the subjects of sustained analysis (Leiss 1972, ch. 8; Nash 1989, ch. 6; Bookchin 1990, pp. 44–7).

[138] The connection is particularly apparent in Bookchin's (1990, p. 44) 'social ecology', the basic tenet of which is that 'the domination of human by human *preceded* the notion of dominating nature. Indeed, human domination of human gave rise to the *idea* of dominating nature.'

[139] Discussing their 'ten key values', the Green Committees of Correspondence in the US (1986, item 7) ask for example, 'How can we replace the . . . ethics of dominance and control with more cooperative ways of interacting?' Similarly, Kirkpatrick Sale (1985, p. 91), urging humanity to model itself on nature, recalls that 'in the natural world . . . nothing is more striking than the absence of any centralized control, any interspeciate domination. . . . "King of the jungle" is *our* description of the lion's status, and quite anthropomorphously perverse; the lion (or better, lioness) is profoundly unware of this role, and the elephant and rhinoceros (not to mention the tsetse fly) would hardly accede to it.'

the setting free of that which was previously subjugated. On the other side, liberation is the opposite of 'alienation'. Liberation is the setting free of the self from internalized inhibitions. These familiar themes are often merged, often in ways that are not altogether clear.[140] Loose talk of 'emancipation' and 'empowerment' is characterisitically left to do the work that really should be done by tight arguments and analysis at this point.[141]

Mystical though it might be in these other respects, however, one thing is tolerably clear about the notion of liberation. We need some further specification of what we are being liberated from, in order to talk sensibly about 'liberation' at all. Liberation is a relational notion. The logic of the relation, whatever its particulars, must always necessarily take the form: 'X is liberated from Y.'[142]

Furthermore, and following on from that, we need some further theory of why it is good that X should be liberated from Y in order to explain what is so good about liberation as such. The goodness of the good of liberation is, in that sense, wholly derivative. Liberation is good only because, and only in so far as, domination or alienation is bad. The case for liberation is thus parasitic on the case against domination or alienation.

Put that way, it is easy to see why I tend to regard 'liberation' as something of an argumentative 'flag of convenience' beneath which sails a rag-tag flotilla of very disparate arguments. There are many diverse forms of domination. Very many different sorts of agents are dominated by very many different other sorts of agents and forces, and that domination works by many very different mechanisms. It is simply not credible to suppose that one and the same argument can be given against these disparate forms of domination. If, as just suggested, the argument for liberation must necessarily be parasitic on arguments against domination, then there must be as many subtly different

[140] For example, Horkheimer and Adorno (1972, p. 3) write, 'Men pay for the increases of their power with alienation from that over which they exercise their power. Enlightenment behaves toward things as a dictator toward men.' Luke (1988, p. 72) adds, 'Deep ecologists want to overthrow this dictatorship of enlightenment . . . [and] overcome man's alienation from domination of Nature.' Habermas's elaboration of this tradition might be the most useful for these purposes (Dryzek 1990b; Eckersley 1991).

[141] Wainwright 1988; Tokar 1987, ch. 7.

[142] In the case of 'liberation as non-domination' Y would refer to the factors responsible for X's domination, in the case of 'liberation as non-alienation' to the factors responsible for X's alienation. The formula is perfectly general, as between those two readings of 'liberation'. To make it more general still, we might – following MacCallum's (1967) similar generalization of the positive/negative liberty debate – write it as 'X is liberated from Y to do Z.'

arguments for liberation as there are against all the varied forms of domination. And likewise with alienation and with notions of liberation cashed out in those terms.

Thus, I do not think that there is one general argument in favour of liberation *tout court*. Instead, there are many different arguments in favour of liberation, depending on the context. What liberation means, and why it is morally important, depends crucially on what it is that is being liberated from what.

The boast that I would make on behalf of the green theory of value that I have advanced is just this: it provides a credible account of the environmentalist part of this larger story. It is no disadvantage that it provides only the environmentalist part of the story. If the argument just sketched is right, it is only to be expected that different sorts of analysis will be required for different parts of the story as to why liberation is morally important. But at least so far as the environmentalist side of the story goes, the green theory of value provides a good explanation of why humanity's domination of nature is wrong and why living in harmony with nature is good.

There is no need to belabour the merits of this account, which are in any case elaborated in section 5 above. The crucial point to be made against a rival analysis which would put notions of 'liberation' rather than the green theory of value at centre stage is simply that, even if the green case can be cast in those terms, there is no standing argument that will justify liberation in all its forms. Those who want to talk in terms of liberating nature will be forced to provide some more specific argument, tailored to the special case of nature and its liberation, that will justify liberation in that context. Nothing is then gained by subsuming environmentalism under a broader liberationist banner, if the liberation of nature will itself have then to be defended in environmentalist terms.

Authenticity

Finally, green theory is sometimes defended in terms of 'authenticity', as contrasted with artificiality and pretence. This certainly figures largely in the symbolism of green politics. When being sworn in as members of the West German Bundestag in 1983, Die Grünen members pointedly refused to wear formal attire and donned instead their colourful, unconventional everyday clothes.[143] But it also appears as an

---

[143] In the words of one pair of observers, 'a river of colorful sweaters, shirts and dresses . . . flowed down the middle of the chamber between the tiers of black-and-white-suited politicians of the conservative Christian Democrats . . . on the one side

argument for certain policies and against others. In *Where the Wasteland Ends*, for example, Roszak's introductory chapter bemoans 'The artificial environment'.[144]

In one way, I have little reason to resist this as an analysis of the green creed. For opposition to artificiality is tantamount to a defence of 'the natural';[145] and according to the green theory of value which I have been defending, value derives precisely from a history of creation through natural processes. So opposition to 'artificiality' is to that extent fully consonant with what I have here been depicting as the core of the green theory.

Where the two arguments fail to dovetail, perhaps, is in their analysis of what is good about natural processes and bad about artificial ones. In so far as authenticity is indeed valued on account of non-artificiality, understood as the naturalness of the processes involved, then there is no problem. But talking in terms of 'authenticity' admits of another interpretation, namely, the absence of pretence.[146] And that rather suggests that it is not so much the naturalness of a thing's history of creation but something else – its simplicity, its lack of affectation of contrivance, its lack of artifice in *that* sense – that is valued.

Much of what I have to say against the value of naturalness in that sense will come in the next section below. That is the sense of naturalness which seems generically to underlie the green recommendations regarding personal lifestyle that I there dismiss as a peripheral part of the green creed. As I shall there argue, there may be nothing particularly valuable about naturalness in that sense. Indeed, valuing naturalness in that sense may empty naturalness of the value that I had earlier (in section 4) found in it.

That argument will be broached shortly. For present purposes, it is enough merely to say that this analysis of naturalness as simplicity straightforwardly mistakes the nature of nature. Nature is complex, not simple. It is elaborate, not plain. It is variegated, not monotone. In short, if there is anything to the absence of pretence at all, it is not 'plain' or 'simple' living as some back-to-nature aesthetics might assert. It is instead the absence of artifice – the absence of humanly imposed creation – and the centrality instead of naturalness and natural creation.

and the liberal-left Social Democrats . . . on the other' (Spretnak and Capra 1986, p. 5).

[144] Roszak 1972, ch. 1.

[145] Mill 1874/1969, p. 375.

[146] For example, Mill writes, 'For my part I can perceive only one sense in which nature, or naturalness, in a human being, are really terms of praise; and then the praise is only negative: namely when used to denote the absence of affectation' which he defines as 'the effort to appear what one is not' (ibid., p. 400).

7   Green Heresies

The long preceding section, with its many subsections, has been devoted to discussing at length what I call 'green corollaries'. Those can be considered broadly 'friendly amendments' to the green theory of value that I have been elaborating. Typically, they are less good ways of making those same basic points – which, after all, is why I prefer my own formulation to those alternatives. But they are, or they can be construed to be, basically in sympathy with the spirit of the value theory I have been trying to set at the core of green political theory.

Despite that long list of broadly friendly amendments, it would be wrong to leave the impression that my green theory of value can accommodate any and all things that green writers have ever wanted to say, though. Some of the analyses advanced by self-styled greens would, in those terms, have to be counted as distinctly 'unfriendly amendments' to my analysis. At the very least, it would have to be said that they cannot easily be subsumed within the green theory of value that I have been developing. If those propositions are to be defended, they must be defended on other grounds altogether, rather than deriving support from any supposed association with the other tenets of green theory derived from the green theory of value as I have described it.

In principle, that list might be as long as the other. But since the work of this section is wholly negative rather than being even partially positive, I shall not elaborate all the things that greens sometimes say that I think cannot be squared with my green theory of value. Suffice it to say, in the most general of terms, that the purely 'personal lifestyle' recommendations that often come from green writers seem to me to be wholly separate issues from their public-policy recommendations.[147] All the latter stem from the green theory of value I have been describing, as I shall argue in chapters 3 and 4 below. None of the former do, for reasons I shall now attempt to sketch.

When feminists adopted as their catchphrase the slogan, 'the personal is political', they were meaning to recognize power politics as a pervasive feature of social life, nowise confined to the formally political

---

[147] I say '*purely* personal lifestyle' because a great many of the public policies that greens recommend are designed to protect the quality of their personnel environment. Thus, clean indoor air – understood as air free of carcinogens or pollutants, ranging from asbestos to cigarette smoke – is an environmental issue of the ordinary sort, even if it does touch upon personal lifestyles. So too are public policies ensuring that foods are free of carcinogenic additives or residues. Those sorts of issues clearly have to be separated from the more purely personal lifestyle recommendations that greens sometimes make, I think.

realm. Greens sometimes say analogous things, like 'we make political statements not so much by the way we vote as by the way we live.'[148] But they say that more in the spirit of downgrading the political element in social life rather than of upgrading it. They tend to regard political action as a cop-out, seeing petition-signing and campaigning as excuses for doing nothing oneself to save the environment. Voting green but living brown is, for them, the height of hypocrisy.[149] Indeed, for many of them it seems that only direct, personal steps to 'save the planet' really ultimately count.

What precise measures greens would have us adopt in our daily lives is somewhat unclear. Green writers make many and varied and sometimes contradictory recommendations concerning personal lifestyles. Diverse though they may be, however, all seem to be inspired by 'holistic' thoughts of one sort or another. This might be dubbed 'whole earthism', in honour of the *Whole Earth Catalogue* that, together with sister publications like *Mother Earth News*, did so much to promulgate the faith.[150] It is by virtue of this holism running through them all that everything from Buddhist philosophy to worship of tree spirits, everything from organic farming, health foods and holistic medicine to attempts to reconcile Newtonian physics with Eastern mysticism can be seen to be manifestations of one and the same basic green creed.[151]

Some of the things we want to say about these further extensions of green theory – like, perhaps, some of the things that ought be said about more core features of green public policy prescriptions – is that they are (or anyway might well be) factually in error. Holistic medicine involves factual claims about how to restore a certain sort of functioning to specific bodily organs. Claims are made on behalf of health foods that should, in principle, be testable in the ordinary way by nutritionists or other scientists specializing in preventive medicine.

While suprisingly many of those factual claims will probably turn out to be true, many more will quite probably prove to be false. Of course, that might just be because the particular practitioner of holistic

[148] Skolimonski 1981, p. 41; see similarly Elgin 1982.

[149] I shall say more about the rationale underlying this position in chapter 4, section 1 below.

[150] Lest these be thought marginal phenomena, recall that the *Whole Earth Catalogue* regularly figures in bestseller lists and that *Mother Earth News* boasted a circulation of half a million by the late 1970s and almost three-quarters of a million by the mid-1980s (Hays 1987, pp. 30, 259).

[151] Roszak 1978; Sale 1985; Devall and Sessions 1985; Capra 1975; 1982; Hays 1987, esp. pp. 29–32, 259–65. Even the basically political face of the green movement talks in such ways; see e.g. the item on 'Personal and social responsibility' in the list of *Ten Key Values* adopted by the umbrella organization representing US greens (Green CoC 1986, item 3).

medicine, for example, is inept or the particular theory of holistic medicine being applied is in error. Particular practitioners or particular versions of the broader theory can be wrong and the broader theory be right nonetheless. Holistic medicine, in particular, has many sceptics, however, who suspect that any version of holistic medicine has to be wrong – or at least that it is in extreme cases, which are the ones that really put alternative theories, of medicine or anything else, to the test.

For present purposes, let us leave those factual and quasi-factual problems to one side. Whether or not holistic medicine is a good cure or subsisting principally on beans is a healthy diet or chanting mantras to tree spirits is a satisfying way to lead one's life are interesting and important questions. But they are not, strictly speaking, the questions properly before us here. The issue here is instead to what extent those personal lifestyle recommendations of greens are part and parcel of some larger theory that embraces their public-policy recommendations as well. Are green lifestyle recommendations logically linked to, or are they logically separable from, green policy recommendations?

This question resolves itself into two others, in turn. First, we must ask whether the green lifestyle recommendations imply green policy recommendations. Do the grounds that the greens have for offering their lifestyle recommendations imply the green theory of value sketched above, which I argue underlies all their policy recommendations? Second, we must ask whether the green lifestyle recommendations are implied by green policy recommendations. Does the green theory of value which grounds green policy recommendations also imply green lifestyle recommendations?

I would answer 'yes' to the first question but 'no' to the second. Green lifestyle recommendations imply, but are not implied by, green policy recommendations. You cannot consistently be a principled green in your personal lifestyle without being a principled green in your policy recommendations. But you can consistently be a principled green in your policy recommendations, grounding them in a properly green theory of value, without necessarily adopting on principle a green personal lifestyle. Or so I shall argue.

The first of these propositions is not difficult to establish. Obviously, such holism as underlies green personal lifestyle recommendations is broadly in accord with the rationale I have offered for the green theory of value. People want to see their lives set in a larger context, I have claimed in defending that theory of value. Seeing their lives as continuous with the larger continuity of nature as a whole seems part and parcel of that. Indeed, it is very hard to imagine what principled grounds you might have for wanting your personal life to be in harmony with nature but for resisting public policies that would bring public aspects of your shared lives into accord with it. There may be pragmatic reasons – you may think that nothing you could do, politically, would make any difference. But in principled terms, the one surely implies the other. Green personal policies imply green public policies, in so far as 'harmony with the larger natural order' is the end in view in both cases.

That thought is presumably what leads to the easy slide between all forms of greenery. It is what leads both greens and their detractors to suppose, quite wrongly as I shall suggest, that all forms of greenery go together. Notice, however, that all that that proposition has actually established is an implication only in one direction. The arrow from green personal policies to green public ones is thereby established. But an arrow in the other direction – from green public to personal policies – remains yet to be established.

I would argue that that is quite a separate issue. There are many reasons that might be given. Perhaps nature's large-scale patterns can tolerate a fair bit of individual-level variation.[152] Or perhaps the larger social order simply impinges so severely on people's personal lives that there is no meaningful sense in which people can pursue individual lives genuinely in harmony with nature without first getting the larger social context right. Those are more empirical questions that I propose to leave to one side here.

Let me here concentrate instead on what I see as the most important principled reason for supposing that it might be consistent for you to be green on public but not on private (personal lifestyle) policies. According to the green theory of value as it has here been developed, recall, the aim in view is to see your life being set in a larger context. Natural processes provide just such a context. That is why, on the green theory of value, we should value natural processes; that is why, on the green theory of value, we should advocate public policies to protect such processes, to secure those larger contexts in which we can set our lives. Having said all that, however, an advocate of the green theory of value might go on to say that one's own life must be separate and distinct from the larger context – outside of it, in some important sense – for its being set in that context to be satisfying or even meaningful.

The objection, in other words, is this. For one thing to be 'in harmony' with another, you need to have two separate things. If people slavishly follow green personal lifestyle recommendations, they will be living their lives so much in harmony with natural processes as to be

---

[152] As greens themselves both acknowledge and welcome, under the heading of 'respect for diversity' within and among human societies (Green CoC 1986, item 8).

wholly subsumed within them. They will not be two separate things in harmony with one another. They will rather be part and parcel of one and the same thing.

Now, according to certain Eastern philosophies much favoured by certain 'deep ecologists', this eclipsing of the self and merging of the individual with the whole of the universe is an independently desirable outcome. Here I shall be taking no stand on the merits of that case. My aim here is merely to emphasize that not all the reasons we might have for assenting to the green theory of value would necessarily require us to presuppose that proposition. Buddhism and its ilk is a separate issue, to be argued for separately.

In the present context, what really matters is just this. It is perfectly possible – logically coherent, ethically defensible – for us to think that it is important for people to have personal identities and personal projects, and for us nonetheless to think that it is important that those fit into some larger (natural) contexts. If that is our view, as I think it is of a great many greens and would-be greens, then that provides a rationale for at one and the same time: (a) pursuing green public policies, to secure the larger natural contexts in which we want to see our own projects set; but (b) refusing to adopt green personal lifestyle recommendations aiming to deprive us of the distinctively personal stance from which harmony with nature would be satisfying or even meaningful. Which is just to say that, depending on why we endorse the green theory of value in the first place, we might have good grounds for pursuing the green public-policy recommendations it prescribes while at the same time refusing to follow apparently analogous green personal lifestyles.

Perhaps it is needlessly tendentious to describe those green personal lifestyle recommendations as 'heresies'. That might seem to suggest that they are necessarily incompatible with the larger green theory – which is not at all true. Those personal lifestyle recommendations might be perfectly compatible with the larger green theory, if you happen to endorse some variant of the Buddhist doctrine described above and to embrace the green theory of value and the public-policy recommendations following from it for that reason.

The heresy I have in mind is simply the heresy of supposing that greens necessarily have to endorse all forms of greenery – in personal lifestyle as well as in public-policy. That proposition is in error. There are perfectly good grounds for endorsing the green theory of value, and green public policies in consequence, that would have almost the opposite logical consequence, permitting one to depart from a green personal lifestyle in almost any given respect and perhaps even requiring one to deviate from it in some respect.

In practical political terms, the error is vastly important. A great many people attracted to the green political message, and willing to bear the very considerable sacrifices that green public policies might entail, simply cannot bring themselves to endorse a position that seems to require them not only to vote for sensible policies but also to adopt what they see as silly beliefs about homeopathic medicine or tree spirits.[153] Politically, their votes may well be lost to the greens altogether unless green public policies and green personal lifestyle recommendations can be shown to be separable items on the larger green menu. I think it is perfectly defensible for them to be so presented.

[153] Untold damage is done the green cause, politically, by its association with various forms of 'New Age' theory, more generally. The limiting case – let us fervently hope – was the press conference convened by David Icke, former spokesman for the Green Party in Britain, announcing himself 'a channel for the Christ spirit'. 'The title', Icke explains, 'was given to me very recently by the Godhead,' who also warned of earthquakes that will leave New Zealand, Cuba, Greece and the Isle of Arran under water by Christmas 1991. The interview goes on to reveal King Arthur to have been an archangel sent to turn off 'the power point at Stonehenge' before Lucifer could use it, and so on in this vein (Cohen 1991). This sort of talk, obviously, does green parties no good at all, a fact to which people like Icke will always however have a ready reply ('It's better to have the Green Party embarrassed in 1991, then the world destroyed in 1997').

3

The Unity of the Green Programme

1 Single-Issue Groups versus Catch-All Parties

Traditionally, established political parties tend to treat single-issue groups in general really rather dismissively. They regard their demands as legitimate, within limits. They might be willing to revise their own programmes at the margins in order to give such groups some of what they want. But they are hardly prepared to honour all their demands, and they are hardly apologetic about that fact.

In a way, that is precisely how genuinely single-issue groups should be treated. Such groups almost always have a point. But, being mono-maniacal, they almost always make too much of it. It is the role of mainstream political parties in such situations to act as brokers between all those narrower, special interests within the larger polity.[1] It is their role, as they would put it, to act as 'responsible parties of government'.

What exactly it is to be a 'responsible' party, in this context, is of course an open issue. Much of the answer turns on one's conception of democratic theory and the notion of 'responsibility' or 'accountability' embodied in it. Some would say that a responsible party is one which tries to incorporate all interests afoot in the community – one which, when in office, tries to be the government of 'all the people' rather than serving merely sectional interests. Others, however, would say that a responsible party is simply one which (a) puts up a distinctive policy statement and (b) faithfully implements that election manifesto once it has been elected on it.[2] On that latter account, it would be perfectly

[1] That, anyway, is the pluralist model James Madison (1787) offered in *The Federalist* number 10 for 'curing the mischiefs of faction', and it has long been the dominant focus of American political science (Dahl 1956, ch. 1; Berry 1984).

[2] The latter model, inspired by Schumpeter (1950, ch. 12), won the endorsement of an official committee of the American Political Science Association (1950), no less.

consistent with a party's being a 'responsible' party of government for it to adopt idiosyncratic stands and selective emphases on the various issues of the day, just so long as it had given the electorate prior notice of what it intended to do once in government.

Still, if being a responsible party of government is consistent with having idiosyncratic stands and selective emphases, it nonetheless requires that the party in question take a stand – however idiosyncratic, however unemphatic – on all the issues of the day. Parties in government must inevitably discharge certain 'housekeeping' responsibilities. They have to tend shop – the whole shop, and not only those bits of it that interest them. It would be irresponsible in the worst sense (wantonly reckless, rather than merely undemocratic) for a party in government to ignore altogether whole swathes of public affairs that come to it for resolution, just because that party does not take any particular interest in or have anything particularly distinctive to say about, for example, economic management or defence policy.

It is perfectly proper for parties to stamp their distinctive marks on policy. It is perfectly proper for them to declare 'theme years', rather like the Year of the Child or Women's Decade. But it would be irresponsible in the worst sense for parties in government to pursue those themes to the exclusion of all the other business of government, which must be kept ticking along in parallel with those special programmes.

It is that sense in which ordinary single-issue groups are deemed unfit to form a government all on their own. It is not merely a matter of the idiosyncratic nature of their stands on most issues of the day; it is not merely a matter of the disproportionate emphasis which they propose to accord their pet projects. If they can persuade a sufficient proportion of the electorate to concur in their possibly peculiar views, there is nothing in notions of democratic responsibility to preclude their being allowed to implement them. What is wrong, however, is their concentrating on their pet projects and pet peeves to the exclusion of all the rest of the necessary business of government. What debars ordinary single-issue groups from forming a government is the well-founded fear that – being as they are utterly monomaniacal, taking as they do absolutely no interest in or views on any issue outside their narrow set of concerns – they will indeed neglect the business of government while riding their own particular hobby-horses.

So long as environmentalist lobbies focused narrowly on environmentalist issues, that criticism applied as much to them as to any other single-issue interest group. They were providing important policy inputs. Together with other sectional interests, they could form part of a larger coalition that could credibly present itself as a party of government. But on their own, single-issue groups – be they environmental or industrial – cannot credibly aspire to forming a government.

All that has now changed, though. Greens now offer full-scale election manifestos touching on all the most important issues of the day. The German Greens' fifty-page 1983 manifesto is proto-typical.[3] It touches on issues of environment and work, foreign policy and questions of the individual and society (including law, health, education, women/children/the aged), in addition to the obvious issues of environment and nature.[4] All other national green parties are now offering similarly ambitious programmes of action.

Obviously, the emphases they accord to various issues differ from those that would be accorded them by other, more mainstream parties, just as the substance of their policy positions differs. But that is neither here nor there: it is for the electorate to judge the merits of those emphases and policy stands. The crucial point, for present purposes, is just that greens in their party political mode now take stands on a comprehensive range of political issues. They are therefore as credible a party of government as any other. There is no formal reason for automatically debarring them from office.

2   A Unified Moral Vision

In one crucial respect, though, the green political programme really is radically different from that of other, more established parties. Those tend to be 'catch-all' parties, alliances of disparate factions with disparate interests.[5] Being so carries important consequences for the sorts of political programmes that they can offer. Specifically, being a catch-all party naturally prevents them from offering programmes displaying any particular clarity of moral vision. That, I argue, is where the greens come into their own.[6]

---

[3] Die Grünen 1983.

[4] See the appendix below for details.

[5] Though the phrase was coined by Kirchheimer (1966) as a description of postwar West European parties, it seems equally apt as a description of the American party organizations described by, e.g., Sorauf (1968).

[6] Of course, some versions of their political strategy – notably, that of Parkin (1988), quoted in chapter 1, section 4 above – would put greens in the same 'catch-all' boat. On that account, there is not any one theory underlying green political positions, which represent instead the confluence of various different theoretical commitments and practical emphases. Various people (among them John Braithwaite, Claus Offe and

It is my claim that the green theory of value elaborated in chapter 2 above is what underlies and unifies the entire green political programme. It is that which gives logical cohesion to the green agenda. It is what makes it illogical and inconsistent for other, more established parties to try picking and choosing some bits off that agenda, without accepting all the rest of its demands as well.[7]

Strictly speaking, to make good that claim I would have to show two things. First, I have to show that there are traces of this green theory of value running throughout all of the core green policy proposals. That is not a difficult task, but it is a laborious one; I have, accordingly, relegated it to an appendix below. Second, I would have to show that that green theory of value is the only thread that could plausibly be running through all the planks of the green political programme. Now, that is a taller order. Indeed, I am unsure how claims of that latter sort could ever be established conclusively. So instead I shall be proceeding rather more impressionistically. Still, the conclusion that this impressionistic account is meant to motivate is that the green theory of value sketched above is uniquely able to account for the coherence of the green public-policy proposals.

There is, of course, little need to belabour the connections between the green theory of value which I have sketched and the standard sorts of environmentalist concerns that give green parties their names. The stauncher sorts of environmentalists – those who would identify most powerfully with the green cause – have always been concerned with the protection of nature for its own sake. Their objections to the waste and destruction of natural resources have always been explicitly based on considerations of the harm done to nature itself, rather than on any derivative harm to human interests.

It is easy enough to see how that sort of concern for nature, and the peculiar value it attaches to nature, is indeed what informs all those planks in the green programme pertaining to matters of pollution,

Albert Weale) tell me that they frankly prefer this style of green politics, with various approaches running simultaneously or in strategic sequence. As Offe (personal correspondence 1991) put it, 'Incoherence and inconsistency may well turn out to be a necessity, if not an outright virtue of political programs. Why not?' The only reason 'why not' is that greens would thereby be forced to forego the strong 'all or nothing' claim which I show, in this section, derives from the fact that all their policies flow from a single theory of the good.

[7] Certain greens – certainly the more strident among them – might despair of such 'logic chopping'. They would regard 'illogical' and 'inconsistent' as woefully inadequate terms of disapprobation, and disapprobation itself as a woefully inadequate response to the situation. But that is simply to say that they despair of reasoned argument altogether, preferring instead 'direct action' (whether on their own part or that of Gaia) to drive home their points.

conservation and the environment. If we respect nature in that way, then clearly we would not want to see the air or water polluted. Clearly, we would want to halt the dumping of wastes – especially highly toxic ones – both on land and especially in the oceans. Clearly, we would want to halt and if possible reverse the destruction of the ozone layer. Clearly, we would want to protect forests and natural landscapes. All of that follows absolutely straightforwardly from the sort of respect for nature that a green theory of value would imply. There is no trick at all in that part of the proof. And while some of the same policy prescriptions might be supportable from other value perspectives as well as that green one, it is hardly much of a trick to show that at least some of the more dramatic ones would not.

The trick – if there is one – lies instead in showing that all the other non-environmentalist planks in the green agenda also fit the same basic template.[8] I have little hope of demonstrating that conclusively, so I shall argue more suggestively instead. My basic strategy is to show simply this: seeing the green position on those other issues as a reflection of the green theory of value and the general respect for nature which it embodies will at least help to solve various puzzles that would otherwise arise; it helps us in interpreting apparently anomalous and inconsistent green attitudes towards those issues.

The simple fact that these green policy positions would appear anomalous and inconsistent suggests that other more standard interpretations of the green creed (such as those canvassed in chapter 2, section 6 above) would not easily explain this conjunction of attitudes. That the green theory of value here developed can dissolve those apparent inconsistencies shows that it can account for aspects of green policy thinking that those other more standard interpretations cannot. None of this provides a knock-down argument for supposing that the green theory of value is the only way of accounting for all green policy prescriptions: there might be other, non-standard ways of reading the green creed; or some of the more standard ways might, with sufficient twisting and turning, fit the same facts. Still, knock-down arguments are not ordinarily to be expected in philosophy. We cannot expect literally to

---

[8] Many, frankly, do not. Included among them are many of the most famous green proposals (for decentralization, grassroots democracy and internal party structure, for example); they embrace up to three out of the 'four pillars' of the Die Grünen (1983, preface) programme and seven out of the 'ten key values' of the US greens (Green CoC 1986, items 2–7, 9). These – together with whole branches of the green movement based on them, such as Bookchin's (1990) 'social ecology' – derive from a 'green theory of agency', which is logically separate from and, even in greens' own terms, evaluatively subsidiary to the 'green theory of value' which unifies green policy proposals. Or so I shall argue in chapter 4 below.

disprove people's claims, but can only hope to drive them into increasingly uncomfortable corners and increasingly implausible epicycles.[9]

This claim can best be elaborated by way of examples. Begin with an example drawn from very near the traditional core of green concerns – the curious anomaly between green attitudes towards animals, individually, and towards species of animals, collectively. Of course, no green worthy of the name would endorse wanton cruelty towards animals: they are necessarily opposed to factory farming, and suchlike.[10] But greens do not necessarily endorse animal rights in their fullest form, either.[11] Far from calling, literally, for animal liberation the German Greens demand merely that 'in agriculture, domestic animals are . . . kept in ways that are fair to their species and nature.'[12] That is apparently to say that they do not necessarily object to animals being kept and killed for human consumption, so long as the conditions are sufficiently humane.

While greens might not necessarily object to the destruction of individual animals, they do object strongly to the destruction of whole species of animals – and they are prepared to go to great lengths to prevent that from happening.[13] This is certainly true of the German Greens, who offer a detailed nine-point plan for 'protection of species'.[14] But it is also true of North American greens, who ask 'how can we guarantee rights of nonhuman species?', apparently oblivious to any rights of individual members of those species.[15] And European Greens are likewise opposed to the 'industrialization of agriculture', less because of the cruelty to animals it entails (although they insist that that

[9] This claim, made famous by Nozick's (1981, pp. 1–26) tirade against 'coercive philosophy', actually depends on nothing more than Quine's (1961, ch. 2) 'Two dogmas of empiricism', as Jack Smart has reminded me.

[10] Which is to say that Bahro (1986, pp. 196–209) was right to resign from the German Greens when they refused to support a total ban on animal experiments, arguing that that was carrying the spirit of compromise too far.

[11] Indeed, should probably avoid casting their case for protecting animals in terms of rights at all, since other inanimate elements of nature which greens are presumably no less anxious to protect clearly cannot be the bearers of rights. For a particularly persuasive development of this familiar theme, see Feinberg's (1974) classic paper on 'The rights of animals and unborn generations'.

[12] Die Grünen (1983, sec. IV.7). The European Greens (1989, sec. 7) similarly call merely for 'protection for animals against industrialized farming and [an end] to the use of chemicals and hormones' in agriculture; though elsewhere (sec. 6) they say, 'We object to the treatment of living beings as objects,' it is clear from context that it is merely the 'patenting' of plant and animal life to which they are there objecting.

[13] On the scientific and philosophical importance of species preservation more generally, see Norton (1986; 1987) and Feinberg (1980, esp. pp. 171–3 and 204–5).

[14] Die Grünen (1983, sec. IV.6).

[15] Green CoC 1986, item 1.

should be curtailed) than because it is 'one of the main reasons for the disappearing of more and more plant species'.[16]

On the face of it, those attitudes would seem to appear anomalous: it is hard to see how species can have any moral claims above and beyond those of the individuals comprising them. The best way of making sense of this apparent anomaly, I submit, is to notice that destroying a whole species interferes with the entire natural order, in a way that destroying an individual specimen does not: destroying types changes things fundamentally, in a way that destroying mere tokens does not. In other words, an important nuance in green attitudes towards animals in general seems to make best sense when seen as a manifestation of the green theory of value's emphasis on the value of nature.

Consider, next, a curious anomaly in green defence policy. Greens are, of course, necessarily opposed to militarism in any form; they oppose armed aggression and even the stationing of troops on foreign soil. But they are not necessarily pacifists in the strictest sense, either. The German Greens specifically endorse 'the fundamental right of self-defence' which, they pointedly add, 'includes social resistance in its various forms'.[17] North American greens display similar ambivalence in asking, 'how can we cut our defense budget while maintaining an adequate defense?'[18]

How much military and quasi-military hardware might be required purely for self-defence is unclear. The examples of the classically neutral nations – Sweden and Switzerland – with defence postures ostensibly directed similarly towards simply repelling aggression suggests quite a bit. So does the work of vaguely greenish bodies like the Alternative Defence Commission in Britain.[19] There are certain types of weapons,

---

[16] European Greens 1989, sec. 7; note that they are even more implacably opposed to biotechnology (sec. 6) on similar grounds.

[17] Elsewhere in its manifesto, *Die Grünen* specifically endorse a policy of 'social defence', by which they mean 'organizing and reorienting our society in such a way (in the direction of civil courage, resistance, alternative and decentralized structures) as to make immediately clear to an aggressive foreign power that attempted occupations and domination would entail more difficulties and a greater burden than the increase in power and profit it might bring'. Not only would they permit such resistance; the German Greens even call, in their itemized list of specific policy proposals, for 'programmes of training and education in [such] nonviolent action'. See Die Grünen (1983, secs. I and III.2 respectively).

[18] Green CoC 1986, item 9. So too with the European Greens (1989, preamble): while campaigning 'for one Europe . . . without military alliances', they nonetheless endorse the idea that "the neutral and non-alligned states, together with the countries of the EFTA . . . develop a new dynamic in the balance of power within today's divided Europe'.

[19] In the Alternative Defence Commission's (1983) report, *Defence without the Bomb*, 'defence by civil resistance' (ch. 7) is indeed discussed, but alongside explicitly 'military options' for both Britain (ch. 4) and West Europe (ch. 5). The same schemes are broadly endorsed in Kemp and Wall's *Green Manifesto* (1990, ch. 9).

though, that greens simply are not prepared to tolerate under any conditions. As the German Greens say, completely without qualification, 'Nuclear, biological and chemical weapons must be destroyed.'[20]

Why those weapons especially? The obvious reason, given later in their programme by the German Greens themselves, is simply that 'With the introduction of nuclear weapons war has reached completely new dimensions. The possibility of destroying the whole Earth several times over has turned war into . . . a crime against life in general.'[21] It is the wholesale destruction of nature, rather than the mere destruction of (even very many) people, that makes the greens necessarily opposed to nuclear, chemical and biological weapons. The green theory of value, with its peculiar emphasis on the value of nature as a whole, thus helps to explain why some weapons matter so very much more than others within the broadly pacifist green programme.

For one final example, consider an anomaly in green energy policy. Greens are not happy with fossil-fuel burning plants, of course; their emissions of nitrous oxides produce the acid rain that kills lakes downwind, and their emissions of carbon dioxide produce potentially catastrophic warming worldwide. Greens would much prefer to see coal- and oil-fired power plants phased out and replaced by energy conservation and an increased reliance on 'renewable' energy sources.

In the short term, though, greens are prepared to tolerate the burning of fossil fuels (provided there is 'improved combustion' and so on), despite its grievous environmental harms. In their energy policy, greens are adamant about only one thing: nuclear electricity generation must be stopped immediately and at all costs.[22]

Why? Once again, because it – and its further geopolitical consequences – threaten wholesale destruction of nature as such, in a way that even the burning of fossil fuels seems not (or not so imminently) to do.[23] Here again, the green theory of value – emphasizing as it does the

[20] Die Grünen 1983, sec. 1. North American greens are only a little more equivocal in asking, 'how can we eliminate nuclear weapons from the face of the Earth without being naive about the intentions of other governments?' (Green CoC 1986, item. 4). See similarly European Greens (1989, secs 4 and 11).

[21] Die Grünen 1983, sec. III.2. Similar themes are sounded in Jonathn Schell's (1982) aptly entitled anti-nuclear tract, *The Fate of the Earth*.

[22] Die Grünen 1983, sec. II.6. European Greens 1989, sec. 4.

[23] In their 1983 manifesto, Die Grünen (1983, sec. II.6) say, variously: 'nuclear power is an energy source directed against the very foundations of life,' nuclear power threatens the future of all life, as the radioactive products of atomic fission are life-endangering,' and 'the export of nuclear installations to all countries of the world creates new military risks and undermines international efforts to restrict the spread of nuclear weapons.' Similarly, the European Greens (1989, sec. 4) 'unequivocally oppose the use of civil or military nuclear technology as an . . . extremely dangerous technology that creates environmental problems persisting for thousands of years'.

peculiar importance of protecting nature as such – explains what would otherwise remain a really rather curious emphasis within the green programme.

3   Claims of Consistency

All the evidence provided by these examples is impressionistic and inconclusive, to be sure. But viewing the green theory of value as the unifying thread running throughout the green agenda does seem to help make sense, in those various ways, of demands and emphases that would otherwise remain somewhat mysterious in the green agenda. Showing that that is true is enough to establish at least a *prima facie* case for supposing that all the planks in the green political programme really are informed by the one and the same green theory of value here identified.

The practical political point of trying to demonstrate the peculiar cohesion of the green political agenda, as I have just done, is to show that the green movement amounts to more than an ordinary single-interest group – and that its agenda deserves more respect accordingly. On the analysis just offered, all the major planks in the green political programme can plausibly be traced to one and the same green theory of value. That being so, there is something *prima facie* wrong with the standard political strategy of embracing some green demands while ignoring others.

The *prima facie* wrongness of a strategy of piecemeal borrowing from the greens is easily explicated. It derives straightforwardly from the logic of consistency. It would be simply wrong to embrace a theory of value – the green theory, or any other – for some purposes while shunning it for others. The truth status of value theories just does not flicker on and off like that.

If a theory of value is true for some purposes, it is equally true for all situations to which it is equally applicable. If you propose to do green things for green reasons in some circumstances, then you are under a *prima facie* obligation of consistency to do equally green things for green reasons on every occasion on which an equally strong green reason for action is equally applicable.

There are grave implications for mainstream political parties trying to steal the greens' political thunder. They hope that, by adopting a few of the less demanding planks of the green agenda, they can buy off the greens. But if the green agenda really is logically as tightly unified as

I have here been suggesting – if it really does all derive from one and the same theory of value, at root – then that strategy of piecemeal borrowing will be logically inconsistent as well as politically unacceptable. Piecemeal borrowing may be not at all inappropriate in the case of a more ordinary interest group or catch-all party. In the case of the greens, however, it really does have to be a matter of all or nothing.

4 Brown Evasions

I have described the strategy of piecemeal borrowing from the greens as *prima facie* wrong. The reason that strategy is wrong only *prima facie* is this: there are various ways in which mainstream parties wishing to adopt green positions on some but not all issues might avoid falling prey to the errors to which that argument points. One approach is for non-green parties to try to 'mimic' green values. The other is for them to try to 'swamp' green values.

The first strategy ('mimicking green values') essentially amounts to endorsing green conclusions for purely brown reasons. Then, while appearing to adopt green causes, mainstream parties would never have actually committed themselves to a green theory of value in the first place. They would therefore be guilty of no inconsistency in refusing to follow the dictates of such a theory elsewhere as well.

Following the second strategy ('swamping green values'), mainstream parties would embrace green values alongside many others. Green values could then be given their full due, in the sense of being applied consistently in all cases to which they are relevant, without necessarily dictating the outcome in each case. Green values would then be only some among many, after all; and they do not necessarily trump all others in cases of conflict. Arguing in this way, mainstream parties might claim that, while green values are always weighed into the balance, they are sometimes (indeed, perhaps most times) outweighed by other competing values also deserving of consideration in such circumstances.

Either of those strategies would allow mainstream parties, with perfect consistency, to endorse green positions in some cases but not in others. In what follows, I shall discuss each of those alternatives in turn. To foreshadow, I shall be relatively dismissive of the first, for the obvious sorts of reasons. While there genuinely are plenty of non-green reasons for adopting green causes, a party which purports to be even partly 'green' when it is actually acting purely from brown motives is fundamentally fraudulent.

I shall be relatively more welcoming of the second, for reasons that are perhaps slightly less obvious. If that strategy is not to amount to an analogous form of fraud, the mainstream parties in question genuinely will have to give full weight to green values at every juncture, instead of disregarding them altogether wherever their implications seem uncomfortable or inconvenient; and even if those values are often ultimately outweighed, giving them genuine consideration in this way will at least sometimes generate victories for green causes that they would not otherwise have won.

Mimicking Green Values

If the green agenda is defined in terms of the practical political demands it contains, others may well come to many of the same conclusions as green activists without in any way necessarily endorsing the same fundamental green values. The green theory of value is, I hope to have shown, what underlies all these practical proposals in the eyes of green activists themselves. And it is, I believe, the best way to make sense of their programme as a whole. But as regards a great many of the items on their agenda, the greens can easily enough form a marriage of convenience with others who have reached the same practical conclusions for very different reasons.

Nowhere is this more apparent than with the classic problems of pollution and resource conservation. Even the narrowest, neoclassical economist is prepared to concede that the 'external costs' associated with pollution must be internalized if social welfare is to be maximized – the polluter must be made to pay, just as greens demand.[24] In so far as the burning of fossil fuels genuinely does threaten to produce global warming sufficient to melt the polar ice and inundate the world's low-lying cities and farmland, or the use of CFC gases threatens to strip away the ozone layer protecting us and our agriculture from damage from the sun's ultraviolet radiation, prudence of a perfectly ordinary sort is all that is involved in support for policies to prevent those outcomes.[25] In so far as current consumption patterns genuinely do threaten to exhaust the earth's material resources before technological substitutes can be found for them, you do not need to be particularly

[24] Die Grünen 1983, sec. IV.1; European Greens 1989, sec. 1. Pigou (1932, pt II, ch. 9) is the classical source. For modern restatements and elaborations, see Mishan (1967); Kneese, Ayres and D'Arge (1970); Freeman, Haveman and Kneese (1973); and Fisher (1981, ch. 6).

[25] Wilson 1970. US NRC 1989. Smith and Tirpak 1989.

green to demand that those resources be conserved – you need only be attached to your present lifestyle.[26]

On all those classically green issues, and many others besides, mainstream political parties may well want to do green-looking things for non-green reasons. They do not have to endorse the green theory of value, as such, in order to justify a concern for reducing pollution, averting catastrophic climate change or avoiding serious resource depletion. They can therefore adopt those particular planks from the green agenda, incorporating them into their own programmes for their own reasons, without necessarily getting committed to the green theory of value and all else that follows from it.

Green parties may, or may not, want to take advantage of that fact. They may, or may not, want to form marriages of convenience with other, more established political parties to do certain things that they all agree, each for its own distinctive reasons, ought be done. Whether they ultimately do is in part a matter of strategic calculation: is it prudent, politically, to let other parties share and perhaps steal your best clothes? In part, though, it is also a matter of principle for many greens who reject the cynical compromises of coalitional politics.

How the greens themselves respond to these coalitional possibilities is of less concern to me here than is how the mainstream parties represent themselves in discussing green issues. There is no objection, presumably, if they admit forthrightly that they are green only in their conclusions and not in their premises. That would be fair enough. It would be perfectly fair for them to go on to try to persuade the electorate that this is as it should be – that the brown reasons are the right reasons for green actions. Or, again, it would be perfectly fair for them to try to persuade the electorate that all that really matters, when it comes to green issues, are the conclusions – premises are of no consequence. But all those further arguments are fair enough only because, in making them, mainstream parties necessarily come clean on the fundamental issue and admit that, although they are proposing green actions, they are definitely not doing so for green reasons.

Mainstream parties are not always prepared to play the game that way, though. They will often argue, imply or allude that they are not only doing green things but that they are also doing them for green

---

[26] That was the practical political hook that doomsday modellers hoped to set with works such as Forrester (1971), Meadows et al. (1972) and US CEQ (1980; 1981); cf. Cole et al. (1973), Simon (1981) and Simon and Kahn (1984). Notice that even economists, who talk quite happily in terms of the 'optimal rate' of exhausting natural resources, would be nonetheless opposed to using them up precipitously; see Dasgupta and Heal (1979) and Fisher (1981, chs 2–5).

reasons. Occasionally they say as much; more often, they merely allow voters to believe as much, without actually saying so themselves. Either way, though, it is a simple form of fraud. That is not the only way mainstream parties might play the game, I should emphasize once again. But in so far as it is the way they choose to play it, it is a morally flawed strategy. If they give (or allow people to get) the impression that they are committed to green causes for green reasons, then they really are morally committed to following the green theory of value wherever it leads. Failing to do so would be inconsistent – or, worse, fraudulent.

Swamping Green Values

The second strategy for mainstream political parties wanting to adopt some green positions without getting committed to the whole green programme is to say that the green theory of value forms part – but only part – of the larger, composite theory of the Good that they embrace. Green values are important, they would say, but so too are various other values as well. Furthermore, they would continue, those other considerations within that larger theory of the Good might always conflict with – and, in any particular case, override – green ones, however deeply we might be committed to them. Hence, on any particular occasion it might always be better, on balance, to do something altogether different from that which a green theory of value recommends.

I would not necessarily care to argue against any of that. In discussing theories of value in general, and the green theory of value in particular, I have been careful to say that there is no reason to suppose that any one theory of value is true to the utter exclusion of all others. And if we are to be prepared to contemplate value pluralism of that sort, we must probably also be prepared to allow values arising in one domain to overweigh values arising from another, from time to time.[27]

Saying that might seem to amount to conspiring with the mainstream parties in evading the full force of the green position. In a way, perhaps it is. We ought nonetheless to recognize the very real achievement involved in merely making mainstream parties give green considerations their full due in each and every case to which they ought to apply. Cynical or incoherent as it may seem, mainstream politicians are all too often tempted to accept the green theory as a source of values in certain situations and yet to ignore it *altogether* in others to which it is equally

---

[27] Unless we choose – implausibly – to give one value domain some form of absolute (e.g. lexical) priority over all others.

applicable. Stopping them from doing that would, in and of itself, be no mean feat.

It is perfectly proper that the conclusions of the green theory of value might sometimes be outweighed. There is nothing inconsistent or incoherent in concluding that, on balance, greens are right to demand that the 'polluters pay' for the damage they have done but that, on balance, it is better not to join greens in insisting unequivocally on the 'elimination of piecework and conveyor-belt work, as well as other forms of production stress'.[28] But in so far as all the greens' demands spring from the same deeper theory of value, all of them ought to be seen to be exerting a similar moral tug on us. They ought be given the same consideration in every case to which they apply, even though countervailing considerations might outweigh them at some times but not at others.

A theory of value – *any* theory of value, be it the green one or any other – cannot legitimately be first embraced and then scorned in quick succession. Even if green values are ultimately outweighed, they ought at the very least to be consistently weighed into the balance on all occasions to which they are relevant. Consistency requires that much, at the very least, if those values are going to be weighed into the balance on any occasions at all.

Forcing mainstream parties to give green values their full due, in this way, carries potentially substantial practical political consequences. For if they genuinely weigh in green values wherever they are appropriate, rather than (as all too often at present) dismissing them in certain contexts right from the start, then the converse is also true. Just as in any credible sort of weighting scheme green values will sometimes be outweighed by other values, so too will those other values at least sometimes be outweighed in some perhaps surprising ways by green ones.

In one of the more fascinating empirical studies of bureaucratic decision-making of recent years, it has been shown that the superficially toothless requirement that US agencies must simply file an Environmental Impact Statement cataloguing the consequences of their plans for the natural environment has actually had an important effect. It has made those agencies more environmentally sensitive. It has made them think of environmental consequences of their actions, in a way that they would otherwise not have done. And in that way it has actually prevented them from wreaking certain forms of damage on the

[28] See Die Grünen 1983, secs. IV.1 and II.4 respectively.

environment that they would almost undoubtedly have inflicted quite without thinking.[29]

It is obviously too much to expect that mainstream political parties, purporting to take green values seriously, will respect their edicts mechanically. But the strains of consistency might at least force mainstream parties to *think* seriously about green values wherever they are applicable, and that might in similar fashion have a very real political effect. Thus, though this latter trick of 'swamping green values' is usually intended as every bit as much of an evasion as the first, the practical effect of implementing it systematically will probably be to secure substantially more respect for green values than is anticipated – by the mainstream parties or by their green critics, either.

5   The Moral Weight of Countervailing Values

There are, of course, a great many values that might be thought to come into conflict with green values. Most of those conflicts arise only from time to time, and on a case-by-case basis. That being so, little of a systematic sort can therefore be said about those conflicts.

There are two values that seem in ongoing conflict with green values, though. One is the value of economic growth (or, perhaps better, 'material prosperity'). It is said that respecting green values above all else necessarily – always and everywhere – retards economic growth and development, impoverishes the community and creates substantial human misery in consequence.

The other value thought to be in constant tension with green values is property rights. It is said that respecting green values above all else necessarily – always and everywhere – interferes with the rights of property owners to do what they will with what is by rights their own.

These two important challenges are well worth considering in their own right. In addition, however, they are also representative of two broader styles of challenge: the first utilitarian, focusing on human happiness; the second libertarian, focusing on people's rights and liberties. The particular challenge in view is, in each case, only one among many possible ones under each of those broader headings, of course. Still, if those two more particular challenges can be repelled, that would provide at least some reason for supposing that in general

---

[29] Taylor 1984. Weiss and Gruber (1984, p. 238) report similarly that simply promulgating information about the extent of discrimination in education has similarly persuasive effects.

green values might be relatively impervious to the whole style of challenge that each of those more particular challenges represents.

Economic Growth

The apparent necessity of a trade-off between economic growth and environmental protection owes more to the rhetoric of environmentalists themselves than to the arguments of their opponents. Their major works bear titles like *The Limits to Growth*;[30] *The Costs of Economic Growth*;[31] 'The no-growth society'.[32] One of their most distinguished spokesmen quotes another, approvingly, as saying 'that anyone who believes exponential growth can go on forever in a finite world is either a madman or an economist.'[33] In light of such rhetoric, those inclined to favour economic growth and to oppose environmental protection as a retardant to growth need not prove that environmental protection retards economic growth. They are tempted to suppose that they need merely take environmentalists at their own word.

That is a good way of scoring debating points, but a bad way of making public policy. Environmentalists themselves seem oddly over-inclined to emphasize the sacrifices that their programme would require – their willingness to bear enormous sacrifices for the sake of their crusade is, apparently, offered as evidence of their moral seriousness. In such circumstances, we cannot simply assume that a major sacrifice of economic goals would be required to secure environmental ones, just because both parties to that dispute agree that that is the case. We need to examine for ourselves whether, why, and to what extent, those two goals really are in conflict.

Passing as it does largely unexamined in ordinary environmentalist-economist debates, the argument for the necessity of such a trade-off is peculiarly weak. It seems to appeal to little more than the intuition that anything that constrains corporate conduct – as environmental regulations unquestionably do – is bad for business. And anything that is bad for business is presumed to be bad for the economy.

[30] Meadows et al. 1972.

[31] Mishan 1967.

[32] Olson 1973.

[33] Olson (ibid., p. 3), quoting Kenneth Boulding. A parallel proposition appears conspicuously in the preamble to the 1983 German Greens' election manifesto: 'The established parties in Bonn behave as if an infinite increase in industrial production was possible on the finite plant Earth. . . . Proceeding from the laws of nature, and especially from the knowledge that unlimited growth is impossible in a limited system, an ecological policy means understanding ourselves and our environment as part of nature' (Die Grünen 1983, p. 7).

It would be a mistake, though, to suppose that all environmentalist regulations are aimed exclusively, or even primarily at constraining corporate conduct. Much of the damage that the environment sustains comes instead through careless consumption. While many of the most important environmental protection measures work through regulations on corporations, their ultimate aim is actually to alter the behaviour of consumers. 'Bottle bills' encourage consumers to recycle glass by requiring companies that sell bottled products to pay a refund to consumers returning those bottles. The US Environmental Protection Agency's 'emission standards' constrain the levels of noxious chemicals that may on average come from any given manufacturer's automobiles, with a view to making consumers drive cleaner cars – an aim which is also pursued more directly through state-by-state emission control laws, requiring consumers themselves to keep their cars' exhaust systems in good shape.

That said, it must nonetheless be agreed that environmentalists are concerned to constrain – first and foremost – the activities of profit-seeking corporations.[34] From that simple fact follows the widespread perception that environmental protection measures are necessarily costly to the larger national economy. It is worth pausing briefly to reflect on the implicit logic underlying this perception, though.

The unstated argument underlying this intuitive response seems to rest on the following propositions. Firstly, we are invited to suppose that, in so far as environmentalist measures constrain corporations at all, that necessarily means that those regulations prevent corporations from doing something that they would otherwise have done. Secondly, we are invited to suppose that corporations are (or try their best to be) profit maximizing. From the conjunction of those propositions we are invited to infer, thirdly, that anything that prevents corporations from doing what they ordinarily would have done (probably) reduces their profits. Fourthly, we are reminded that anything which reduces corporate profits reduces the nation's economic prosperity.

Of course, almost all those propositions are highly debatable. There is, for example, no reason to suppose that 'corporations know best', in so far as opportunities for profits are concerned. They are not perfect profit maximizers. Much recent work on the theory of the firm questions whether they even really try to be.[35] In any case, firms hardly show

---

[34] In capitalist countries. In command economies, their concern is to constrain managers who are anxious to meet or beat the targets set for them in the Plan, and who are prepared in the course of so doing to cut any (environmental, or other) corners that they can.

[35] Marris 1964; Marris and Mueller 1980; Cyert and March 1963.

themselves to be perfect judges of what would best maximize profits. They market a great many products that simply fall flat, and they are often initially reluctant to market products that then take off. Hence, preventing corporations from doing something that would damage the environment, even if it does prevent them from doing something they would otherwise have done, does not necessarily cut into their profits.

Neither, it must be said, does whatever cuts into corporate profits necessarily reduce national economic prosperity. It may well be true that whatever reduces corporate profits reduces a country's gross national product (GNP). Indeed, that sometimes seems to count as a veritable analytic truth, given how those figures are compiled. Remember, however, that what we are supposed to be maximizing here is national economic prosperity. GNP is only a measure – an indicator – of that. If it were a perfect measure, then GNP maximization would be equivalent to maximizing the goal in view. But no indicator is perfect, and GNP is less perfect than most.[36] And in so far as it leaves important elements of people's economic well-being out of account, a course of action that maximizes GNP will deviate from a course of action that maximizes the real goal, national economic prosperity.

That, in fact, is the crux of the environmental economists' case.[37] Environmental economists are died-in-the-wool economists. They are as anxious as the next economist to maximize human happiness (or sum-total social utility, or people's preference satisfaction – progressively more modern expressions of the same root idea). Their point is merely that GNP maximization is an inadequate proxy for maximizing preference satisfaction.

Their key analytic notion, in making that case, is that of economic 'externalities'.[38] The basic idea underlying that notion is that, for one reason or another, people do not always get to reap the full benefits or – more importantly – have to pay the full costs of their activities. In the classic case of a positive externality, orchard-keepers do not have to pay bee-keepers for the services of their bees in cross-pollinating apple trees. In the classic case of a negative externality, factory owners do not have to pay the full costs of disposing of their wastes if they can dump them free of charge into the air or water.[39]

---

[36] The classic critique from within the economics profession itself is of course Morgenstern's (1963).

[37] For excellent summaries of this massive literature, see Fisher (1981); Freeman, Haveman and Kneese (1973); Kneese, Ayres and D'Arge (1970). On the limits to their models, see especially Sagoff (1988).

[38] Mishan (1967, esp. pt 2).

[39] Meade 1952; Scitovsky 1954.

Profit-maximizing factory owners would, of course, seize any such opportunities gladly. It would enable them to cut their costs of production, and with them their prices; and that in turn would enable them to maximize their sales, and hence their profits. They would have done so, however, not by genuinely reducing their costs of production but merely by passing part of them off on to someone else. When profits are maximized in this way, what is being maximized is not some unambiguous measure of how much better off others who buy those products have been made. What is being maximized is instead some deeply ambiguous measure, combining how well off producers have made some (their shareholders and customers) and how badly off they have made others (those who are forced to carry the external costs associated with such a mode of production). There is a genuine difference between the two, and an important one to anyone concerned to maximize people's prosperity, preference satisfaction, or material well-being. In terms of GNP calculations, though, these two very different sources of profits are indistinguishable.

In the presence of external economies, there is always going to be a systematic deviation between private cost and social cost of production. Profit maximizers will always maximize private rates of return. That means passing off the external costs of their activities on to others whenever they can, and carrying on with activities only part of whose costs they bear long after it would have been socially optimal for them to stop.[40]

In such circumstances, if we want to maximize net social welfare we must find some way to force people to 'internalize' externalities, to take them fully into account in their own decision-making. One slightly ham-fisted way of doing that is the traditional political response of imposing social regulations that prohibit or limit or circumscribe such activities.[41] Economists propose instead that we ought simply to impose a special 'tax' on externally-generating activities, equivalent to the sum that those activities actually cost others in society. If the polluter can afford to pay the tax and still make a profit, then that is proof positive, they say, that the activity yields more social profit than loss and hence should continue.[42] We may or may not like such proposals in general.[43] The

---

[40] Pigou 1932, pt 2.

[41] Lave 1981.

[42] Originally suggested in Pigou (1932), the pollution tax proposal has been picked up by Kneese and Schultze (1975) and, through them, most of the economics profession. Recent advocates include Pearce, Markandya and Barbier 1989; Pearce 1991; Kemball-Cook, Bauer and Mattingly 1991.

[43] We may, for example, think that it is important to talk in terms of 'fining' polluters

important thing to notice about those proposals in the present context, though, is the wedge that they drive between maximizing corporate profits and maximizing national prosperity: to maximize the latter we must cut into the former, the welfare economists themselves are telling us.

A similar critique can be mounted against growth maximization as a national goal, more generally. The real goal is to maximize not growth rates but rather national well-being. The indicators we use to measure growth, or prosperity, do not take into account all the factors which are genuinely relevant to people's sense of prosperity or well-being. People may be earning more but enjoying it less, because leisure time has gone down or crime rates gone up as a consequence of the higher growth rate. Standard economic indicators, picking up the increase in earnings, will say that people are unambiguously better off. They are wrong in that. But they are wrong in ways that we can demonstrate only by conjoining 'social' indicators to those more standard economic ones. Yet after fully a quarter-century of trying, we have still fully to master techniques for doing so.[44]

All this is merely to say that there will be less of a conflict between green values and growth values than might at first appear. Much of the apparent disparity comes simply from miscalculations of growth rates. Much of what is involved in calculating them properly, and making them genuinely reflect the underlying values that they are supposed to be tapping, actually involves adjusting them for previously uncosted environmental effects. Adjustments of that sort will obviously reduce the scope of conflict between the two sets of values.

To say there will be less conflict between the adjusted values is not to say that there will be none, though. For countries that are poor, or even for the poorer members of relatively rich countries, genuine improvement in their material economic circumstances may well be worth the sacrifice of some – maybe much – environmental amenity. Mishan caustically remarks, 'Like a national flag and a national airline, a national plan for economic growth is deemed an essential item in the paraphernalia of every new nation state.'[45] And it is undeniably true that the only way we can persuade the very poor to attach any high priority to a wide range of values – ranging from social equity to environmental quality – is to show that they are consistent with continuously high rates of economic

(with the implication that they are doing something wrong) rather than in terms of a 'tax' or a 'fee' (which seems to suggest that polluters are being sold a licence to pollute).

[44] US Department of Health, Education and Welfare 1969; Rose 1989.

[45] Mishan 1967, p. 27.

growth.[46] It would be wrong to pretend that, for the poor especially, this trade-off literally disappears once economic prosperity is construed more broadly than mere GNP.

Let us not leap to hasty policy conclusions, though. Being willing to sacrifice environment for economic growth is one thing; being able to do so is another. Much though we may wish we could make that trade, it may well be that there is no way to do so. We might just end up with a despoiled environment, without any compensating economic gains. Or we might end up with an environment that was unnecessarily despoiled, in that there was another less environmentally destructive way to achieve the same economic ends.

So the second fundamental point to be made with respect to the economy-environment trade-off is that we must be careful to engage in no gratuitous sacrifices. We must not simply assume that, by sacrificing something, we will be buying ourselves something.[47] We must demand to see the details of the economic model on the basis of which we are being told that environmental despoilation will yield economic dividends. We must make sure that that model works – that it is a good representation of the real economy. We must inspect that model to see what additional conditions must obtain in order for the proposed environmental sacrifices actually to yield the promised economic rewards; and we must then consider how likely those further conditions are, and how sensitive the model's predictions are to variations in them. Finally, we must inspect that model to see whether there might not be some other way to obtain equivalent economic gains with fewer environmental or other sacrifices.

Again, this is not to say that it will never prove possible to trade economic gains for environmental losses. In some – maybe in most standard – economic circumstances that may well prove possible. But we must not simply assume that it will be so. Nor, even where it is, should we simply assume that environmental sacrifice is the only way to make those economic gains, just because it is one way to do so.

[46] The World Bank had to cast its arguments for social equity as a strategy for *Redistribution with Growth* (Chenery et al. 1974). Similarly, the Brundtland Commission could sell environmental protection to the Third World only with the aid of the catchphrase 'sustainable development' (World Commission on Environment and Development 1987).

[47] As we typically do in other areas where social values are being sacrificed to economic growth. Consider the case of human rights. It is often said that there is a trade-off between respect for human rights and promoting economic development. But cross-national empirical evidence reveals no systematic relationship of that sort (Frohock and Sylvan 1983). And none of the economic theory that might be relevant to that issue seems to argue in that direction either (Goodin 1979).

The conjunction of these points substantially narrows the scope of the environment–economy, green–growth trade-off. The first set of considerations suggests that – purely as a value proposition – we ought be willing to make the trade less often than it might seem we should. 'Economic growth', as traditionally measured, poorly captures the values we care about under such headings. And economic prosperity properly conceived incorporates all the considerations that environmentalists are wanting to press.

The second set of considerations suggests that – purely as an empirical proposition – we will have less opportunity or less need to make the trade than it might seem that we do.[48] Lower wages might translate automatically into higher profits, within any plausible economic model. But lower environmental standards do not automatically translate into higher economic growth in any so straightforward a way. And, of course, unless the sacrifice of environmental values to economic ones is both efficacious and necessary, then we ought not sacrifice those values.

Property Rights

When governments slap a preservation order on a listed building of great historical or architectural interest, or when they enact measures prohibiting farmers from draining wetlands or tearing up hedgerows, it is standardly said by libertarians opposed to such measures that the government is thereby interfering with people's property rights. Some go so far as to say that the government has actually 'taken' people's property, at least in part, for public purposes whenever it enacts environmental protection legislation restricting what people can do with their property.[49] Whether or not it has taken the property, certainly it has restricted some of the rights that owners formerly enjoyed with respect to that property.[50]

Such restrictions on property rights might, on balance, be justifiable, these commentators are quick to concede. What they demand in return

[48] For one particularly dramatic example of the way in which empirical facts about the economy might belie very confident predictions of theoretical models of it, note Tobey's (1990) demonstration that empirically 'the introduction of stringent environmental control measures' cannot be shown to have worked to disadvantage those nations adopting them in international trade.

[49] Epstein 1985, esp. chs 5 and 11. But, as environmentalists would be quick to point out, the original act of acquisition – removing something from nature and appropriating it to oneself – is an act of 'taking' too, and one which must be justified just as surely as any other (Rodgers 1982).

[50] Honoré (1961, pp. 146–7), referring to the 1947 British Agricultural Act that imposed a 'duty of good husbandry' upon cultivators.

is a concession that such measures genuinely do restrict property rights. Their main claim is just that there is always a countervailing value – the legitimate claims of property owners – to be weighed in the balance against any environmental protection measure of this sort.

It is tempting to concede that point. Indeed, it seems churlish not to do so. It seems to amount to little more than meeting the opposition halfway. Before conceding the necessity of conflict between green values and property rights too quickly, though, it pays to reflect for a moment. Exactly which right of property is it, after all, that is necessarily compromised by laying on people a duty to preserve?

Property owners here are implicitly asserting a 'right to destroy'. But that right is nowhere to be found in any of the standard lists of the main components of property rights. According to that standard catalogue, a property right is an amalgam of, basically: (1) a right to use; (2) a right to use exclusively; and (3) a right to transfer.[51] The putative 'right to destroy' is mentioned nowhere on that list, and it appears only incidentally and very much in passing on the far longer and less systematic lists sometimes favoured by lawyers.[52]

Trying to think how we might ground such a right to destroy in property rights of a more ordinary sort, all the obvious strategies fail us. It is not analytically implicit in any of those more standard components of property rights. Some might say that you cannot have a right to use without having a right to abuse and hence to destroy; but renters of hired cars enjoy precisely such a right to use but not destroy the car that they hire.[53] Some might say that you cannot have a right to use something exclusively or to transfer it without having a right to destroy it; but, again, owners of a building under a preservation order enjoy precisely such rights to use exclusively and to transfer the building to others, without having a right to destroy it. That is not to say that all buildings necessarily should be under preservation orders, or that all property is or should consist just in leaseholds, of course. The point is merely that there is no necessary, analytic connection between a right to destroy and any of those other more standard rights of property.

---

[51] Together with various subsidiary rights and duties (liability rules, etc.) required for the enforcement of those others. See Snare (1972) and Macpherson (1977a), echoing, after a fashion, Blackstone (1765, bk 1, ch. 1, sec. 3).

[52] See e.g. Honoré (1961) and, following him, philosophers such as Becker (1977, pp. 19–20).

[53] At most, a right to use might entail a right to use up, if the thing we have a right to use is something (like food or firewood, for example) that can only be used by using it up. But even that right to use up would be consistent with a quasi-preservationist duty, such as a duty to replace what you used up (saving and planting some seed corn or saplings, in the examples just mentioned).

Neither, it seems, would any of the standard justifications for giving people property rights in the first place justify giving them a right to destroy. Suppose, following Locke, we think that the reason you must be given ownership of some previously unowned natural object is that, through your labour, some truly essential part of yourself has become inextricably intertwined with it. But why, through that mixing, do you gain what was previously no one's rather than losing what was previously yours?[54] Presumably whatever you mixed was such an essential bit of yourself that it would be wrong to allow you to separate yourself from it by frittering it away. But if it is so important a bit of yourself as all that, then it would be wrong to allow you to destroy that bit of yourself, either. For the same reason we give property rights to people who have mixed their labour with unowned things, therefore, we should presumably prohibit rather than allow them to destroy those things.

Locke's is only one particular – and particularly metaphorical – version of a broader style of desert-based justifications for property rights, of course. But, more generally, there seems nothing in the general notion of a 'fitting reward' for labour expended that people should be given a right to destroy the products of their labour. Of course, the language of 'fitting reward' is itself metaphor laden, and it is therefore often hard to pin down precisely what a 'fitting' reward would be. But the general point can be made perfectly well by appeal to the sort of sporting analogy to which notions of 'desert' seem most typically to appeal ('the fastest runner deserves to win the race' and so on). When winners of a challenge cup are awarded the prize, they are not allowed to melt it down; instead, they are required to return the cup for presentation to the winner of next year's contest. The cup is no less fitting, as a reward for their efforts, for their having no right to destroy it. The notion of a 'fitting reward' – and hence the desert-based justification for property rights more generally – thus does not seem to entail a right to destroy.

Neither does the other main class of utility-based justifications for property rights. The reason for giving people private property rights, on that account, is that that is the way to maximize social utility derived from the objects of the natural world. Everyone's business is no one's, in the classic phrase: common property resources get overused without some particular individual who has a special interest in protecting and preserving them. Cultivated land is ten times more productive than

---

[54] In Nozick's (1974, p. 175) classic example, when you dump a can of tomato juice which was indisputably yours into the ocean, which is no one's, you do not come to own the ocean in consequence.

uncultivated, Locke tells us, and people will only sow if they can be sure that they will be the ones to reap. If increasing the general social usefulness of objects is the reason for assigning private property rights in them, though, that again would seem not to ground a right to destroy. Destroying something destroys its future usefulness, after all.[55]

This is a brief precis of what would ultimately have to be a much longer argument, of course.[56] The upshot is simple enough, though. If arguments along these lines succeed, then they will have succeeded in showing there is no reason to suppose that there is any necessary conflict between property rights and preservationist duties at all. Greens can impose preservationist duties on property owners without apology, and without fear that some countervailing value of property rights might always trump green values in any particular case. Hence there is far less need than is commonly thought to trade off green values for libertarian ones, either.

6   Compromising Green Values

In section 2 of this chapter, I argued strongly against piecemeal borrowing by mainstream parties from the green agenda. There I argued that, since all the items on it are informed by one and the same moral vision, politicians are logically committed to accepting it on something akin to an all-or-nothing basis. It is simply inconsistent for them to embrace any theory of value – the green one or any other – for some purposes but not for others to which it applies with equal force. And, although there are ways for them to try evading that charge of inconsistency, none of those evasions are likely to prove altogether successful if the arguments of the intervening sections are broadly right.

I see this principally as a problem for mainstream parties trying to capture the green position, though. It might be thought that analogous problems arise for greens themselves, in so far as they are obliged by the logic of coalition politics to cut deals with mainstream parties who are

---

[55] Of course, the utility from destroying something might always exceed the sum total of utility that would have been produced, now or later, through any alternative use that those things might have been put to. That may be true at any time of any good, and must be true at some time of those goods that can be used only by being used up. So on utilitarian grounds it may be right for people to destroy a thing at some particular moment. But giving them a right to destroy is a queer way of institutionalizing that rule. It gives people a blanket right to destroy at any time what, on utilitarian grounds, they may properly destroy only at one particular time.

[56] It is elaborated in Goodin 1990b.

prepared to accept some but not all of their demands. In trading away some but not all of their demands, green negotiators might seem to have fallen into the same inconsistency as I have alleged plagues their reluctant mainstream suitors.

Whether or not to form coalitions with other parties at all is a larger issue, and one on which greens themselves are split. This debate has particularly divided the German greens, with self-styled Fundis (fundamentalists) insisting that greens should remain pure but seemingly perpetually in opposition. Realos (realists), in contrast, are committed to making a genuine difference, even if that means joining a coalition and making the inevitable compromises that that would necessarily entail.[57]

This is not a problem peculiar to parliamentary politics, it ought be noted. The same sort of calculation faces the green more generally, in deciding whether to press for thoroughly green policies or whether to accept, for the time being, the best compromise that they are likely to get others to make. Jonathan Porritt tells the salutary tale of a British Friends of the Earth campaign to persuade consumers to shun aerosols that employed as propellants ozone-destroying chlorofluorocarbons. 'Greener-than-greens absolutists', he recalls, 'were quick to castigate Friends of the Earth for not campaigning against aerosols in general, inasmuch as they are indisputably unnecessary, wasteful and far from environmentally benign even if they don't use CFCs. . . . As Director of Friends of the Earth, [though,] I know that we were right to campaign in the way we did. We would have made little, if any, headway with an anti-aerosol campaign.'[58] Thinking in terms of 'the long-term implications of what we were doing', the self-indulgence of that greener-than-thou stance just could not be justified. So long as no one mistakes – or allows others to mistake or misrepresent – such provisional compromises as 'the end of the road', green movements outside parliament as well as inside it ought regard them as both morally permissible and, often, morally required.

As a pure matter of electoral prudence, though, coalition formation always involves tricky calculations. It is always doubtful whether any group – green or otherwise – is wise to merge its corporate identity with that of another. In so far as coalitions agree a single stand on contentious issues, parties cease taking distinctive stands on important

[57] For commentaries, see Cohen and Arato 1984; Spretnak and Capra 1986, p. 7; Hülsberg 1988, chs 8 and 9; Kelly 1988; Offe 1990; Dobson 1990, pp. 132–9. For the point of view of the principal Fundi involved in the rift, see Bahro (1986, pp. 51–9, 159–88 and esp. 196–211).

[58] Porritt 1988, pp. 200–1.

policy questions. The separate identities of coalition partners are merged, and the distinctiveness of smaller and more marginal partners all too often submerged, within the larger parliamentary union. And being deprived of their distinctiveness can have obvious electoral consequences, especially for those larger and more marginal parties, in turn. There is, therefore, always something to be said, as a matter of pure electoral prudence, for standing aloof from coalition politics.

But if greens should shun coalition politics, that can in my view only be for reasons of political prudence. The principled objection we have to a mainstream party picking and choosing items off the green agenda has to do with the inconsistency of adopting a green theory of value for some purposes but not others. But that objection simply does not apply to Realo greens themselves. They truly do try to apply one and the same theory of the Good – one and the same green theory of value – consistently across all cases.

They are, of course, stymied in their attempts to do so by coalition partners who refuse to accept that theory's implications in certain applications. But the refusal to apply the green theory of value consistently is a refusal on the part of the mainstream coalition partner, not of Realo greens themselves. At most, they are consenting – reluctantly and under protest – to trade away some green positions, as needs be, to attain some others. They are, as it were, in the same position as a missionary confronting many starving mouths and only a few morsels of food: they would dearly love to satisfy all, but they are only able to satisfy a few; still, it is better that few be satisfied than none.

Perhaps, Fundis might say, it is wrong for them to be prepared to do even that. Their argument is in part pragmatic. By compromising, Realos are letting mainstream parties off the hook that the green theory of value should have them on. They are allowing them to embrace the parts of the green agenda that they find congenial while shunning the bits that they find more challenging.

But the Fundi argument is in part principled, as well. The Realos are not merely unwise to consent to the compromises entailed in coalition politics, the Fundis would say: they are wrong to do so. The inconsistency involved in their coalition's accepting some green positions but not others is an inconsistency forced on Realo greens by their mainstream coalition partners, to be sure. But that necessity of acting inconsistently was itself accepted by Realos, in their consenting to enter a coalition in the first place.

The question, in essence, is whether the compromises are genuinely necessary. 'Accepting necessity' is realism in its best, most incontrovertible sense. Even Fundis do not seem to dispute the wisdom of that policy:

Compromising Green Values　　　　　111

they do not demand the repeal of the law of gravity, or even of the second law of thermodynamics. The issue that divides the Fundis and Realos seems instead to be merely an question of whether – or, more precisely, in what sense – the compromises entailed in coalition politics are genuinely necessary ones.

The sense in which Realos think that they are necessary is clear enough. They are necessary, Realos would assert, in order to make any practical difference to public policy in the foreseeable future. They might be right or wrong in their political calculations on that score – that is the matter of electoral prudence, to which I have already alluded. But let us suppose for the sake of argument that they are right in those calculations, and the compromises of coalition politics really are necessary in order for the green agenda to be even partially implemented. Would that then justify the compromises?

Here, it just comes down to a question of how consequentialistic we want our green ethic to be. Fundis are purists. Like deontologists in the classic moral divide, they pride themselves on their clean hands. They would have us do right, though the heavens may fall. Realos are pragmatists, in contrast. Like consequentialists more generally, they would have us do as much good as we can in the circumstances.

There is no agreement, and little prospect of agreement, on those larger issues of deontology versus consequentialism, of the Right versus the Good. But we can, without resolving those larger issues, nonetheless resolve the more particular one here before us. The question here is not which style of ethic is right in general, but which is the correct characterization of the green ethic in particular.

On the account I have given in chapter 2 above, the green ethic is built around a particular 'green theory of value'. And that theory of value in turn is a distinctively consequentialistic one. It is a theory of the Good, rather than a theory of the Right. The green ethic, thus characterized, is a theory that tells us to promote and to protect things of value, understood as things that have been produced through natural processes.

There are elements of a theory of the Right, to be sure, in the 'green theory of agency', to be developed in chapter 4 below. So it might seem that which group is right – Fundis or Realos – in their characterization of the green ethic's implications for coalition politics just depends on the relative weights accorded to these two separate parts of the green ethic. But that would be to suppose that the green theory of agency and the green theory of value are morally on a par with one another.

Within the green ethic, though, the theory of agency is – as I shall argue shortly – subsidiary to the theory of value. That may or may not be an apt characterization of relations between theories of agency and of value in general. But it is true of their relations in green theory, at least. The green theory of agency is a theory about how to go about pursuing green values. It sets constraints on how to pursue them, perhaps. But it does not take the place of them, nor within green political theory does it seriously compromise the pursuit of them. Or so I shall argue in chapter 4, section 1 below.

4

The Green Theory of Agency

1 Theories of Value and Theories of Agency

The discussion in previous sections of this book has focused largely if not exclusively on the substance of green public-policy positions and the outcomes that they are designed to promote. Those policy positions, I hope to have shown, all flow from one and the same green theory of value. The role of that theory of value – like that of any theory of value or any theory of the Good – is essentially to tell us which outcomes are desirable and why.

Like all theories of value in general, however, that green theory of value is not self-implementing. Instead it is a theory that is addressed to moral agents, in hopes that they might themselves use it in guiding their conduct. It is through the deliberate actions and choices of those agents that the recommendations of our theory of value will be implemented, if they are to be implemented at all. Hence any theory of value or any theory of the Good needs to be conjoined with a theory of agency, analysing the nature of the mechanisms by which its recommendations are to be given practical meaning.[1]

The need for a theory of agency is, if anything, greater when the recommendations of the theory of value in view are not purely personal but also interpersonal and, indeed, largely political in nature. Then we will need not only a theory of agency of the ordinary sort – a theory about the nature of (individual) human action. We will also need a theory of agency that embraces interactions between individuals – a

---

[1] For a sample of recent philosophical work on agency and action theory in general, see e.g. Goldman 1970; Hornsby 1980; Taylor 1985, esp. ch. 1; and White 1968. For an excellent adaptation of such theories to allied problems, see O'Neill (1986, esp. ch. 3).

theory for analysing coordination of actions among various individuals. And we will also need a theory of agency that embraces notions of genuinely collective agency – a theory for analysing an entirely new sort of collective moral agent (clubs, cadres, firms, parties), which is created by the intentional actions of individuals but which then goes on to acquire something of an independent moral life all its own.[2]

Philosophical analyses of agency often tend to confine themselves to questions of the nature of individual agency. In a way, that emphasis is perfectly proper. Before we can properly address questions of the nature of coordinated or collective action among individuals, we must first get clear on the logically prior question of the nature of individual human agency itself. But we cannot stop there. Many (perhaps most) theories of value have important interpersonal and, indeed, distinctly political implications. In so far as they do, what is crucially required in framing a strategy for implementing them will be some analysis of the coordination and collectivization of individual agency.[3]

Such an account of agency might, in the first instance, be a purely positive theory. It might analyse what human agents are really like, what actually makes them tick, without passing any normative judgement on the matter either way. To a certain extent, any decent theory of agency is going to have to be like this. In so far as there are any hard and fast empirical truths about the nature of different sorts of agents, then a theory of agency must of course report those facts fully and faithfully; and it must respect them as best it can, consistently with respecting other facts of similar standing, in its theorization of the phenomenon.[4]

A theory of agency need not and usually does not stop with that, though. It is partly an empirical theory, to be sure. But it is an empirical theory with normative overtones. In part, those derive from the normative concerns – the desire to get someone to act on our theory of value – that set us looking for a theory of agency in the first place.

Quite apart from that, however, a theory of agency is also often normatively charged in so far as it commends certain forms of agency as being morally especially worthy and condemns others as being morally

---

[2] On coordination, cooperation and the nature of collective agency in general see Lewis 1969; Goodin 1976, esp. pt 2; Regan 1980; French 1984; Snidal 1985.

[3] O'Neill's (1986, ch. 3) discussion of problems of agency as applied to problems of famine relief differs strikingly from standard philosophical accounts in just this way, for example.

[4] Likewise, brute empirical (if only institutional) facts constrain the sorts of collective agency that green parties can manifest, as when Die Grünen proposed that the constituency party's mandate should bind MPs whose independence from just such influences is enshrined in the Federal Republic's very constitution (Poguntke 1987).

reprehensible. Furthermore, it commends or condemns those forms of agency at least in part independently of their characteristic consequences, and hence independently of the values or disvalues that would be assigned to them on that account by a theory of value alone.

Some might say, at this juncture, that what is really happening here is that we are finding that we need to conjoin a theory of the Right with our theory of the Good. It is all too tempting to try to cash out the present point in terms of that familiar contrast. A theory of the Good is standardly said to be a theory of value, to be used in assessing outcomes and consequences; a theory of the Right, in contrast, is standardly said to be a largely independent theory of right action, to be used in assessing people's actions and choices regardless of their consequences. Each has an important role in overall moral assessment, most commentators would have to agree.[5]

Notice, however, that what a theory of the Right delivers is not quite what a theory of agency requires. A theory of the Right specifies right actions, whereas what a theory of agency requires is an analysis of the nature of the actors who are supposed to be performing those actions. In that sense, then, a theory of the Right itself needs a theory of agency every bit as much as does a theory of value or a theory of the Good. The prescriptions of a theory of the Right are addressed to agents, every bit as much as are the prescriptions of those other sorts of theories. And it therefore needs an analysis of the nature of the agents it is addressing, every bit as much as do those other theories.

All that is simply to say that theories of value and theories of agency are really rather different sorts of theories. They take as their focus different subjects – outcomes and their values in the former case, actions and choices and the mechanisms producing them in the latter. In that sense, at the very least, they are philosophically separate issues, at least in the sense that they have to be considered separately.

A Separate Issue?

To say that theories of value and of agency are *logically* separate issues, however, is not necessarily to deny that arguments that bear on the one issue might also bear on the other as well. And if they do, then our answers to those two genuinely separate questions might, in such ways, be indirectly connected. Both might derive from some deeper common theories of humanity and society, for example. The same thing that

---

[5] Some might suppose one could be reduced to the other, however. See chapter 2, section 1.

makes us think that certain outcomes are valuable and to be desired might lead us to prefer certain sorts of human agent and certain sorts of social structure, as well. The fact that the two are logically separate issues, philosophically, ought not automatically to preclude us from giving one and the same style of answer to both sorts of questions.

Green theorists seem to think – or hope or imagine or pretend or presume – that this is the case. They themselves draw no sharp distinction between the arguments that they offer for their theory of agency and those that they offer for their theory of value. That is in part because they rarely appreciate the difference between the two sorts of theory, supposing both are part and parcel of one and the same larger theory. Or if they do see that there is a separate theory of agency at work within their larger theory at all, they do not see the need to offer any separate defence of it. They seem just to presume that whatever they say in defence of their theory of value will apply, *mutatis mutandis*, as a defence of their theory of agency.

I can see only one plausible way to justify this traditionally unargued-for conflation of green theories of agency and green theories of value. That would involve a further unstated premise, postulating the uniquely natural status of small-scale primitive (prototypically, hunter-gatherer) human societies. Suppose it were true that those, and those alone, were the uniquely natural forms of human organization. Then the green theory of value would accord value to those, and only those, forms of human agency which are characteristically embodied in such societies. We would thereby be led to praise, among other things: simple living and plain dealing; societies that are small in scale, modest in material possessions and broadly egalitarian in character; loose authority structures internally, and even looser links between communities.

Greens are of course sensitive to the charge that they are essentially involved in romanticizing a primitive past. They are quick to deny that they are doing any such thing. But there is much to suggest that, for many greens, some such Rousseauian vision is indeed what bridges the gap between their theories of value and their theories of agency. It is not only that green recommendations hauntingly echo Rousseau's discourses.[6]

---

[6] Luke (1988, p. 74) effectively evokes the deep-ecology myth of man's fall: 'Once upon a time, or elsewhere in more primitive regions of the world, humanity lived in a state of innocence. But now, due to technological domination, humanity lives in a state of corruption or alienation. For deep ecology, however, redemption is possible, in accord with examples set by primal societies, by attaining correct moral consciousness.' Although this is obviously an unsympathetic characterization, it is far from an inaccurate one, is apparent from a comparison of e.g., Bookchin (1990) and Roszak (1978) with Rousseau (1750; 1755); see similarly Bahro's (1986, pp. 87–8) description of small-scale communes as 'anthropologically favourable', in the sense

Among the more distinguished green writers, commentaries on ideal green social forms followed from – and one can only presume were at least partly inspired by – studies of primitive societies.[7]

If that is the argument, there is a good reason for its having long remained unstated, for it is obviously a highly suspect one. It amounts to privileging, seemingly arbitrarily, one particular stage in human social development over all others. For the argument to go through, we would need some reason for believing what this argument merely asserts – namely, that hunter-gatherer society (or some such) is a uniquely natural social form.

On the face of it, that claim seems highly implausible. The shifts in social evolution that led from hunter-gatherer society to the social forms which followed it are seemingly of a cloth with the shifts in social evolution which led up to hunter-gatherer society from the social forms that preceded it. If the one sort of shift is 'natural', the other must be likewise. The only way we can deem one natural and the other not is by arbitrarily stipulating what is and is not to be included in the category of the 'natural' for these purposes.

Presumably even greens themselves, trying to argue that hunter-gatherer society and the social forms associated with it are recommended on the same basis as the green theory of value, would not want to argue that hunter-gatherer society is, literally, *uniquely* natural. They may well want to argue that at some point social evolution was artificially pushed off its natural course.[8] Everything that happened after that false turning might be non-natural, or less natural, than everything that went before. But greens wanting to argue in this way would not, presumably, be so bold as to claim that hunter-gatherer society is more natural, somehow, than all the even more primitive social forms that *preceded* it. They may want to say that later stages in that process of social evolution

that they correspond better to crucial aspects of 'human nature'. Note also green arguments in favour of 'authenticity' and the 'simple' life, discussed briefly in chapter 2, sections 6 and 7 above.

[7] At the risk of an *ad hominen* argument, reflect upon the fact that Kirkpatrick Sale's *Human Scale* (1980) – which is without doubt the best argument in the existing literature for green decentralization – carries opposite its title page a list of the author's previous books, headed by *The Land and People of Ghana*. Lest that be thought a quirk of personal history, notice that Sale (1980, p. 488) actually leans heavily upon anthropological literature about stateless societies – the Dinka, especially, but also the Mandavi, the Amba, the Lugbara, the Konkomba, the Tupi and so on – in his crucial discussion of the optimal size of local communities. See similarly the appeals to the examples of American Indian tribal society in Devall and Sessions (1985) and Tokar (1987, ch. 1).

[8] In Rousseau's (1755) tale, with the introduction of notions of private property, for example.

count as 'higher' forms of social organization. But up to the crucial wrong turning, they are all equally 'natural' forms of social organization, surely.

On what basis, though, could hunter-gatherer society even be said to be a 'higher' – if not necessarily any more natural – form of social organization? Surely it cannot just be that it is a 'later' stage in social evolution. Then whatever followed hunter-gatherer society must be a yet 'higher' stage.[9] And that, of course, is precisely the result that greens want to avoid.

Similarly, though, they run the very real risk that any other basis on which they end up commending hunter-gatherer society as superior to earlier forms of social organization will lead to the conclusion that other, subsequent forms are superior to hunter-gatherer society, in turn. Suppose we fix on some particular consequence of the evolutionary step in view – greater efficiency in procuring food, for example – as the basis for saying it has led to a 'higher' form of social life. Well, certainly hunter-gatherer society is superior to what preceded it by those standards. But settled agriculture is yet better still, by those standards, than is chasing after herds of itinerate animals or seasonal berries. And so it is likely to go with any criterion we might consider: complexity of cultural artefacts, increasing human knowledge, or what have you.[10]

Ultimately, it seems, the ostensible unity of the green theory of value and the green theory of agency really does have to rest on a claim that there is something uniquely natural about the processes that led to hunter-gatherer society and something peculiarly artificial about the processes that led beyond it. Then and only then will greens have good grounds for stopping with hunter-gatherer society – for praising it as uniquely natural and the form of social organization that it embodies as being uniquely commended by a green theory of value.

I cannot, for my part, see how such a claim can be sustained. The processes of banding together for the hunt, of shaping tools and of the

[9] Perhaps we should add: 'just so long as it followed equally natural processes of social evolution'.

[10] The one candidate that might conceivably be credible – both as an account of what hunter-gatherer groups manifest among themselves and as an account of what greens value societies of broadly that sort – is 'diversity'. That, too, may be a romanticized account of hunter-gatherer societies. (Pressures towards standardization undoubtedly increase in all stages of social development from settled agriculture onwards; but it is, I take it, an open and essentially empirical question just how diverse hunter-gatherer bands themselves actually were.) And, in any case, we need to know what it was about hunter-gatherer societies that made them diverse: in the absence of any strong theoretical understanding of that, we have no good grounds for supposing that replicating some (but, inevitably, not all) attributes of such societies will actually yield the desired levels of diversity.

division of labour within the hunter-gatherer society seem of a cloth – no more and no less artificial human contrivances – than the processes of banding together for agricultural cultivation, and shaping tools and dividing labour in that connection. Both are human artifices of a peculiarly low level, agreed. Both might even be considered 'natural' artifices, in the sense of being artifices that come somehow 'naturally' to agents equipped with the ordinary sort of mental machinery standardly possessed by humans. My point is merely that neither of those stages in social evolution – nor any others adjacent to them – involve human artifices that are obviously different in kind from others that immediately precede or follow them.

True, I have offered in chapter 2, section 5 an argument to the effect that some social forms are more 'natural' than others. But the argument there, it should be noted, is that social forms are more natural if they are more 'in harmony' with nature. And that is consistent with a great variety of forms of agency. Or, at the very least, that certainly does not necessarily have the ordinary implications that greens would wish for, dictating the form of agency that they particularly prefer.

Living in harmony with nature does not necessarily require egalitarian communities of the standardly green sort, for example. One of the paradigm cases discussed earlier – the medieval English village – was characterized by great disparities of status and wealth between lords and peasants. The great 'wool churches' from Lavenham to Ely stand in silent testament to the fact. Nor does living in harmony with nature necessarily imply small-scale societies. Such medieval English villages as contemporary greens hold up as models were themselves originally set in the context of a moderately strong Tudor state. Likewise, we can presumably live more or less in harmony with nature even in advanced industrial and postindustrial societies, without necessarily dropping out of those societies altogether.[11]

In short, I agree that there are some forms of society which are to be preferred, on the green theory of value. Those are societies that are living 'in harmony with nature'. But such societies are characterized merely by a certain attitude towards nature. And that has no necessary implications for any particular forms of social agency. Certainly it does not imply the forms of agency ordinarily recommended by green theorists. The green theory of value and those theories of agency really do have to be regarded as separate, not only in the weaker sense that they are logically separable but also in the stronger sense that genuinely different arguments must be given in support of each.

---

[11] Indeed, the green political agenda would be even more pointless than its worst critic imagines were that not the case.

Priorities

Of course it is true to say that there are principled concerns, not just pragmatic calculations, underlying greens' preferences among alternative forms of agency. Still, it seems to me it must be said, the core green concerns are consequentialistic at root. In cases of conflict, I shall argue, the green theory of value – and the ends that it would have us promote – simply must, within the logic of the greens' own theory, take priority over the green theory of agency, and the principles of right action, agency and structure that that would recommend.

It is the greens' ardent hope, of course, that this is a conflict that they will never need to face. They ardently hope that the best way to pursue green values will always prove to be through their preferred green mechanisms. And in this respect greens tend to let the wish be the father of the thought: hoping there will be no contradiction between the two strands of their theory, they all too often tend simply to presume that there will be no such conflict. And through their reluctance to acknowledge that there might ever be a hard choice of what to do in the (hopefully rare) case in which the two components of their political theory do come into irreconcilable conflict, greens themselves fail to provide any guidance as to how we should go about resolving such a conflict.

In addressing such issues, we are therefore left largely putting words in the greens' mouths. Or, rather, we are left drawing inferences from their theories that greens do not themselves care to contemplate. Still, I think we can answer pretty confidently on their behalf – giving the answer that they would themselves have to give, in light of the basic structure of their moral theory.

Let us begin by reflecting on what lies at the core of green thinking. That, as I understand it, is an abiding concern that natural values be promoted, protected and preserved. Given that as the logical primitive in their moral system, I think we would have to say – and I think that reflective greens would have to agree – that it is more important that the right things be done than that they be done in any particular way or through any particular agency.[12] Greens would genuinely and rightly

---

[12] It has been suggested to me that a stronger demonstration might be possible. The consequences which greens are striving to promote sometimes amount to nothing less than underwriting the preconditions of (even just human) life on earth; and the green theory of agency presupposes ultimately some form of human agency. From that it is right to infer that the consequences there in view must be secured (temporarily) before there are agents to whom a green theory of agency can be

regret having to forsake their preferred political forms, in a way that others with no principled theory of agency might not. But at the end of the day, forsake it they should, if doing so were truly necessary in order to secure certain highly valued green outcomes.

That proposal to give the green theory of value priority, in cases of inevitable conflict, over the green theory of agency will of course run contrary to the predilections of a great many greens themselves. As I said earlier, many greens accord heavy emphasis to personal gestures and appropriate lifestyles. Indeed, many of them think it more important to engage in those sorts of direct personal actions than it is to engage in political action.[13] Voting green but living brown would, for them, be the purest form of hypocrisy.

To see why they are wrong – wrong, even in terms of the actual implications of green theory itself – we need to see why they say what they say. The rationale underlying their position is straightforward enough. The basic idea seems to be that voting green is cheap, almost an empty gesture.[14] Reorienting one's personal life, on the other hand, is costly. It often entails considerable personal sacrifices. If what we are concerned to test is one's commitment to the cause, then the willingness to bear costs in pursuit of the cause is crucial. And testing the depth of one another's commitment is indeed what primarily concerns those who would accord high priority to issues of agency.

There is another side to this calculation, though. Collective action can make a real difference to the state of the world, in a way that individual action cannot.[15] Carrying the green cause to electoral triumph might

addressed. But it is wrong to infer from that that the prescriptions for consequences are somehow morally more important than the prescriptions for agents. Logically, it is perfectly possible (though, I would argue, in the green ethic contingently untrue) that those consequences might have only derivative value, being morally important only by virtue of their role in facilitating agency of that sort.

[13] See chapter 2, section 7 above.

[14] Certainly the act itself entails virtually no direct, immediate costs to voters themselves. Furthermore, any costs that might come from the green cause actually prevailing electorally are, in all probability, costs that you would have to bear independently of how you yourself vote; the probability of any one voter being decisive are, in a large electorate, next to nil. That, after all, is the thought that in other contexts gives rise to the 'logic of collective action' (Olson 1965; Hardin 1982).

[15] Or, anyway, usually cannot. Greens delight in stories like 'how . . . the Zen poet Gary Snyder stopped the war in Vietnam. In the mid 1960s, Gary was sitting in a bar in Tokyo and fell into conversation with a fellow American who was on his way to Saigon to do a government study of the war. The stranger was so surprised and fascinated to find that Gary thought the war a bad idea that he postponed his trip to Saigon and they talked for three days about the war, about values and philosophy. . . . Some years later, having moved back to California and lived in several places, Gary got word on the grapevine that someone on a motorcycle had been looking for him,

affect the fate of the earth; deciding to live a thoroughly green lifestyle oneself most definitely will not.[16] As Kirkpatrick Sale writes,

> What I find truly pernicious about such [lifestyle] solutions is that they get people thinking they are actually making a difference and doing their part to halt the destruction of the earth: 'There, I've taken all the bottles to the recycling center and used my string bag at the grocery store; I guess that'll take care of global warming.' It is the kind of thing that diverts people from the hard truths and hard choices and hard actions, from the recognition that they have to take on the larger forces of society – corporate and governmental – where true power, and true destructiveness, lie.[17]

The difference between those who would emphasize personal over political actions and those who would adopt the opposite emphasis can therefore be recast in the following terms. Those emphasizing personal actions are inclined to accord substantial weight to the demonstrated willingness of a person to bear sacrifices, even probably gratuitous ones, for the sake of the cause.[18] Those emphasizing political actions are inclined to accord substantial weight to the outcomes that the action will produce and to encourage sacrifice only if the sacrifice has some hope of making a material difference to the outcome.[19]

chasing him from one old address to the next. The searcher had finally sent forward a message to Gary, saying, "I'm the guy you met in that bar in Tokyo. That conversation changed my life. Watch your newspaper." A few weeks later, the Pentagon Papers story broke. The guy was Dan Ellsberg' (Lovins and Lovins 1987, p. 21). Such stories are few and far between, however.

[16] Some might say that the comparison is unfairly formulated. Voting green yourself is as unlikely to make a difference to the fate of the earth as is adopting an ecological lifestyle yourself: voting green can change the fate of the earth only if enough others do likewise that the greens win elections. But so too might eating only vegetables rather than meat affect the fate of the earth (or at least those portions of it dedicated to fattening cows) if, similarly, enough others did likewise. The difference, I take it, is that in voting one is (if one is even a moderately tactical voter) sensitive to how many others actually are going to do likewise, while in adopting an ecological lifestyle one characteristically is indifferent to how many others are doing the same.

[17] Sale 1990, p. 54.

[18] In a clever turnabout of this argument, greens calling for political rather than personal solutions sometimes say that it is their opponents, not themselves, who are unwilling to make any real sacrifices. Donella Meadows (1991), for example, writes, 'Sometimes I think we get enthusiastic about low-flow faucets and high-mileage cars because they give us the feeling of doing good without seriously challenging our lifestyle.'

[19] Not surprisingly, green parties and political movements themselves emphasize the latter, as well. European Greens (1989, sec. 12) campaigning for seats in the European parliament, for example, insist that 'voting Green is probably the only way to get the message across. Staying at home or voting for another party means that the message will be lost – a vote will have been wasted.'

Some greens emphasize the ecological equivalent of 'clean hands' (personal actions, appropriate lifestyles and suchlike) at the expense of political action that might carry far greater ecological consequences. Those who do, though, are in effect giving considerations of agency priority over considerations of value and consequences. That, I think, is an error. That it is an error is plainly demonstrable in terms of the selfsame argument used by those greens themselves in discounting the value of political action.

The objection to 'voting green but living brown', recall, is in part premised on the assertion that voting is all too often an 'empty gesture'. There are of course two senses in which the gesture is empty. On the one side, voting green is an empty gesture because any costs that are going to be imposed politically on us will be imposed very largely independently of how we ourselves vote in the matter. But on the other side, and by the same logic, our own vote will make only a negligible difference towards tilting the eventual electoral outcome in a greener direction.

In both respects, the complaint that voting is an 'empty gesture' might fairly be represented as a complaint that our vote will make no difference. But if the complaint is couched in terms of 'making a difference', then the complaint is one couched primarily in terms of outcomes and consequences rather than purely in terms of the 'clean hands' principles of personal rectitude that according priority to theories of agency would suggest. Thus, even those greens who are at first inclined to attach more importance to questions of agency than value and consequences seem eventually to end up advocating the opposite emphasis.

2   Principles of Green Political Action

Theories of agency, as I have said, operate first and foremost at the level of individual human agents. Those are not the only sorts of agents that exist, of course. There are also properly constituted groups of people (clubs, movements, parties, states) that have all the properties that would be required for them to count as fully fledged moral agents. Some sufficiently complex automata – super-smart robots and the like – might do likewise. The point about all those artificially created agents, though, is that they are artificial human creations. Logically as well as causally, individual human agency comes first. It is that which any theory of agency must address, first and foremost.

In most respects, there is nothing special – or anyway nothing peculiar – about the green theory of individual human agency. By and large, at the level of individual human actors, it just takes over pretty standard assumptions about the nature of human action and intention, powers and purposes.[20] In taking over those standard analyses rather unreflectively, as a job lot, it runs the risk of embracing contradictory positions and failing to confront tricky issues. But the contradictions that it incorporates are just those that are 'in the air' anyway. In failing to resolve them, the green theory of agency is no worse off than any other which piggybacks on the received wisdom in this way.

It is in the more value-laden aspects of its analysis of individual agency that the green theory shows its distinctive colours, and it is on those that I shall therefore primarily focus in the present discussion. I shall discuss, specifically, the importance which the green theory of agency accords to democratic participation in the life of one's society (which is arguably the central plank in the whole green theory of agency) and the importance that that theory accords to nonviolent action (which, even according to many greens themselves, arguably does not belong there at all).

Democratic Participation

Above all else, the green theory treats individual human beings as agents who naturally are, and morally ought to be, autonomous and self-governing entities. Politically, that pretty directly implies the central theme of the green political theory of agency: the importance of the full, free, active participation by everyone in democratically shaping their personal and social circumstances.

Thus, the canonical 1983 manifesto of the German Greens conspicuously and repeatedly claims that the present 'ecological, economic and social crisis can be countered only by the self-determination of those affected. . . .[W]e stand for self-determination and the free development of each human being. . . . [W]e want people to shape their lives creatively together in solidarity, in harmony with their natural environment, their own wishes and needs, and free from external threat.' In consequence, the German Greens 'take a radical stand for human rights and far-reaching democratic rights both at home and abroad.'[21] Their manifesto

[20] Represented by Goldman (1970), Davidson (1980) and Taylor (1985), to name just three of the most distinguished exemplars.

[21] Die Grünen 1983, sec. 1, p. 8. Among the *Ten Key Values* enunciated by the Green Committees of Correspondence in the US (1986, item 2) we find similar concerns: 'How can we develop systems that allow and encourage us to control the

calls for the increased 'use of referenda and plebiscites to strengthen direct democracy'.[22] It urges that large industrial combines 'be broken down into surveyable units which can be run democratically by those working in them'.[23] And so on.

The same phrases recur in several contexts, thus giving the impression of consistency. The images of 'democracy' and 'self-determination' at work in these various propositions are themselves many and varied, though.[24] Perhaps certain background conditions are presupposed by all of them – conditions like freedom from external compulsion, whether physical or economic, for example. Still, green theories on the broader subjects of democracy and self-determination more generally seem to share the same problems as most theories of participatory democracy, self-management or self-determination.

All such theories seem systematically ambivalent as between the following:

a) Choice of oneself On this reading, aspirations of self-determination refer to character formation, to choosing one's personality, preferences and deepest character traits for oneself.[25] This might (indeed, it almost inevitably will) have implications for one's relations with the larger community. But basically self-determination, on this understanding, is restricted to very personal concerns.

b) Choice for oneself The most standard reading of 'self-determination', familiar from Kant and Rousseau, understands it as being 'self-legislating', obeying only those commands which one has given to oneself.[26] On this understanding, the scope of self-determination extends well beyond the purely personal to embrace matters of collective concern. Yet it is unclear how individuals who are self-legislating in this strong sense could yield to any collective determination of

decisions that affect our lives? . . . How can we develop planning mechanisms that would allow citizens to develop and implement their own preferences for policies and spending priorities?'

[22] Die Grünen 1983, sec. 5, p. 37.

[23] Ibid., sec. II.3, p. 11. See similarly the Green Committees of Correspondence in the US (1986, item 6).

[24] The best single attempt at unravelling them is, in my view, Berg (1978).

[25] Issues of 'choice of self' have recently been discussed, in very different contexts, by Charles Taylor (1976) and John Rawls (1982).

[26] Rousseau 1762; Kant 1785. Even today, the standard analysis of 'autonomy' is still couched very much in such terms (Benn 1988; Dworkin 1988).

these common concerns.[27] This brings us to our third reading of self-determination:

c) Choice by oneself   A final way of construing 'self-determination' puts the emphasis on determining whatever it is to be determined all by oneself. On this interpretation, what is to be determined is left largely open: certainly it is not confined to purely personal matters of 'self-formation' as on the first interpretation; and in principle it is allowed to range as widely as you please. What is crucial to self-determination, on this reading, is simply that one should do the determining all by oneself.

These distinctions make a very real difference. Many of the best philosophical arguments for moral autonomy imply self-determination largely, if not exclusively, in the first ('choice of oneself') sense alone. As such, they have next to no political implications.[28] Certainly they would not, on their face, necessarily dictate active participation in the political institutions of direct democracy as being the best – still less the only – way of achieving self-determination.[29]

That conclusion emerges only if we construe self-determination in the second sense ('choice for oneself'). Seeing self-determination as a matter of obeying only such commands as one has given to oneself might lead us to suppose that only those who have directly and actively participated in the making of laws can obey those laws and at the same time be self-determining, in the sense of being purely self-legislating.

But then self-determination in the second sense shades dangerously over into the third. For how can we pretend that one is obeying a law that one has given to oneself if one were on the losing side of the contest? Only in the rare case of unanimity can we plausibly pretend that we are obeying 'only ourselves' when obeying laws that have been collectively enacted.

[27] It is a notoriously tricky problem in political theory how a person can, at one and the same time, connive to obey only oneself and yield to the collective will. The problem has driven at least one reluctant theorist to philosophical anarchism (Wolff 1970). And it seems that the problem really is just about insoluble, absent fortuitous unanimity or some peculiar theory of a 'real will' (in Rousseau, uncorrupted by self-interest) or a 'split will' ('I vote for X, and in that way will for it to be implemented; but above all, I will to be implemented whatever policy the majority votes for').

[28] 'Next to no', rather than literally 'none', in deference to familiar arguments for democratic participation as a means of self-development (Pateman 1970, ch. 2; Macpherson 1977b, ch. 3).

[29] And, indeed, models emphasizing participation as a means of self-development tend to concentrate primarily on shopfloor democracy in the workplace (Pateman 1970, chs 3–5; Vanek 1975; Greenberg 1986).

In the context of collective decision-making, self-determination in the second sense ('choice for oneself') would therefore seem to require self-determination in the third ('choice by oneself') sense. Each person must be decisive – in effect, each must have a veto – over the ultimate collective outcome.

Notice, however, that the institutions implied by giving everyone a veto are very different from those characteristically associated with participatory democracy. There is not much democracy (certainly not in its majoritarian form, at least) in any of this. Nor is there even much of a case for active participation. (The rule could be phrased, 'We propose that this law should be enacted: if you agree, you need do nothing; only if you disagree do you need to take action to register your veto.') In short, what is implied by self-determination in the 'choice by-and-for oneself' mode is more what Macpherson dubs 'protective democracy' rather than genuinely 'participatory democracy'.

I happen to think that such arguments are both true and important. But all of that, it might fairly be said, amounts to little more than philosophical point-scoring. Arguments conducted on such a plane of conceptual purity and intellectual abstraction are always in danger of missing – sometimes, one suspects, of stubbornly refusing to see – the point which real-world actors are trying, however imprecisely, to make. So let us stand back from such logic-chopping to see what might really lie behind demands for participatory democracy, from a green perspective in particular.

The goal of participatory democracy, as greens (among others) espouse it, is for example to give workers more say in what happens on the shopfloor, rather than having all production decisions being dictated from on high by a handful of managers.[30] Or, for another example, the goal is to give local communities more say in what happens in their own neighbourhoods, rather than having all decisions handed down from on high by a handful of politicians or corporate executives. Or, for yet another example, the goal is to give the local branches of green parties a genuine voice in the affairs of the party, rather than having all policy dictated from some central office.

---

[30] Still less do greens – or democrats of any other tint, come to that – want the democratically determined decisions of the community at large negated by the actions of powerful private corporations. That is another reason for market-socialist institutions of workers's ownership and control of the firms in which they work. To the minds of many, it is a far more important reason than the considerations of 'self-development' and 'self-expression' to which theorists of participatory democracy typically point. See e.g. Dahl (1970, ch. 3; 1985). Lindblom (1977) and Walzer (1980, ch. 17).

Clearly, there is a common theme running through all those propositions. What greens are objecting to is, essentially, the concentration of power in the hands of the few. The root idea running through all their demands for 'participatory democracy' is not, as is often claimed, that everyone should be self-determining completely and in all respects. Rather, it is that more people should have more say over more of what happens to them.

That aim, however, is consistent with various different sorts of decision rules. Interminable discussions designed to evoke unanimous agreement is one, but far from the only one, which is consistent with that larger goal. Furthermore, that aim is consistent with a rationale for promoting widespread political participation which is purely pragmatic – and which may well be all the stronger for being so. The idea behind encouraging widespread, active political participation might be no more than this: mass mobilization simply makes it harder for the powers-that-be to resist popular demands. The green theory of democracy might, in those crucial respects, be better characterized as 'populist' – if the term can still be used in its original non-technical, non-pejorative sense – rather than as 'participatory', strictly speaking.

Participation, thus rationalized, would not be an end in itself but instead merely a means designed to promote substantively better decisions. They would be 'substantively better' simply in the sense that they would have to take more seriously into account a larger proportion of the community's self-conceived interests. Of course, people still might conceive their interests incorrectly, and morally there might be more to good public policy than mere interest satisfaction. So widespread, active public participation might not guarantee morally perfect outcomes. But at least in that restricted sense, it is quite likely to promote morally better ones.

What exactly is required to promote widespread public participation in politics is an empirical question, though. Happily, it is one on which political scientists have by now built up considerable expertise. First and foremost, what is required is the elimination of all manner of formal barriers to participation, ranging from the literal disenfranchisement of certain groups (women, blacks, guest workers) to mere deterrents to participating (literacy tests, poll taxes). Merely legally granting everyone the right to vote is not enough in itself, of course; arrangements must also be made for that legal right to be effectively secured (so there are no lynch parties gathering to greet any blacks who appear at the polling station, for example). But once all of that has been done, various requisites of a more sociological sort come to the fore.

Once the right legal structure is in place, it is less a question of whether people are able to vote and participate more generally than of whether they are willing to do so.[31] At this point, political sociologists point to the importance of a wide range of sociological factors (like socioeconomic status, education, group ties) in addition to more transparently political ones (like the activities of political parties) in mobilizing people to participate.

All those things are undeniably important, but they are probably important for reasons other than the social-psychological ones which political sociologists usually tend to suggest.[32] They are right to suppose that all those sociological factors work to increase people's propensity to participate in politics by increasing their 'sense of efficacy'. It stands to reason that people will only bother participating if they think that they can, through their participation, make some real difference to the outcome.

True to their social-psychological groundings, though, political sociologists standardly treat that 'sense of efficacy' as essentially an illusion. People with a good education, high social standing and links to the local elite score highly on 'ego strength'. They feel good about themselves. And that, on this essentially psychological account, is why they are inclined to have a greater 'sense of efficacy' and hence to participate more vigorously.

The model that I, and I suspect most greens (and indeed most radical-left commentators more generally), would want to counterpose to that one interprets the same facts differently. True, people with better education, higher social standing and links to the local elite tend to participate in politics more vigorously. And true, that is because they have a stronger sense of their own efficacy. But their greater efficacy is, on the radical-green account, real rather than illusory. Far from being 'all in their head' – a psychological residue of happy early childhood socialization experiences, or some such – the rich and powerful participate more often because through their participation they can win more often. They have more weight to throw around.[33]

That finding has important implications for political and social structures more generally. Suppose we think that it is important for people to participate actively in the making of decisions that affect

---

[31] And to participate more generally. Voting, though only one mode of political participation (and in many respects a peculiar one), will here be used as a proxy for all others. Everything I say here applies, *mutatis mutandis*, to all other modes as well.

[32] Verba, Nie and Kim (1978) represent the culmination of a research tradition. For critiques, see Goodin and Dryzek (1980) and references therein.

[33] Pateman (1971; 1974) suggests this model. Goodin and Dryzek (1980) put it to the empirical test, and find it at least as good on all accounts and better on some than the more standard social-psychological analysis.

them, if only to ensure that their interests are protected. Then we should strive to ensure not only that formal legal institutions allow participation but also that actual social circumstances facilitate it.

That means various things. Minimally, it means ensuring that questions are put to people in terms that they can understand. More demandingly, it requires a generous provision of public education. Those are the easy corollaries of any belief in even a moderately strong democracy. And, if those demands are not necessarily always easy to satisfy, they are at least easy enough to recognize and acknowledge as corollaries of a genuine belief in democratic government.

There are other corollaries to a genuine belief in democratic rule that are perhaps harder to recognize and harder yet again to realize. Creating social circumstances that facilitate democratic rule also mean, for example, that the decision units should be small enough for people to comprehend the issues facing the polity, preferably from firsthand experience. (That gives rise to green proposals for decentralization, workplace democracy, and suchlike.) It also means, more importantly still, that there must be at least rough socioeconomic equality within the decision units.[34] For then and only then will people have the sort of rationally well-grounded sense of political efficacy that is required for them to bother participating at all. (That provides yet another reason for the regime of greater social equality which greens would prefer on other, quite separate grounds as well.)

Both of those latter two prescriptions might seem wildly idealistic. Neither decentralization nor radical equalization of social resources is likely to happen any time soon. Greens might of course reply that they have room to compromise on these points. Although they would ideally like both decentralization and equalization worldwide, they can make do with either one or the other. Specifically, if rough equality of socioeconomic resources worldwide is too much to hope for, then it might be enough (so far as promoting participation is concerned, anyway) to decentralize decision-making powers to small communities of socially a relatively homogeneous character. Rough equality within communities will be enough to ensure high levels of participation within those communities themselves, even if substantial inequalities across communities remain.

Of course, no green theorist would say that gross inequalities across communities would be in any way ideal. Furthermore, green theorists would still need some way of deciding issues that straddle communities –

---

[34] As Rousseau (1762, bk 2, ch. 11) puts it, 'no citizen shall ever be wealthy enough to buy another, and none poor enough to be forced to sell himself.' This theme is picked up by Pateman (1970, ch. 2), in particular.

and the smaller the communities, the more that will fall between the cracks in those ways. (I shall have more to say on those matters in section 4 of this chapter.) The thing to notice here is merely that green theory is only half as unrealistic as it sounds, at least in the sociopolitical structural reforms it would would advocate as a spur to democratic participation.

Nonviolence

A second principle that green theory commends to individual agents is nonviolence. Although nowhere near as central to the green theory of agency as the principle of democratic participation, nonviolence is nonetheless undoubtedly central in many respects. Green politics grew out of, and enjoys continuingly close links with, the politics of peace and opposition to nuclear armaments. Greens profess respect for all living things. Many of them count Gandhi among their intellectual progenitors, professing deepest respect for his views on nonviolent resistance in particular.[35]

Thus it should come as no surprise that nonviolence appears as one of the four main principles of the canonical 1983 German Green manifesto.[36] Nor does it come as a surprise that similar propositions should reappear in virtually every subsequent list of green values.[37] It must also be said, however, that that principle was undoubtedly the most contentious among those adopted by the German Greens in 1983, and that in the minds of many it undoubtedly remains an 'optional extra' on that list.[38]

Discussions of nonviolence among greens themselves focus very largely on the defence policies that they would implement, were they ever to win office, and on the tactics that they should deploy against nuclear weapons deployments in the meanwhile. In those contexts, especially, it is important to emphasize that nonviolence is not the same

[35] Devall and Sessions 1985, pp. 199–202; Naess 1989, pp. 193–6.

[36] We aim at a nonviolent society where the oppression of one person by another is abolished. Our foremost principle is that humane goals cannot be achieved by inhumane means. Nonviolence should prevail between all human beings without exception, within social groups and within society as a whole, between population groups and between nations' (Die Grünen 1983, sec. I, p. 9). 'Nonviolence' similarly figures as the fourth of the *Ten Key Values* enunciated by the Green Committees of Correspondence in the US (1986).

[37] See the *Ten Key Values* of the Green Committees of Correspondence (1986, sec. 4), for example.

[38] Spretnak and Capra (1986, pp. 43–7) detail the opposition of the Group-Z faction, in particular.

as passivity, that nonviolence is consistent with active (albeit nonviolent) forms of resistance, that alternative defence strategies and civil disobedience organized along those lines have proven highly effective in the past and can be expected to do so again in the future.[39]

It is important to emphasize all those things in debates over defence policies and military strategies, lest it appear that the greens' commitment to nonviolence means, in effect, that they have nothing (or anyway nothing at all credible) to say on those important issues. Greens do have a variety of ingenious – in many cases, wonderfully mischievous – ideas about how to implement a strategy of resistance that is at one and the same time active and yet nonviolent.[40] They can point to the historical record for evidence of such strategies working well in the past.[41] They can point to a wealth of evidence that violence leads only to further violence.[42] In short, there is much greens might say to convince doubters that, on grounds of pure pragmatism, nonviolence of the sort that they recommend may well be the best policy for defending the nation, after all.

Important though it is that greens be seen to have a position on issues of national defence, it is nonetheless an error to confine discussions of green nonviolence to those applications. Certainly that is not the only realm of application of such principles. It is not even the best worked-out application of them. After all, greens have yet to enter into a national governing coalition anywhere in the world; so green discussions of defence policy and military strategy are necessarily hypothetical. Elsewhere, though, greens have been forced to confront in more meaningful ways what exactly nonviolence means and why they think it is important.

Let us, therefore, concentrate on green principles of nonviolence as they apply to one of those other areas – the defence of the forests being my preferred example here. That is not the only area in which they have been put to the practical test. But it is an area where greens have been particularly accused of employing terrorist tactics, and in which they have therefore been most forcefully challenged to work out the implications of principles of nonviolence in practice.[43]

---

[39] Die Grünen 1983, sec. I, p. 9. On civil disobedience in particular, see Goodin (1987).

[40] Alternative Defence Commission 1983.

[41] Sharp 1973; 1990.

[42] Spretnak and Capra 1986, p. 47.

[43] Animal liberation is another such area. I prefer to concentrate here upon the fight for the forests, on the grounds that activists there are more thoroughgoingly and self-consciously green than are animal liberationists, who often see themselves as at most mere fellow-travellers with greens.

The logic behind a green preference for nonviolence in defence of the forests is obvious enough. If the essence of green philosophy is reverence for natural processes and their products, then their destruction is a bad thing. That applies to people every bit as much as to trees. It is important to the greens that they protect the trees. But it is also important that they do so, if they can, without inflicting injury on things (such as people) that are at least as valuable as trees.

The countervailing logic against such a principle is equally obvious, though. People are important, but so too are trees. Even if people are in some sense more important than trees, there must be some point at which a little harm to a few people might be justified in order to prevent a lot of harm to a lot of trees. Such trade-offs might seem licensed by our green theory of value. But were we to adopt a principle of nonviolence, it would prevent us from making any such trade-offs.[44]

Now, as it happens, there is much that green advocates of nonviolence can say to reduce the pragmatic incompatibility between those positions. In the fight for the forests, as elsewhere, nonviolence does not necessarily commit us to sitting back passively and watching the chainsaws rip through the wood. Here, as elsewhere, there are many suitably nonviolent things that we might do – many effective actions we might take – to block the activities of the despoilers. Furthermore, violent defence of the environment, like violence in other contexts, may well prove counterproductive. Politically, the damage done by alienating potential supporters may well outweigh any good that a violent act might directly achieve; and, conversely, many of the most effective things we can do to protect the environment, as to achieve other goals, are perfectly compatible with principles of nonviolence.

Interestingly enough, those very arguments are advanced by the most notoriously violence-prone defenders of the environment, the self-styled 'Monkeywrenchers' of the American West. They get a decidedly bad press. They are – not without cause – branded 'eco-terrorists'.[45] But notice that the first principle enunciated in the semi-official monkey-wrenching manual is this:

> *Monkeywrenching is non-violent.* Monkeywrenching is non-violent resistance to the destruction of natural diversity and wilderness. It is not directed towards harming human beings or other forms of life. It is aimed at inanimate machines and tools. Care is always taken to minimize any possible threat to other people . . .[46]

[44] At least it would do so if we adopted the principle in the 'absolutist' form in which it is ordinarily commended, by greens among others.

[45] Indeed, they often revel in the label: see Manes's (1990) description of *Green Rage*.

[46] Foreman and Haywood 1987, p. 14 (emphasis in original).

Some may suppose that those are just so many pious words. Such cynicism fades, though, once we begin looking at the more specific tactics recommended in that manual. Among the suggestions are spiking roads and flattening tyres and disabling vehicles through the simple expedient of putting sugar in their fuel tanks or unscrewing crucial bolts. Those acts are all nonviolent in the relevant sense. No doubt they are destructive. No doubt they damage private property. But the point is that they harm machines, not people. And that is standardly seen to be the proper and primary concern for advocates of nonviolence.

That is even true of the practice that has done the most to earn monkeywrenchers their reputation as eco-terrorists. Tree-spiking involves driving large (six-inch long) nails deeply into living trees. The trees themselves are undamaged by the process. But anyone trying to saw through the tree – either to chop it down in the forest or to mill it in the lumber yard – will find that their saw's blade is destroyed as it strikes those nails. So unless the nails can be located and removed beforehand (which is hard, once their heads have been cut off, as monkeywrenchers recommend) the tree is commercially useless. If nothing else, the down time taken to sharpen or replace damaged saw blades would typically make the whole operation uneconomic.[47]

What is particularly important in the present context is the care that that monkeywrenching manual recommends be taken to avoid harming timber workers. 'There are two basic philosophies of tree-spiking. Some people like to spike the base of each tree, so the sawyer, in felling the tree, will almost certainly encounter one of the spikes with the chainsaw. This would at the very least require the sawyer to stop and sharpen the saw and might require the replacement of the chain.' But the manual reports, as a telling objection to this type of spiking, 'the possibility, however remote, that the sawyer might be injured, either by the kickback of the saw striking the nail, or by the chain, should it break when striking the spike'; and 'because of this possibility, we do not recommend this type of spiking.' Instead, the manual 'favors placing the spikes in the trees well above the area where the fellers will cut. . . . The object of the spiking in this case is to destroy the blades in the sawmill. Since in large mills the blades are either operated from a control booth some distance from the actual cutting, or are protected by a plexiglass shield, this method is unlikely to cause anyone physical injury even should a blade shatter on striking a spike, which is an unlikely event.'[48]

---

[47] Ibid., ch. 3.

[48] Ibid., pp. 26–7. This monkeywrenching manual continues, 'It is true that in small, "backyard" sawmills the operator might be standing close to the blade, but we would assume that anyone contemplating spiking would never consider doing it on

So even in their fiercest guise, 'eco-terrorists' seem to conform pretty well to canons of nonviolence.

There is a second thing to notice about the tactic of tree-spiking. Suppose sawyers or mill operators actually were hurt by the spikes that monkeywrenchers drove into trees, despite all the precautions that monkeywrenchers take to avoid this happening. Regret though they may that harm done to sawyers or mill operators, monkeywrenchers could rightly claim that at least the harm thus inflicted conforms to the classical canons of measured retaliation in a just war.

Tree-spiking is, to borrow the terminology of nuclear deterrence, a decidedly 'counter-force' strategy. A nail pounded into a tree will harm no one until someone starts harming the tree. Even then, it is tightly 'targeted' retaliation. It will harm only those who are actually cutting on that particular tree. And it is retaliation that satisfies the traditional conditions of 'proportionality'. The injury inflicted on the sawyer or miller is in various ways roughly commensurate with the injury that they are proposing to inflict on the tree: they would be cut by the same blade, they would be injured by recoil from their own weapons, and so on.

There is of course a small problem of agency involved in this argument. The injury that the sawyer is proposing to inflict is on the tree, not the monkeywrencher; yet it is the monkeywrencher whose spike would injure the sawyer. So it is not, literally, a case of self-defence. Rather, it is a case of a third party defending someone else (here, a tree) against attack. And the question in such cases is by what right C (monkeywrenchers) can inflict harms on B (sawyers) to prevent B from engaging in activities that would harm A (trees) but not C themselves.

Now, for some purposes there is no doubt whatsoever that other agents can act on behalf of inanimate objects. Certainly people can legitimately speak up for the interests of animals or even trees, in the course of moral debates and perhaps even in the course of legal proceedings.[49] Whether other agents may legitimately act on trees' behalves for the purposes here in view is more doubtful. In legal debates about the nature of the 'self-defence', such extensions are standardly blocked. It is one thing for me to injure someone defending myself

other than the largest timber [plantations], where the trees are destined for a corporate, rather than a small, family-operated mill. Locally owned and operated sawmills are seldom a major threat to wilderness. It is usually the big, multi-national corporations whose "cut-and-run" philosophy devastates the land and leaves the local economy in shambles when all the big trees are cut and the main office decides to pull out and move to greener pastures.'

[49] Stone 1972; Feinberg 1974.

against attack; it is quite another for me to inflict gratuitous injury on another who is not attacking me, even if I do so in order to stop an attack on some third party. (At the very least, it certainly is not a case of self-defence any more.)

There is another, nastier problem of agency traditionally involved in discussions of nonviolence quite generally. Injunctions to behave 'nonviolently' are sometimes said necessarily turn crucially on a distinction between 'positive' and 'negative' agency: between acting and omitting, between actively doing something and passively merely letting something happen (between killing and letting die, in the classical application). Nonviolence, on this understanding, is taken to be an injunction not to be *actively* violent, not to *do* anything violent oneself.

But in so far as it is a counsel of passivity, the injunction to refrain from violence oneself is consistent with letting something equally bad happen at the hands of another. Indeed, enjoining nonviolence would, on that traditional understanding, often require us to let happen things that are as violent, or perhaps even more violent, than would be any measures that we would have to take to prevent them from happening.[50]

The upshot of all this is just that a rule of nonviolence, as standardly understood, would not be a rule aimed at violence minimization at all. It is instead a rule aimed at minimization of the agent's own violence. But why should there be such a big moral difference between lifting a finger to make something bad happen and not lifting a finger to stop something bad from happening?

That problem plagues all theories in which an active/passive, positive/negative, act/omission distinction figures at all largely. But it would be a peculiarly difficult problem for the larger green theory, dominated as it is by the green theory of value. In a different sort of theory – one that values clean hands and righteous agents above all else – there may be some scope for defending the importance of not doing evil oneself. There is less scope for defending that proposition in a theory, like the green theory, which attaches value primarily to outcomes and consequences. Within such logic, surely consequences that come about through avoidable omissions are no better or worse than the same consequences that come about through an agent's active interventions. If consequences count heavily, then it is hard to see how the distinction between active and passive agency – between doing violence and letting violence be done – can count at all.

Thus it is highly appropriate that greens flatly reject this conventional equating of nonviolence with passivity. It is right – truer to the core of

---

[50] Honderich (1980) develops these themes in a rather different connection.

their own theory – that they should deny the relevance of the active/ passive, act/omission distinction in this context.[51] It is right, in that sense, that they should advocate instead resistance, where appropriate, which while always nonviolent might sometimes be active nonetheless.[52]

It is perfectly possible for greens to sustain a distinction between violence and nonviolence, cashed out in terms of the intentional harms directly inflicted on others, without recourse to the active/passive act/ omission distinction. An act can be active but still nonviolent, just so long as it entails no harm to others. We might want to qualify that formula in various ways. We may want to add, for example, 'no direct intentional harm', to allow us to engage in acts that indirectly or unintentionally harm others (if they insist on continuing to chop down the tree that has a note pinned to it that says it has been spiked , for example). And we may want to include, among the 'others' who are not to be harmed, things other than just other human beings – ranging from sentient beings more generally through living ecosystems all the way to valued parts of the utterly inanimate world. But however we elaborate that basic formula, the basic point is just that we can pin our criterion of nonviolence essentially to an injunction requiring 'no harm' rather than 'no active harming'.

That is enough to avoid the allegation that nonviolence requires, in a way that green principles arguably do not permit, passivity in the face of grievous wrong. Action is permitted; the ban is just on causing harm. A further problem still remains, though. Green principles might even license deliberately harm-causing action, were that the only way to avoid greater harms being inflicted by others. The green focus, as I have presented it, is on consequences above all else. If very evil consequences can be avoided by doing just a little harm to the evildoers, then consequentialist reckoning would on the face of it permit the infliction of such harm. And the calculus is all the easier if it is a case of a little violence being required to stop the infliction of greater violence – whether against oppressed peoples or endangered species.[53]

All of that, of course, leaves all the pragmatic arguments for nonviolence firmly in place. Nonviolent resistance often produces the best consequences, for green causes just as for so many others. When it does, then of course greens should obviously adhere to principles of

[51] A distinction which is in any case philosophy suspect. See Bennett (1966; 1983), Glover (1977) and Goodin (1982b, pp. 14–15).

[52] Die Grünen 1983, sec. 1, p. 9; Routley 1984.

[53] Greens further appeal to notions of 'structural violence' (Spretnak and Capra 1986, p. 47) to bring much oppression of a vaguely impersonal sort within that broader ambit. On that concept, see more generally Galtung (1969).

nonviolence out of pure pragmatism. And here as elsewhere, it is a farsighted pragmatism that greens (like all other agents) should have in view. So they may well, for pragmatic reasons, adopt a rule of nonviolence as a general guiding principle in their actions. Still, if greens are primarily concerned about consequences – as I have argued that they should be – then they should be prepared to renounce principles of nonviolence, *in extremis*, whenever adhering to them would lead to really catastrophic consequences for the environment and those inhabiting it.

Let us be clear on the precise terms of that conclusion, though. That is not to say that nonviolence is not properly included among the central tenets of a green theory of agency. It is as deserving of inclusion on that list as is any other principle of action. The point is merely that the green theory of agency in general – and its constituent principles, among them nonviolence, in particular – must take a subsidiary role in the larger green political theory. It is the green theory of value, and the consequences that it would have us promote, that enjoys priority in cases where it conflicts with the green theory of agency.

3   Principles of Green Party Organization

A theory of agency, especially one that is meant for political application, must apply to artificially created collective agents as well as to natural human individuals. One such artificially created collective agent is the community as a whole. What the green theory of agency implies for green communities as a whole will be discussed in section 4 below. Another artificially created collective agent is the green political party itself. What the green theory of agency implies for it is the subject of the present discussion.

Theories of collective agency rest, of course, on theories of individual-level agency. All artificial agents have been created through the efforts of natural individuals, operating with the powers and purposes and principles that our theory of agency says do (or should) characterize such individuals. Analytically, their nature – powers, purposes and principles – are derivative (albeit, perhaps, in an awfully complicated way) from those of the individuals whose interactions were responsible for giving rise to them in the first place. Operationally, their actions are (at least in principle) wholly reducible to the actions and inactions of natural human individuals working through them.

Once created, though, it is nonetheless true that those artificially created collective entities take on something of a life of their own. Or, more precisely, individuals operating within them and in response to them do things (and induce others to do things) that they would not have done had that artificial agent not existed or had it taken a different form. (All references in what follows to collective agents acting ought be understood as a shorthand way of referring to individuals acting within them in this way.) Hence it is clear that any theory of agency aspiring to political application ought have something to say about how those artificial agents do – and especially about how they ought to – conduct their affairs.

Certainly the green theory of agency passes this test. It prescribes a variety of principles to be used both in analysing and, more importantly, in shaping both green political communities as a whole and green political parties more specifically. All, at root, grow out of the green concern for democratic participation quite generally. As applied to party organization, that translates particularly powerfully into a pair of injunctions on the party. The first is to practise 'grassroots democracy' – to consult local party units regularly and meaningfully. The second is to take measures to avoid cultivating an elite within the party which is cut off from the party's grassroots, by devices designed to ensure 'rotation in office' among the party's leaders. Each will be discussed in turn.

Grassroots Democracy

The 1983 manifesto of the German Greens boasts, 'Our internal organisational life and our relationship to the people who support and vote for us is the exact opposite of that of the established parties in Bonn', resting as it does on 'a new type of party organisation, the basic structures of which are set up in a grassroots-democratic and decentralised way'. They add, 'the two things cannot in fact be separated.'[54]

This principle clearly derives from the more general green concern with promoting democratic participation in all aspects of social life. Just as they want to democratize the polity, the civil service and the firm, so too do they want to ensure democratic practices internally within political parties – their own included.

At least they want to democratize internal party life in so far as political parties are going to exist at all. There is nothing in green principles that leads to the conclusion that a political structure built around a system of organized political parties is an ideal state of affairs. There is nothing to suggest that it will necessarily persist into a thoroughly green future. Parties may – and quite possibly will – pass

[54] Die Grünen 1983, sec. 1, p. 8.

away, in the same manner that greens hope that large-scale political units and the representative forms of government that they necessitate will pass away, in the ideally green world.

All of that is still some way in the future, though. In the meanwhile, there will remain some substantial role for political parties – especially green political parties – to play in bringing about that sort of future.[55] And so long as they are going to be needed at all, it is important to greens that those parties be governed, internally, according to the most democratic possible of procedures.

What exactly that entails is perhaps unclear. But given the green focus on the active participation by everyone in decisions that shape their lives, that would seem to dictate, minimally, that in a green party 'meetings and committees at all levels are [ought be] open to party members' in general.[56] Of course, merely being open to all is a very minimal requirement indeed. It is compatible with the onlookers having no formal powers at all – not even the right to address the meeting, much less a right to vote on issues coming before it.

In practice, though, the requirement of openness of all meetings is probably more potent than it at first appears. Simply having to justify their stand before their fellows forces people to internalize the point of view of the other, and to alter their own position accordingly.[57] Even if the others have no formal say in the matter – even if there is no practical reason to bother to try winning them over – people will nonetheless inevitably try to do so out of a deepseated desire to attempt to appear reasonable in the eyes of others. And that desire will be particularly strong when the others in question are seen as one's fellows, as would presumably be the case with fellow party members.

The downside to grassroots party democracy, even when operationalized as no more than a requirement that all party meetings be open to all members, is just this. The more people taking part in meetings, and the more meetings strive for unanimity, the longer – and the more meetings – it takes to make any decision.[58] We might

---

[55] There is scope for such parties, even in the absence of representative government, in organizing to get questions put to the public through national referenda and in coordinating public information campaigns to secure the 'right' results in those referenda.

[56] Die Grünen 1983, sec. V.1.3, p. 37.

[57] On these themes see Habermas (1976, pt 3), Barber (1984, esp. pp. 167–98) and Dryzek (1990a); cf. Elster (1986) and Goodin (1992b, chap. 4).

[58] 'Strong democracy' of the sort Barber (1984, p. 270) has in mind would entail weekly meetings of neighbourhood assemblies, alternating between Saturday afternoons and Wednesday evenings. Walzer (1980, ch. 7) tries to convince us that that ought to be regarded as a happy prospect. Few, I suspect, would concur.

therefore say, paraphrasing Oscar Wilde's famous quip about socialism, that the trouble with green politics is that it would take up too many evenings.[59] Or, rather, the not altogether happy prospect of committing all that much time to green politicking would reduce participation in those meetings to a small and highly unrepresentative subset of green party members.

That problem is bad enough even if you just give every party member the right to attend all meetings. It gets worse still if you give everyone a vote. Of course, giving everyone a vote might be quicker than giving everyone a say, so long as you were prepared to cut off debate sharply and press the issue to a vote. But presumably greens will not ordinarily be prepared to do that: they would want everyone both to have a say and to have a vote. Again, giving everyone a vote as well as a say would not necessarily take very much longer than just giving everyone a say, if we were prepared to let the issue ultimately be settled by a simple majority (or plurality) vote. But, again, greens will presumably not be prepared to do that, either. Eschewing notions of 'adversarial democracy', greens would presumably prefer to talk matters out until there was no need for a vote.[60] And if an issue had to be taken to a vote at all, they would presumably insist on super-large (two-thirds, three-quarters, some even suggest up to nine-tenths) majorities before declaring a matter settled.[61]

---

[59] 'Participatory democracy is not for the impatient,' say two leading green theorists (Spretnak and Capra 1986, p. 125), who proceed to hold up – apparently for approbation – the model of the Hesse Greens, who convened 'a statewide party assembly [that] met for six consecutive weekends to discuss the various points in contention and to agree upon a final draft of the [1983 Die Grünen] program'. And it is not just settling big issues for the first time like that takes time. As one prominent Die Grünen member complains quite generally, grassroots democracy 'easily degenerates into endless discussion. Whoever wants to come comes and whoever is there votes, without any responsibility for the consequences. So nothing comes out of such meetings most of the time' (Joseph Huber, quoted in Hülsberg 1988, p. 123).

[60] Mansbridge 1980.

[61] A central principle of organization of the German Green party, Die Grünen, holds that 'in as much as possible decisions have to be arrived at by consensus rather than majority vote', in order to ensure that 'minorities are protected' (Hülsberg 1988, p. 120). Tokar reports, similarly, that 'most . . . Green groups, both in Europe and in North America, operate according to a consensual decision-making process . . . originally adapted by peace and anti-nuclear activists from the processes developed by American Quaker councils over the past three centuries' (1987, p. 104). In 'larger, more diverse organizations', where literal consensus might be hard to obtain, the 'spirit of consensus is [nonetheless] protected' by requiring a large majority (two thirds to 90%) . . . to break serious deadlocks' as well as by other institutional devices, like 'waiting for the next meeting before a vote can be taken; allocating time for people on the opposite sides of an issue to try resolving their differences in private; or requiring a larger majority to proceed with the vote than is needed to pass

All of that would, of course, take even longer. Consider the process used by Die Grünen in the state of Hesse to draft their 1983 campaign manifesto – a process which some influential green writers particularly extol as a paradigm to be replicated wherever possible.[62] There the state party

> selected a program committee who invited suggestions from members on [various specified] issues. . . . When the committee members had compiled the ideas from the general membership, they sent the program back to the one hundred local groups in their state, asking for refinements, changes, and further ideas. After the committee had incorporated the changes, a statewide party assembly met for six consecutive weekends to discuss the various points in contention and to agree on a final draft of the program.

Now, asking people to give up six consecutive weekends – even if it is to draft a crucial election manifesto – is asking an awfully lot from them. And of course the longer it takes the group to make a decision, the more party members drift away in the meanwhile. So not only does the green vision of grassroots democracy threaten to impose awfully large demands on party members' time. By so doing, it threatens even to undercut the democratic character of the process that it was intended to ensure. By guaranteeing that everyone can come, talk for as long as they like and that no decision will be taken until nearly everyone has been talked around, green theorists guarantee that only a small and unrepresentative sample of party members will be left in the room by the time the final decision is taken.

This is not a problem peculiar to green theories of grassroots democracy, I hasten to add. All socialist, New Left, utopian and radical communities, organized on a thoroughly participatory basis, encounter the same problem. But while the problem is not peculiar to greens, neither do greens have any particularly convincing account of how this familiar problem with such organizational structures is to be avoided. And that failing is all the more glaring for the problem's being so very familiar.

In practice, of course, greens have plenty of ideas of how to avoid such problems commonly associated with mass meetings of any sort. In practice what greens most often do is, in effect, to work through a tiered system of consultation with local, grassroots groups.

One problem with that scheme is that, while undoubtedly more practical, it is also unprincipled. Or at least it is not nearly so obviously a

the final decision, [as] a way of assuring that even people in the minority agree that an irresolvable deadlock exists' (p. 105).
[62] The following description is from Spretnak and Capra (1986, p. 125), who regard the process in this way.

corollary of a concern for direct, active participation in the decisions that affect them. Open meetings which all may – and hopefully most will – attend is one clear way of giving meaning to that value. Consulting people from on high does not do so, or anyway not nearly so obviously.[63]

Much of course depends on how the higher tier handles the local inputs.[64] But presumably the suggestions of all the various local groups will always be somewhat contradictory; and presumably the central body responsible for collating their comments will not be expected to go back and forth to them all until absolutely everyone agrees with literally everything.

If so, though, the higher tier of party representatives responsible for collating local responses will be doing much more than merely collating responses. They will be exercising real power: they will be taking some suggestions and rejecting others. In short, the party's positions will be settled, at least in part, in 'smoke-filled rooms' far from the grassroots party members.

That, anyway, seems to be the upshot if the party, *qua* party, is to take any unified stand on issues. The alternative – which is also embodied in the rules of the German Green party, Die Grünen – is to say that each parliamentary representative is bound by the 'imperative mandate' of his or her constituency party.[65] But in so far as green constituency parties differ among themselves, green MPs thus bound will be voting different ways on the same issues, thus blunting their parliamentary power.

Greens would of course reply that a national parliament is not their preferred political institution, anyway. They would rather have all these matters decided on a community-by-community basis. Still, in so far as they are in the business of party politics at all, even if only for the time being, it must surely be a telling objection to their theory of party politics to say that it would prevent their parties from doing what parties must necessarily try to do, which is to seize and exercise political power.

---

[63] Macpherson (1977b, p. 109), who canvasses this as one 'abstract first approximation' to what participatory democracy might involve, comments, 'This may seem a far cry from democratic control. But I think it is the best we can do.'

[64] The task of coordinating local branches of the green party is just a special case of the problem (discussed in section 4 below) of providing coordination among decentralized decision units more generally.

[65] Cohen and Arato 1984, p. 330; Hülsberg 1988, p. 120.

Rotation in Office

A second central premise of green party organization is the principle of rotation in office. The German Greens, for example, stipulated in their 1983 election manifesto that members can only serve two successive terms in office before being required to stand down.[66]

Such rules are clearly a response to the familiar problem of entrenched party elites growing increasingly distant from the party's grassroots. Michels refers to this as the 'iron law of oligarchy', and he demonstrates its powerfully law-like character by showing that it holds true even in some of the most notionally egalitarian organizations around: socialist parties and trade unions.[67] Greens, forming their new parties, clearly supposed that they were not immune and attempted to institutionalize devices to protect them from the same fate.

The measures which the German Greens adopted amount, though, to periodic decapitation of the party. Those rules guarantee that, at the end of every term, there will be a massive (on average, 50 per cent) turnover in the green leadership. Now presumably there are certain political skills and certain forms of political capital that can only be acquired on the job. If so, the massive leadership turnover imposed on green parties by rules requiring rotation in office threatens to reduce severely the practical political impact of green parties. Or so the conventional wisdom would have it.[68]

It may well be that the problems of leadership turnover are exaggerated, of course. Perhaps the learning curve is a steep one: after six months or so, new leaders might be just as politically adept as were their predecessors. Perhaps political capital accrues to incumbents quickly: after a few months, new members might have as many political IOUs to call in as did their predecessors. Such propositions may well be true. Whether or not they are is clearly an empirical question. It is also quite probably one that is highly sensitive to variations in local political cultures, rules, practices and traditions.

Such evidence as we do have – from the recently reformed US Congress, for example – is not altogether encouraging, though. In

---

[66] Die Grünen 1983, sec. V.1.3, p. 37.

[67] Michels (1915); cf. Hands (1971) and Plamenatz (1973, ch. 3).

[68] It is a point which German Greens themselves came to accept, when two of their most famous MPs – Petra Kelly and the former general, Gert Bastian – refused to rotate out of office on the grounds that too much 'parliamentary skill and effectiveness . . . would be lost to the movement if they relinquished their seats as planned' (Tokar 1987, p. 106).

assemblies full of newcomers with real power, some very different practices prevail; and by almost any standard business gets done far less effectively, largely because norms of reciprocity fail to function when there is no reason to suppose that the other will still be there when it comes time for him or her to reciprocate a past favour.[69] Furthermore, from what we know of how the old, unreformed Congress worked it is clear that in an assembly dominated by powerful old-timers, the newcomers took an awfully long time to acquire any real power.[70]

Either way, frequent newcomers to office is something to be avoided. But that latter fact gives green parties trying to push their ways into hidebound legislatures a particularly powerful reason, of a purely pragmatic kind, for avoiding frequent turnover in their leadership. Even if it does not hinder their electoral chances to be constantly presenting a cast of unfamiliar faces to the electorate, it certainly will hinder their legislative effectiveness once elected.

Perhaps there are benefits of frequent leadership turnover to offset those costs. There certainly is something to be said for building up a pool of talent within the party. The more people there are with leadership experience, the less the party's prospects will depend on what might happen to any particular leader; and the better positioned the party will be to occupy the offices of state, should it ever find itself in a position to form or join a government. But of course all of that presumes that people with past leadership experience are to be eligible for another turn in leadership, once they have sat out one or two terms.

It is not clear whether or not the green principle of rotation in office is intended to allow to allow past leaders to rotate back into office in that way. If it does allow that, then the party risks being dominated by a small, oligarchic elite whose members take turns in the leadership. George Wallace, when constitutionally debarred from serving another consecutive term as Governor of Georgia, installed his wife in the office for a term until he was eligible to stand again. In that way, he avoided even the need to move out of the Governor's Mansion.

Few would be quite so blatant about it as that, perhaps. But if greens allow their leaders to rotate back into office, having rotated out of it, the spectre of some such revolving door recirculating a small oligarchic elite is something genuinely to be feared. Yet if greens decide not to allow their leaders, having gained experience in office, to rotate back into it

---

[69] Contrast the picture painted by Matthews in 1959 with that of Uslaner in 1990; on the effects of Congressional reform more generally see Dodd and Oppenheimer (1981) and Rieselbach (1986).

[70] Hinckley 1971.

they compromise their effectiveness by always having leaders who are only just 'learning on the job'. Rotation in office would then be all costs and no benefits.

Or, rather, the only benefits from the practice would be purely in terms of principle. Such benefits are not to be denigrated. People are often prepared to pay dearly for their principles; and the principle of rotation in office may well be one for which greens are prepared to sacrifice a fair bit of political effectiveness. The point here is not that they should not do so. It is merely that, if they do do so, the sort of collective that they will have succeeded in creating in their green political party is only a very weak one.

Worse, it would be a weak agent set in the context where its weakness would actually matter. Green parties will inevitably be pitted in political struggle with other parties that are stronger in a great many ways. Being encumbered by any such principled constraints on effective leadership, in a way that those other, stronger parties are not, only exacerbates those strategic disadvantage of green parties.

That impinges, in turn, on the attainment of green policy goals. If what I have argued in section 1 of this chapter is correct – if the green theory of value really does take priority, within green theory itself, over the green theory of agency – then in insisting on rotation in office greens might be pursuing a lower priority goal in preference to a higher priority one. Depending on just how seriously the practice of rotation in office compromises their political effectiveness, green parties might therefore have to consider abandoning that practice in deference to the greater good of implementing green values.

4 Principles of Green Political Structures

Greens aim to reform not just party politics but also to alter the communities which those parties govern. If anything, the green theory of value applies more powerfully to the latter than to the former sorts of collective agents. In the ideal world to which greens aspire, a world of decentralized communities governed by direct democracy, the role of parties – green or otherwise – would largely fade away.[71] So while green

---

[71] Whether this is a realistic ambition is another issue, to which I shall return in chapter 5, section 1 below. For now simply note that many commentators would share Macpherson's (1977b, p. 112) judgement that the persistence of political parties of some sort within participatory democracies is 'probably unavoidable' and 'may be positively desirable'.

theorists have perforce devoted a fair bit of attention to questions of internal party organization, their principal focus has always been on the broader social canvas. It has always been the organization of whole societies rather than of mere political parties with which greens are most concerned. It has always been clear to their sympathizers and their critics alike that the green theory of agency will stand or fall on the cogency of its scheme for reorganizing the political community as a whole.

Decentralization

If there is anything truly distinctive about green politics, most commentators would concur, it must surely be its emphasis on decentralization. As Theodore Roszak puts it in his influential book, *Person/Planet*,

> both person and planet are threatened by the same enemy. *The bigness of things*. The bigness of industrial structures, world markets, financial networks, mass political organizations, public institutions, military establishments, cities, bureaucracies. It is the insensitive colossalism of these systems that endangers the rights of the person and the rights of the planet. The inordinate scale of industrial enterprise that must grind people into statistical grist for the market place and the work force simultaneously shatters the biosphere in a thousand unforeseen ways.[72]

The greens seek to substitute for all that 'a decentralized, democratic society with . . . political, economic, and social institutions locating power on the smallest scale (closest to home) that is efficient and practical'.[73] Their 'guiding principle . . . is that no authority be held at a higher level than is absolutely necessary.'[74] They want to see 'politics on a human scale'.[75] They call for decision-making power to be devolved to units that are 'surveyable' – capable of being scanned and understood by ordinary mortals.[76]

In the words of the canonical 1983 manifesto of the German Greens, the basic principle of green politics is that 'decentralized basic units

[72] Roszak 1978, p. 33.
[73] This is the fifth of the *Ten Key Values* enunciated by the Green Committees of Correspondence in the US (1986).
[74] European Greens 1989, preamble.
[75] Sale 1980, esp. pp. 419–518.
[76] Die Grünen 1983, sec. 1, p. 8. Similarly, in their policy on the economy, the German Greens call for 'decentralized and surveyable production units and a new and democratically controllable application of technology. Large combines are to be broken down into surveyable units which can be run democratically by those working in them' (Die Grünen 1983, sec. 2.3, p. 11).

(local community, district) should be given extensive autonomy and rights of self-government.'[77] They propose, more specifically, things like:

- The establishment of democratically controllable self-administration close to the citizens, in place of the increasing monopolisation of economic power and the steadily increasing central administrative apparatus.
- Thorough-going decentralization and simplification of units of administration.
- The rights of administration and self-determination for states, regions, districts, local authorities and urban districts are to be increased, as well as their share of financial resources. . . .
- Citizens' initiatives and associations must have the right to be heard by the relevant [federal and state] parliaments and authorities, and to obtain information. They must be given plaintiff rights against administrative measures, even across state borders.
- The vast flood of consultation, far removed from the citizens and without clearly defined responsibilities, is to be replaced by combined consultation and decision-making boards (economic and social councils) at all levels. These boards must be given a hearing everywhere (local authority, county, district, state and federal) that economically important planning and decision-making takes place. They are to make decisions about public investment policy, and be responsible in conjunction with the relevant political authority for the economic sphere of the budget.[78]

While all those specific demands are drawn from the 1983 German Green manifesto, they are nowise peculiar to that document. Decentralism of roughly that sort has been a central theme in green thinking right from the outset of the renewed wave of environmentalist concern in the early 1970s. And similar demands are found being echoed, *mutatis mutandis*, in almost any green manifesto.[79]

---

[77] Ibid., sec. 1, p. 8.

[78] Ibid., sec. 5, p. 37.

[79] The consensus statement among European Greens (1989, preface) describes decentralization as their 'guiding principle'. The Green Committees of Correspondence in the US (1986, item 5) demand, more particularly, that we 'redesign our institutions so that fewer decisions and less regulation over money are granted as one moves from the community toward the national level'. The exception to this rule is the British Green Party's 1987 manifesto (quoted in Dobson 1990, p. 127), proposing merely to shift responsibility for many services (taxation and benefits, social services, housing, education, health care, land reform, policing, transportation and pollution control) to decentralized district level, while leaving central government in place to tend to others (foreign affairs, defence, customs and excise, international trade and transboundary aspects of justice, transportation and pollution). It is unclear whether those more modest goals are embraced by British Greens on grounds of principle or merely on grounds of political pragmatism, however.

Voicing sentiments that have been echoed many times since, signatories to *The Ecologist*'s famous 1972 'Blueprint for survival', for example, commended decentralization as an aid to social control, to industrial responsiveness, and to lowering per capita strains on the environment by decanting urban dwellers to rural areas. 'We have no hard and fast views on the size of the [ideal] communities,' say the signatories of that document, 'but for the moment we suggest neighbourhoods of 500, represented in communities of 5,000, in regions of 500,000', which will be 'represented nationally, which in turn as today should be represented globally'.[80] The numbers, although obviously somewhat arbitrary, actually seem pretty well to have stuck.[81] But for present purposes it is the general idea rather than precise numbers that matter most anyway.

Green proposals for reducing the size of the political community are clearly inspired by the greens' democratic impulses, combined with certain theories of an empirical sort about what is required to implement those goals. The root ideas, clearly, are something like these. People must feel a part of their community in order to participate meaningfully in deliberations regarding its future. They must be able to meet together with all other members of their community, face to face, to discuss the problems and options before them.[82] They must be confident that their participation might make some material difference to the outcome. They must be able to comprehend, reasonably fully and completely, what is actually going on within their community; and they must understand its workings well enough to form a reasonable estimate of how various alterations might affect it. Finally, they must be able to

[80] Goldsmith et al. 1972, pp. 14–15.

[81] Kirkpatrick Sale (1980, p. 504; 1985, p. 64), for example, similarly commends neighbourhoods of 500 to 1,000, aggregated into cities of 8,000 to 10,000, set in turn in 'bioregions' (Sale 1984; 1985) of more variable size. 'A bioregion', Sale writes, 'is a part of the earth's surface whose rough boundaries are determined by natural rather than human dictates, distinguishable from other areas by attributes of flora, fauna, water, climate, soils and land-forms, and the human settlements and cultures those attributes have given rise to' (1984, p. 168). That rather woolly suggestion is sometimes made more precise by saying that boundaries should be drawn so as to encapsulate certain self-contained physical and biological processes of nature, such as airsheds and watersheds (to which Sale himself at one point refers in describing a bioregion (1985, p. 107). See further Ostrom, Tiebout and Warren (1961) and, especially, Haefele (1973, ch. 4).

[82] There is actually a considerable literature – in part philosophical, in part empirical – upon the importance of face-to-face meetings in making participatory democracy work. (See e.g. Laslett 1956; Mansbridge 1980, chs 19–20; and Barber 1984, ch. 19). That is why democracy in the workplace, where interactions are more standardly face to face, is such an important model for advocates of participatory democracy (Pateman 1970; Greenberg 1986).

survey the community as a whole, rather than just having a sense of their own small corner of it, if they are to judge the general good rather than pursue narrow sectional interests. In all ways, broadly democratic sentiments combine with pretty standard empirical hypotheses to lead greens to favour devolution of ultimate decision-making power to really pretty small-scale political units.[83]

One of the more important ideas behind decentralization is that people will be encouraged to participate more in the political life of their community if the community is made small enough to ensure that their participation makes a difference. But there is a familiar flaw with that general strategy. True enough, decentralization gives each member of the community more control over that community's decisions. But the smaller the community, the less and less the community decisions will ordinarily matter to the ultimate outcome.[84] People are being given more and more power over less and less.[85]

Or, more precisely, more and more of what really matters will now ordinarily cut across communities and therefore lies in the hands of those who are to be responsible for negotiations with other communities. Hence, decreasing the size of the political unit increases members' control over internal affairs only at the cost of decreasing the relative importance of internal affairs and of increasing the relative importance of external negotiations – which are, of necessity, entrusted to community representatives rather than being conducted through mechanisms of direct democracy.[86]

---

[83] Here is the justification given by Sale (1985, pp. 94–5) for why 'the primary location of decision-making, and of political and economic control, should be the . . . more-or-less intimate grouping' of between 1,000 and 5,000–10,000: 'Here, where people know one another and the essentials of the environment they share, where at least the most basic information or problem-solving is known or readily available, . . . decisions . . . stand at least a fair chance of being correct and a reasonable likelihood of being carried out competently; and even if the choice is misguided or the implementation faulty, the damage to either the society or the ecosphere is likely to be insignificant.'

[84] Thus, Dahl (1970, p. 86) says that a 'nation [that] . . . dissolves itself into tiny states in order to create a multiplicity of primary democracies . . . would be very much worse off than before with respect to a vast range of problems,' naming 'pollution' as primary among them. See further Dahl and Tufte 1973.

[85] Of course, on balance it might still make more sense for people to participate in smaller-scale decisions, if people gain proportionately more power over community decisions than the community loses over ultimate outcomes. My point here is just that matters are less clearcut than 'power to the people' advocates of decentralization pretend.

[86] Frankel (1987, p. 270) similarly bases his critique of 'postindustrial utopians' – greens among them – on the proposition that 'stateless, decentralized, moneyless, small-scale communes or other informal alternatives are not viable without the

It ought to be obvious that the smaller the individual communities, the more crucial becomes coordination between the communities.[87] What green theorists clearly have in mind is that the principal focus of political action is to be very local indeed. It is the 500-person neighbourhoods and, to a lesser extent, the 5,000-person communities that are to be the focus of direct political action. It is they which are to be well-integrated, tightly-knit social units. It is they which are to display the properties of internal organization and collective capacity that are taken to characterize 'collective agents', properly speaking – collective agents capable of deliberative choice and purposive action directed towards chosen ends.[88]

Those properties would, apparently, be markedly lacking among any of the larger aggregates that greens envisage emerging out of the combination of those smaller neighbourhoods and communities into bioregions. They are still more markedly lacking among any national- or international-level combination of those bioregional units. The smaller units – neighbourhoods and to a lesser extent communities – are supposed to become proper collective entities, with which people identify and in which they invest decision-taking and decision-implementing powers. The interactions between two or more of those smaller units are not supposed to be like that at all.

Describing the proper relations between decentralized local communities, greens employ terms like 'self-sufficient collaboration'.[89] They talk of 'the joining together of free communities to exchange goods and solve common problems'.[90] The 'federations of communities' thus formed should and would, therefore, be both 'entirely voluntary' and ephemeral rather than enduring. They would have been 'formed for specific purposes' and would pass when those purposes passed.[91]

---

complex administrative and social structures necessary to guarantee democratic participation, civil rights and egalitarian co-ordination of economic resources.'

[87] Greens themselves would hope to minimize the need for such coordination by making the communities self-sufficient and environmentally friendly. The first attribute obviates the necessity to negotiate with other communities to secure needed positive inputs, the latter the necessity to negotiate an end to negative externalities. Try as greens might to minimize such cross-boundary flows, there are always bound to be some of them and hence some need for coordination across different communities. Furthermore, the smaller those communities are, the larger those cross-boundary flows will ordinarily, of necessity, be.

[88] French 1984.

[89] Sale 1984, p. 170. A better description might be 'self-reliant' rather than 'self-sufficient' (Dobson 1990, pp. 104–7).

[90] Tokar 1987, p. 98.

[91] Ibid. They should also greens say, be 'subject to popular control' (ibid.) – thus making them more ephemeral still.

All of that is merely to say that when local communities come together to negotiate common approaches to shared problems, they should do so as independent agents negotiating arrangements that are mutually agreeable to all concerned. To do that, they need not – and greens would say should not – create a new collective entity in the process to oversee the arrangements. They can, and greens would say should, merely coordinate their behaviour while remaining free and independent moral agents, rather like two individuals coming together to negotiate mutually agreeable terms for the sale and purchase of a house.

In greens' theoretical writings, the preferred image of relations between a large set of decentralized communities is that of a 'network'.[92] Examples standardly offered include inter-library loan schemes and arrangements for interfacing between independent national rail or telecommunications systems. From the green point of view, of course, the salient features of such examples is that they involve free and equal parties meeting to agree mutually desirable arrangements among themselves, without the intervention of any superior authority.[93]

All of that is just to say that greens are basically libertarians-cum-anarchists, at least as regards relations between communities if not necessarily within them. They think that decentralized communities can and should negotiate voluntary agreements coordinating their activities in various respects. But they think that there need not be – and that there should not be – any central coordinating agency overseeing that process.[94]

They say that not because greens think coordination between decentralized communities is does not really matter. On the contrary,

---

[92] In their practical political writings, they take a similarly lackadaisical attitude towards coordination among the various constituent parts of the larger green movement. Sara Parkin (1988, p. 176), co-spokesperson for the British Green Party, claims in an otherwise astute essay on 'Green strategy' that 'there is no need for rigid or formal battle plans. . . . The most successful sort of co-ordination in these cases takes place in bars and restaurant.' That is fine for modest movements whose effective leadership can all fit around the same table. But it is an obviously unpromising model for any movement of a scale sufficient to capture national government.

[93] Sale 1980, p. 513.

[94] Bookchin (1990, pp. 182, 193), for example, advocates what he calls 'libertarian municipalism', with each 'humanly scaled, self-governing municipality freely and confederally associat[ing] with other humanly scaled, self-governing municipalities' – 'a confederal Commune of communes', as it were. Other anarchist strands in green thought are effectively evoked by O'Riordan (1976, chs 1 and 9), Dobson (1990, pp. 83–4), Sale (1980, pp. 466–81), Tokar (1987, chs 1, 2 and 7) and Woodcock (1974), as well as by Bookchin's (1971; 1982) own earlier writings.

greens are the first to recognize the importance of this process. Signatories to *The Ecologist*'s 1972 'Blueprint for survival' wax lyrical on the subject:

> Although we believe that the small community should be the basic unit of society and that each community should be as self-sufficient and self-regulating as possible, we would like to stress that we are not proposing that they be inward-looking, self-obsessed or in any way closed to the rest of the world. Basic precepts of ecology, such as the interrelatedness of all things and the far-reaching effects of ecological processes and their disruption, should influence community decision-making . . .[95]

The question is simply how, exactly, that aim is to be achieved absent the agency of a state.

Some greens see the 'basic precepts of ecology' to which the 'blueprint' refers as providing the solution as well as posing the problem.[96] There is, after all, no central organization imposing order on nature. Rather, the plants and animals of each area simply adapt to their own locality, while at the same time incidentally feeding into the larger scheme of things. Ecologically, the global order emerges out of these local adaptations and interactions between them. And it does so 'naturally', without any self-conscious, intentional interventions on the part of any central coordinating agency or even on the part of any of the local constituents of nature.[97]

Sometimes green writers offer that ecological analogy as a model of coordination among the decentralized political units that they are proposing. They seem to suppose that a 'natural order' will similarly emerge there, too. But the analogy is just an analogy – no more – until they specify the precise mechanism by which order will be imposed, politically. In nature, the mechanism serving that purpose is the familiar one of natural selection. The automatic workings of that mechanism are what obviates the need for any intentional coordination in the ecological

---

[95] Goldsmith et al. 1972, p. 15. Similarly, the 1983 German Green manifesto emphasizes that 'Grassroots democracy . . . requires comprehensive organisation and coordination if an ecological policy is to be carried through at the level of public decision-making against strong opposition' (Die Grünen 1983, sec. 1, p. 8). And the Green Committees of Correspondence in the US (1986, item 5) speak of the need to 'reconcile the need for community and regional self-determination with the need for appropriate centralized regulation in certain [unspecified] matters'.

[96] The authors of 'A blueprint for survival' are not among them, I hasten to add. But something rather like the following argument is vaguely suggested by Bookchin's (1971, p. 80) remarks on the theme that 'an anarchist community would approximate an ecosystem.'

[97] Or at least so the standard models would have it. But this proposition is itself the subject of some controversy among natural scientists themselves. See e.g. the debate between Engelberg and Boyarsky (1979) and Patten and Odum (1981).

setting. Greens appealing to that ecological analogy as a model of political coordination neglect to specify what would on their theory serve as the functional equivalent, in politics, of natural selection in nature.[98]

There is a possible answer here, perhaps, but greens are not likely to be tempted by it. Many writers foresee just such a 'naturally occurring order' in the social world and have a very clear idea as to how that order will come about. The mechanism that they nominate is, of course, the market. Without any intentional interventions on the part of any superior forces, the 'hidden hand' of the market coordinates the activities of all the individual agents involved. For the likes of Hayek and Nozick, this 'spontaneous order' that emerges from the uncoerced market interactions among free individuals is something morally to be cherished.[99]

Greens would usually think otherwise. It is part of their programme that they must be highly sensitive to distributive injustices and exploitative social relations. Both, all too often, come in the wake of markets. So I think we can safely presume that that is not a mechanism that greens can rely on for coordinating decentralized decision-making. Neither, though, is it clear what other mechanism greens could nominate in its place. Until some such mechanism has been specified and its workings adequately explained, we must dismiss the idea of a 'natural order' emerging among decentralized political units that is in any important respect analogous to the 'natural order' that natural selection causes to emerge among decentralized ecological units.

Having emphasized that their decentralized communities must not 'be inward-looking, self-obsessed or in any way closed to the rest of the world', the authors of 'A blueprint for survival' proceed to a relatively limp conclusion. 'Therefore,' they write, 'there must be an efficient and sensitive communications network between all communities. There must be procedures whereby community actions that affect regions can be discussed at global level.'[100]

Clearly communications between the decentralized communities is a necessary condition for effective coordination among them.[101] But to suggest that that will be sufficient to ensure adequate coordination seems little more than a pious hope. Recall that we are supposed to be dealing here with completely independent communities subject to no

[98] The importance of specifying mechanisms to validate non-intentional, non-causal explanations is powerfully brought home by Elster (1983, chs 1 and 2).

[99] Hayek 1960; 1973–9; Nozick 1974.

[100] Goldsmith et al. 1972, p. 15.

[101] Goodin 1976, ch. 5.

common power. So what is being proposed is communications without sanctions – a pure 'talking shop'.

The best single green text on the subject of green decentralization, Kirkpatrick Sale's *Human Scale*, offers an example of how this all might work. He points to the practices of the New England Clamshell Alliance, which is 'based on small "affinity groups" of ten or twenty people, who meet with some regularity and make all decisions by consensus; these are then conveyed to a central committee by non-voting delegates – "spokes" – and this committee then coordinates the results into a fixed policy, sending word back and forth to various affinity groups until general agreement is reached'. From this experience, Sale concludes that 'federation of consensus-taking groups is certainly a workable organizational form.'[102]

But the Clamshell Alliance was being rent asunder even as Sale was busy singing its praises, as Sale himself freely admits. That that happened should have come as no surprise to anyone. Even with the best will in the world, a consensus cannot hold forever. In effect, a consensus rule gives each member the power of veto over all group decisions. That veto will naturally be used as a bargaining lever. What it is one is bargaining for, with it, is variable. In politics-as-usual, the lever is characteristically employed by those with most to win or least to lose to feather their own nests.[103] In more highminded politics, it will be used by those wanting to press their particular vision of the public good on others in the group with a different vision. The motives are different, but the resulting deadlock is the same. And such deadlocks will be the inevitable results of adopting consensus rules among groups of people with divergent goals or even just divergent opinions about how best to pursue goals that they all share.

Perhaps in appreciation of those plain truths, the German Greens seem to place their faith instead in institutions of direct democracy. Their 1983 manifesto declares, 'In all political spheres we support the idea of strengthening the participation of the people affected by introducing elements of direct democracy for deciding on major schemes with regional, state and federal referenda.'[104] That is how they propose to secure the 'comprehensive organisation and coordination' that they acknowledge will be required 'if an ecological policy is to be carried through . . . against strong opposition'.[105]

[102] Sale 1980, pp. 503–4. Elsewhere, Sale (1984) has written that 'bioregions' – a substantially larger unit than the decentralized local communities – should also develop in 'relative autonomy' from each other.
[103] Barry 1965, pp. 243–50.
[104] Die Grünen 1983, sec. 1, p. 8; see similarly sec. 5.1.2, p. 37.
[105] Ibid., sec. 1, p. 8.

Notice, though, that conducting a referendum at the national, state or even regional level is in stark contrast to green proposals for radical decentralization of decision-making powers to very small, local-level political units.[106] Direct democracy within these larger political units may well be an alternative – another way to achieve the same goals that decentralization was supposed to serve, goals of increasing people's control over what happens to them or whatever. Or, again, direct democracy at the national, state or regional levels may be just an interim measure – a second-best stopgap useful only until such time as the sort of genuine decentralization greens most desire can actually be arranged. Still, it must be said that conducting a referendum at the national, state or even regional level is dramatically different from deciding everything at the sort of small-scale neighbourhood or town meetings which greens seemed originally to be proposing.

'Think Globally, Act Locally'

The catchphrase that at one and the same time best encapsulates both green objectives and preferred green strategies for obtaining them is, 'Think globally, act locally.'[107] Greens are strong on the need to overcome traditional constraints of national sovereignty in solving pressing concerns of the global environment. *Only One Earth* was the title of the book that served as an unofficial manifesto for the 1972 Stockholm Conference on the Human Environment that led to the founding of the United Nations Environmental Programme.[108] Similar themes run throughout virtually all contemporary green manifestos.[109]

Certainly it is true that greens are concerned with life on earth as

---

[106] Direct democracy on the local level is, of course, quite another matter. That is not only consistent with green proposals for decentralization but also at least arguably presupposes them. There is much reason to believe that direct democracy works only among groups small enough for everyone to meet face to face (Sale 1980, pp. 492–507).

[107] The phrase is commonly attributed to René Dubois (Tokar 1987, p. 138). The idea obviously predates green parties themselves. In the section of the 1972 'Blueprint for survival' dedicated to decentralization, for example, the signatories are at pains to 'emphasize that our goal should be to create *community* feeling and *global* awareness . . .' (Goldsmith et al. 1972, p. 15).

[108] Ward and Dubois 1972.

[109] The 1983 German Green manifesto, for example, reads, 'The future of life on our planet Earth can only be safeguarded if a survival community of all peoples and nations is formed. For this reason, cooperation in partnership with all nations of the world is the uppermost principle of our foreign policy' (Die Grünen 1983, sec. 3.1, p. 24).

such, quite independently of artificial national boundaries. Certainly they are anti-statist, in that sense. But being anti-statist in that sense is not necessarily equivalent to being 'internationalist', in the Stockholm Conference sense of being in favour of strong international organizations (of which the UNEP is, at most, a feeble precursor) capable of securing protection for the global environment.

On the contrary, greens are more typically concerned with how to 'reshape world order without creating just another enormous nation-state'.[110] Green anti-statism characteristically emanates in proposals not for strong suprastate political institutions but rather in proposals for breaking states up and devolving their powers to smaller units, organized around bioregions or some such. That is the message that is so effectively signalled in the latter half of the slogan, 'Think globally, act locally.'[111]

But of course what gives impetus to the contemporary green movement in its present form is the supposition that we can no longer afford purely local remedies.[112] The problems now before us are genuinely global, in the sense of requiring concerted action worldwide. The paradigmatically contemporary problems of climate change and ozone depletion, unlike the earlier problems of pollution and population control, simply cannot reliably be solved through actions by nations (still less bioregions) one at a time. The systematic, coordinated efforts of all are required.

It is at this international level that the failure of greens to provide any coherent account of coordination among smaller political units is perhaps most serious.[113] What makes the green message especially

[110] That counts as one of the *Ten Key Values* enunciated by the Green Committees of Correspondence in the US (1986, item 9).

[111] The German Greens (Die Grünen 1983, sec. 3.1, pp. 24–5) are systematically ambivalent on this score. On the one hand, they write, 'Though we all undoubtedly live in one world, it would be quite contrary to the principles of an ecological policy if we were to try and solve all problems uniformly and centralistically. Our aim is to maintain the viability of particular regions of the Earth even if they have to depend upon themselves [alone]. This corresponds to our principle of decentralization within the state'. On the other hand they write, 'As many of the important tasks of the future can only be achieved by a worldwide organisation, we Greens support the strengthening of the United Nations'.

[112] As I said right at the outset of chapter 1 above.

[113] Some comfort might be drawn from considerable evidence of norms of 'comity' at work in international law (Paul 1991). But it is an open question how far that will generalize: it is one thing to be willing to apply standards set elsewhere in the relatively rare case of a foreign national standing in the dock in your own jurisdiction; it is quite another to alienate power to set standards for yourselves, at all. The absence of traditions of comity in private international law – where commerce and contracts are concerned – suggests that the model is not likely to generalize very far.

appealing is that it points to the need for concerted global action. What makes it especially unsatisfying is that it provides no account – apart from the apparently vacuous suggestion to 'think globally' – as to how that concerted global action is to be achieved.

The suggestion to 'think globally' might be less vacuous than it at first appears, though. Perhaps what it is meant to suggest is the proposition that, among communities organized around properly green values, there is a different logic at work – and that there is less need for heavyhanded coordination among those communities, in consequence.

Here I shall summarize four different models of the basic dynamics underlying efforts to coordinate environmental protection worldwide.[114] The first two models are more descriptions of current reality. They serve to explain why it is so standardly supposed that some sort of relatively centralized coordination (binding agreements, if not world governments) will be required to secure the desired goals. The latter two models are, perhaps, more apt characterizations of the sorts of dynamics that greens suppose will be operating among decentralized green communities. Greens would presumably hope that they would show how, given these new dynamics, coordination might emerge more automatically without the intervention of any centralized authority. In the end, though, I think I can show that there is still a substantial role for centralized agencies to facilitate that coordination. They will be undoubtedly handy, even if they are not strictly essential.

The basic logic underlying environmental disputes, whether between separate communities or between separate individuals, is ordinarily represented as a Polluter's Dilemma, modelled on the infamous Prisoner's Dilemma. That is the first model I shall be discussing.

In a Polluter's-cum-Prisoner's Dilemma, polluting and environmental degradation more generally is represented as a cheap solution to the otherwise expensive problem of waste disposal. Each side, desiring to minimize costs to itself, is therefore presumed to prefer polluting to not polluting whatever the other side does. As in all Prisoner's Dilemmas, though, each is worse off if all pollute than if none pollutes. Hence each would be willing to be bound to some anti-pollution regulations, if that is the only way that it can ensure that others stop dumping their wastes on it.[115] But since it would be in the narrow interests of each to defect

[114] For a fuller discussion of coordination problems in general and of the social mechanisms appropriate to solving them, see Goodin (1976, chs 4 and 5 respectively).

[115] The Polluter's Dilemma is thus represented in Goodin 1976, ch. 15 and extended to the international environment in ch. 17. On such models of collective action in general, see Olson (1965), Hardin (1982). For an extended application to international environmental regimes, see Ostrom (1991).

from this regime if it could – polluting others without being polluted by them – these regulations require enforcement.[116] This enforcement might in principle come in any of a variety of forms; most commonly, though, it must come in the form of sanctions imposed by some superior legal authority.[117]

The second model is essentially just a variation on that basic Polluter's-cum-Prisoner's Dilemma logic. The story as just told is a story about a two-person game. But in the real world, environmental protection games involve more than just two players: it is, in the language of game theory, an *n*-person game rather than just a two-person game. Now, let us suppose that the goal in view – protection of a fishery from being overfished, protection of the air or oceans from being overpolluted, or whatever – requires the cooperation of most but not quite all of those *n* players in the game. Suppose that if eighty out of a hundred nations did it, the goal would be achieved.

Well, the basic structure of the situation may still be that of a Polluter's-cum-Prisoner's Dilemma. Each nation would certainly rather that others bear the sacrifices, to be sure. But now we have a game within a game. Suppose the world's air, oceans or fisheries can afford for twenty nations to continue polluting. There will be a mad scramble in which each nation tries to lock itself inexorably into a policy of polluting, thereby forcing others to pay the costs of environmental protection that they have avoided. And this attempt to force the other to play cooperatively by locking yourself firmly into a policy of noncooperation is, of course, the defining feature of a Chicken Game.[118] So we might say that, on this second model, there is a Chicken Game nesting inside a Polluter's-cum-Prisoner's Dilemma.

This second model might, on its face, seem to bode even worse for international environmental protection than does the basic Polluter's-cum-Prisoner's Dilemma. But, in fact, it bodes marginally better. For whereas in a Polluter's-cum-Prisoner's Dilemma noncooperation (polluting) is a strictly dominant strategy, better for each whatever the others do, in a Chicken Game there is no strictly dominant strategy. What each side does depends on what it thinks the others are going to do. Specifically, if one side thinks that the others really are locked into a

---

[116] This is what Garrett Hardin (1968) refers to as 'mutual coercion mutually agreen upon' in his classic paper on 'The tragedy of the commons'; the point, indeed the phrase, is echoed in Schelling (1971).

[117] I say 'most commonly' in deference to the possibility that self-enforcement might be possible, on a 'tit-for-tat' basis, among a small group of agents locked into an indefinitely long series of such games with each other (Luce and Raiffa 1957, pp. 97–102; M. Taylor 1976; 1987; Axelrod 1984).

[118] Taylor and Ward 1982; Taylor 1987, ch. 2; Ward 1987.

pattern of noncooperative behaviour, then it will itself play cooperatively.[119] In the example above, if we think that twenty other nations
really are locked into a policy of polluting and if we think that the world
really can afford only twenty polluting nations, then we will sign on to a
policy of not polluting ourselves. And we will do so as a matter of pure
prudence, without any external sanctioning agency to force us to abide
by that agreement.[120]

Of course, mistakes will happen. We will occasionally find ourselves
'calling the bluff' of others who were not bluffing at all – they really were
locked into a noncooperative strategy, and they cannot now get out of it
even if we try to force them to do so by playing noncooperatively
ourselves. Sometimes, in the mad rush to lock themselves into
noncooperative policies and thereby secure their place as one of the
twenty polluting countries that the world can afford, more than twenty
nations might get locked into pollution-intensive policies.[121] And
sometimes there might be disagreement – genuine, or more often
strategically motivated – about how many polluters the world can really
afford. In all these ways, there might still be some substantial scope for a
centralized authority to coordinate environmental protection policies
even on the nested Chicken Game.

Both of those first two models – the Polluter's-cum-Prisoner's
Dilemma and the nested Chicken Game – are essentially attempts to
represent the world as it presently is. Both are essentially models of
problems facing us in our attempt to coordinate environmental policies
of presently existing nations and their presently existing political
leaders. And both point to the need for centralized coordination backed
by sanctions: enforceable international agreements, if not a world
government.

All that is true, however, only in so far as people have the peculiar
sorts of preferences characterizing those particular sorts of games. In
particular, it is absolutely essential to have a superior legal authority to
enforce agreements only if each side thinks it is better off polluting
others than not, just so long it can succeed in doing so without being
polluted by them in turn.[122] Not everyone manifests such peculiarly

[119] For a theoretically elaborated empirical example, see Ward and Edwards 1990.
[120] Ward 1987.
[121] Taylor and Ward 1982; Taylor 1987, ch. 2; Ward 1987.
[122] Indeed, in the peculiar structure of a Polluter's-cum-Prisoner's Dilemma
Game, each is better off polluting whatever others do. One would rather pollute if
they do not: that way one enjoys the comparative advantage over them of disposing
of one's wastes cheaply, whereas they must pay to dispose of them properly. But one
would also rather pollute even if they do: certainly one would not want to put oneself
at the comparative disadvantage of being the only one to pay to dispose of one's own

beggar-my-neighbour attitudes, though. And in so far as they do not, other models of the situation might be more appropriate.

A third model builds on the observation that – at least sometimes and at least on some issues – most people would actually prefer to behave cooperatively, just so long as others do likewise. Certainly that seems to describe the behaviour of people working on Chinese communal farms, for example. They seem happy enough to work hard without any special rewards or punishments, just so long as others are working hard too. All that they seem to ask is that they not be 'played for suckers', working hard themselves while others loll about. Amartya Sen has coined the term 'Assurance Game' to represent this phenomenon.[123]

In formal terms, this Assurance Game differs from that of the Prisoner's Dilemma in basically just one essential respect. The first choice of everyone with Prisoner's Dilemma preferences is to idle while others work. The first choice of everyone with Assurance Game preferences, in contrast, is to work while others work.

That one small change has important consequences for the need for enforcement, in turn. In a Prisoner's Dilemma there will always be a need for sanctions, usually imposed via some superior legal authority, to induce people to abide by agreements that are best for all concerned. The reason is simply that each would prefer to defect from such agreements whatever others did. In an Assurance Game there may be no need for sanctions. The reason is simply that each would prefer to abide by agreements – in the Chinese commune case, to work hard – if others did likewise.

That Assurance Game model is easily enough adapted to serve as a story about environmental protection. On the Assurance Game model of environmental protection, we are asked to imagine that everyone wants – genuinely wants, as their most preferred outcome – for everyone, themselves included, to do their bit to protect the environment. Everyone is prepared to bear their fair share of those costs, so long as others are likewise. The only reason that it might seem otherwise is that no one wants to be played for a sucker. It is only because of the (mis)perception that others will take advantage of our cooperative behaviour that any of us ever fail to cooperate in these realms.

wastes properly. The peculiarity of the Prisoner's Dilemma is that each following this 'strictly dominant strategy' and doing what is best for each, whatever others do, leads to everyone doing something – polluting – which is worse for everyone than everyone not polluting. But since it is best for each to pollute whatever others do, there is no way to get to that socially preferred world of no pollution, absent some mechanism of enforcing the no-pollution agreement. Individual interests, narrowly calculated, will not naturally yield that result.

[123] Sen 1966; 1967.

Now, that may or may not seem like a particularly plausible model of international environmental politics among currently existing nation-states and their present political leaders. Indeed, as a model of that, most would probably dismiss it as really awfully implausible. But remember, the greens are offering this model not as an account of present political preferences but rather as a model of how coordination ought to work among a set of decentralized communities guided by genuinely green principles and values. So the fact that the present rulers of Brazil or Britain or wherever might clearly manifest the beggar-my-neighbour environmental preferences characteristic of a Polluter's-cum-Prisoner's Dilemma ought not be taken as criticism of the green model of how to coordinate transboundary environmental policy among green communities characterized by much more environmentally friendly preferences.

Even setting that obvious but erroneous objection aside, however, there nonetheless remain very real problems with the Assurance Game account of coordination among genuinely green communities. One of them, internal to the logic of the Assurance Game itself, is just that within an Assurance Game such cooperation as naturally emerges is really rather fragile. And in overcoming that fragility, there is a substantial role for a superior legal authority to play.

The source of the fragility of voluntary cooperation in an Assurance Game is that, in such games, people do not want to be 'played for a sucker'. If for any reason they get the idea that not enough others are going to cooperate, then they themselves will not cooperate. Hence, in an Assurance Game there has to be some mechanism for assuring people that enough others are going to cooperate to induce them to cooperate themselves.

Among small groups, perhaps each can assure the other adequately through verbal signals or previous plays in the game. But those mechanisms are unlikely to work among large groups – and if greens decentralize decision-making powers as thoroughly as they say they will, the group of communities to be thus coordinated will be very large indeed.[124]

The most plausible source of the needed assurances among such a large group would, once again, probably be some superior authority

---

[124] The same is broadly true of the self-enforcement of cooperative agreements in Polluter's-cum-Prisoner's Dilemmas via strategies of tit-for-tat reciprocity. While that is still possible even among a large number of players, the conditions required for that strategy to work are less likely to be satisfied with many players (Taylor 1987, pp. 104–5; see further Taylor and Ward 1982 and Hardin 1982, ch. 3).

with the power to impose sanctions on those who do not cooperate. So long as that superior authority can threaten sufficiently severe sanctions against noncooperative behaviour, everyone will be thereby assured of others' cooperative behaviour. And having Assurance Game preferences, each will want to play cooperatively so long as there is sufficient confidence that everyone else is going to play cooperatively likewise. That certainly is one way – among a large group of players, probably the best way – of providing the assurance, crucial for evoking cooperation in an Assurance Game, that others are not going to play you for a sucker.

Of course it is perfectly true that, if everything works according to that plan, the upshot would be that sanctions will never actually need to be imposed on anyone. Their mere existence will have been enough to induce cooperative play from everyone in a genuinely Assurance Game. That does not mean that the sanctions have been superfluous, however. Quite the contrary, the threat of sanctions will have played a crucial role in inducing cooperative behaviour from each by providing the crucial assurance that all others will do likewise.

That is just to say that, even in an Assurance Game, there may well be a substantial role for some central legal authority, superior to and with sanctioning power over all the players in that game. Nationally, that constitutes a case for the state. Internationally, that constitutes a case for, if not a world government, at least treaties with teeth. On neither level does the Assurance Game model provide any support for green suppositions that the needed coordination between decentralized jurisdictions will emerge naturally, if only the people within them 'think globally', in an Assurance Game sense.

Thus, even if relations between decentralized green communities are properly characterized as an Assurance Game, that does not necessarily mean that we can count on the needed coordination among all the various players emerging automatically without any central coordinating mechanism. Superior authorities with sanctioning power would still be useful, and may even prove essential.

There is a further, fatal problem with the Assurance Game model as an account of the green theory of policy coordination among decentralized communities. The problem, simply stated, is that people who genuinely embrace green theories of value or agency have no business harbouring Assurance Game preferences at all. Certainly the desire to cooperate in protecting the environment so long as others do likewise is consistent with those fundamentally green values. But the willingness to do so *only* as long as others do likewise is not. The desire not to be 'played for a sucker' simply cannot, on the face of it, be squared with green values. Surely if you really care about environmental protection, the fact that no one else is not going to do it is *prima facie* more of a reason – not less of one – for you to do it.

Of course, there might be special facts about the situation such that it makes sense for you to refuse to try singlehandedly to protect the environment, even if you care about the environment deeply. (Perhaps it simply will not do any good for just one person or for just a few people to do it, for example; or perhaps you reckon, strategically, that by refusing to do their job for them this time you will get more people to make more of a contribution on lots of future occasions.) The green theory of intercommunal coordination here in view, though, predicates Assurance Game preferences of green players in general – not merely in those peculiar situations where they make that special kind of sense. And I, for one, cannot see any rationale within green theory that would justify people with genuinely green values in refusing to save the environment when they can, just because others who could and should help refuse to do so.[125]

That observation leads to our fourth and final model of policy coordination among decentralized green communities. Suppose that those communities are all thoroughly green. Suppose that they are so infused with green values that everyone within them 'thinks globally' about what is good for the earth, quite regardless of self-interest of any sort. Suppose that none of them would mind in the least being 'played for a sucker', or at least that brown actions from others would not lead them to deviate from their own truly green course of action. Indeed, suppose that, on the contrary, the less that others are prepared to do to save the planet the more they are themselves prepared to do.

That is, in my view, the most credible account of what the greens have in mind with the first half of their injunction to 'think globally, act locally'.[126] Certainly it would represent the strongest possible sense of

[125] At most, the refusal to be 'played for a sucker' might be excused rather than justified on green principles. As in the standard analysis of 'saints and heroes' (Urmson 1958), perhaps it is just more than standard human psychology can bear to let others continually take advantage of you. But then the fact that greens have Assurance Game attitudes towards environmental protection is a sad fact, permissible and excusable perhaps but certainly not in any way justifiable.

[126] In other respects, it must be said, this model is wildly at odds with green theory – especially the emphasis it places upon 'diversity'. Sale (1985, p. 107) is particularly forthright in acknowledging that, while a 'certain homogeneity would exist' within a bioregion, 'a certain divergence would be bound to exist there also. . . . it would be the purpose of a bioregional polity . . . to find agreement between quarrelsome communities.' He goes on to say that 'of course . . . agreement at the cost of squelching variety or imposing uniformity comes at too high a price,' and he adds that the stable bioregion, like the stable econiche, 'permits – even, in a sense, encourages – a certain amount of disharmony and conflict . . .' Whether or not this

'thinking globally' – shaping your preferences in accordance with global environmental demands, and those alone. Greens hope that this strongest sort of 'thinking globally' would underwrite the conditions under which 'acting purely locally' would be prove feasible. They want to devolve decision-making powers to really very small political units, and they want those powers to remain there rather than being taken back by some centralized coordination mechanisms with strong powers all their own. Greens hope that 'thinking globally' in this strong sense can avoid the need for any such agency. Among such totally self-effacing communities, they trust, coordination will prove easy enough.

It is standardly said that pure altruists would have as much trouble with coordination as egoists. Some go so far as to concoct an Altruist's Dilemma, perfectly parallel to the Prisoner's Dilemma.[127] And certainly it is formally true that if you fully internalize my pay-offs and I yours, then the structure of the game remains the same: you just take my place and I yours in the game-theoretic matrix used to represent the game. Then we see the scenario, familiar from vaudeville, of two overly polite people insisting on holding the door for the other: one says, 'After you', the other, 'No, after you'; neither ever gets through the door in consequence.

That problem arises, though, only when – and only because – each party internalizes the other's pay-offs completely, to the exclusion of their own. That is not the situation here in view. What greens propose is that each should 'think globally'. That amounts to saying that each should internalize, not the pay-offs of any particular other, but of everyone taken altogether. And in a Prisoner's Dilemma, when each internalizes sum-total pay-offs (one's own plus the other's), you do not get an Altruist's Dilemma. On the contrary, you will characteristically get each regarding cooperative – in the case at hand, pro-environmental – action strategies as being strictly dominant, the best for them regardless of what the other does.[128]

There do however remain other, more serious problems with the green proposal to avoid the need for organized coordination among

ecological model offers a viable model for containing political conflict, it is clear that on Sale's model conflict between communities is not expected to disappear in the ways here being contemplated.

[127] Buchanan 1975.

[128] 'Characteristically', because of course in this formulation things depend on the precise numbers in each cell. The 'sum total' phrasing of this point presupposes interpersonal comparability and additivity, which many would suppose cannot be done; but I put it that way just for expository convenience, and those who find the phrase objectionable should just think in terms of a 'collective rank ordering of outcomes' which each individual player then internalizes.

decentralized units merely by 'thinking globally'. In environmental protection applications just as in so many others, exactly what you should do (as well as how much you should do) depends on how many others are going to cooperate and in what ways.[129]

Adjusting at the margins – doing a little, seeing how it goes, then doing a little more or a little less as needs be – is fine if it is a matter of just increasing or decreasing some homogeneous commodity. It works just fine, for example, in the standard economic settings, where the 'marginal adjustments' in view amount to no more than slight increases or decreases in price or output.

But sometimes the change in view is not just a marginal quantitative adjustment to quantity. The change in view is, rather, an alteration to the kind or quality of the inputs you make.[130] Then it is far from clear that the desired sort of coordination can come from a large number of decentralized actors adjusting to each other at the margins. If it comes at all, certainly it will not come smoothly but rather in fits and starts as each retools radically in response to each act (and again in response each subsequent response) from every other.

Here again, there might be a very useful role to be served by a centralized coordinating mechanism. There might be little need for sanctions to enforce agreements, perhaps; everyone who really does 'think globally' in this totally self-effacing way may well be prepared to bear whatever sacrifices are required quite willingly, without threat of sanction. But there would still be a need for a central coordinating mechanism to collate everyone's action plans.

Each community needs to know how much of what sort of action every other community plans to undertake, in order to choose the right kind and quantity of action itself. And while in principle they could find this out by trial and error, lots of resources would be wasted (and irreversible decisions might have been taken) in the process. Surely it would be better for there to be some centralized agency collecting and disseminating information about everyone's plans and provisional intentions.

Furthermore, since those plans will – in ways just described – naturally change in response to the plans of others, there will be a useful role for a collective forum in which representatives of all the

[129] This is formalized by economists as the 'general theory of second best' (Lipsey and Lancaster 1956).

[130] For an example that might prove less fanciful than one would like, our community might be happy to reduce our emissions of greenhouse gases if everyone else is going to do likewise, but be inclined to dump lots of carbon-dioxide eating algae in the world's oceans if not enought others are going to cooperate in controlling emissions at source.

communities can meet and negotiate these responses-to-responses-to-responses. Of course, here again, if everyone is 'thinking globally' in this completely self-effacing way these 'negotiations' may be far friendlier than those characterizing present international forums. In a way, that might mean that there is less need for negotiations. In another, though, it means that there is more point to them.

In ordinary negotiations, even where a negotiated settlement would be better for all concerned, negotiations often break down because nobody knows how much to discount for bluff and bluster. The only way you can find out if others really mean what they say is to call their bluff and force them to act on it. In negotiations among the totally self-effacing agents of green theory, however, there will be no bluff or bluster. Everyone can be trusted to report fully and honestly on what they would actually do in response to whatever the others propose doing. Everyone can be taken at their word. And precisely because there is no need to test anyone's word, the potentially costly business of mutual adjustment can all be played out virtually costlessly, on paper or in conversations.

In short, even among representatives of totally self-effacing green communities, there may well be a substantial role for a central coordinating mechanism. It may need to amount to little more than a 'talking shop', perhaps. But it is essential that it should be a centralized talking shop, where all parties are represented.

Of course, many would suppose that such totally self-effacing actors are pure figments of green fantasy. No real individuals – certainly no actual communities – can ever be realistically expected to internalize quite so thoroughly as that the green injunction to 'think globally' so totally to the exclusion of local interests and concerns. If those suspicions are right, then there will always be elements of the other three models at work in coordination among decentralized green communities.

The point to notice is just this. On any plausible model of policy coordination among decentralized green communities, there will be a role for centralized coordinating mechanisms. The role will be greater, the need for sanctioning powers more urgent, the more the situation resembles the Polluter's-cum-Prisoner's Dilemma. But even if it is only a relatively tame Assurance Game, sanctions in support of green policies worldwide will prove useful. And even if green communities manage to be as self-effacing as greens imagine only in their fondest dreams, organized information-pooling through a central agency will still prove essential.[131]

[131] These conclusions parallel the insights of Herring (1990, p. 65) concerning the

This is just to say that greens simply cannot have it both ways. It cannot be true, at one and the same time, that (a) green issues ought to be of pressing concern because only concerted global action is capable of solving them, but that (b) the best way of responding to those issues is to devolve all decision-making powers down to very small political units who lack any way of acting in concert with one another. If green issues are important for the reasons and in the ways that they say they are, then it is essential that greens provide a coherent account of policy coordination among those decentralized communities. And all such accounts, I would argue, must necessarily involve revesting at least some of those powers in centralized coordinating agencies at the global level.

5   Conclusion

All of this, in a way, just amounts to variations on this one central theme. If the green theory of agency cannot be *derived from* the green theory of value – as I argue it cannot[132] – then how can we be sure that the agency thereby created would actually serve the values the other half of the green theory specifies?

This conundrum is most apparent, perhaps, in connection with green support for grassroots democracy. To advocate democracy is to advocate procedures, to advocate environmentalism is to advocate substantive outcomes: what guarantee can we have that the former procedures will yield the latter sorts of outcomes?[133] More generally, how can we guarantee that localized, or nonviolent, action will always best protect the global environment?

Intuitively, greens feel that both dimensions – both process and substance – must surely matter. But much more remains to be done to show that those two dimensions reinforce rather than cut across one another. For now, pending demonstration of some such necessary linkage, we must conclude that the green theory of agency is a separate issue from the green theory of value that truly lies at the core of the green political agenda.

second-order 'role of supra-local authority in providing or denying space for local solutions, mediating between local institutions on overlapping commons dilemmas, and responding to dilemmas which are beyond the reach of any local response'. I am grateful to Claus Offe for drawing this valuable source to my attention.

[132] Section 1 above.
[133] Saward 1991.

5
Conclusions

1 The Fate of Green Politics

In principle, greens have the potential to reshape politics as we know it. Purely in terms of political style, their highly participatory methods are radically at odds with the internal governance of most other, more established parties. If those prove catching, some very great changes indeed will be in store for the way those other parties conduct their own internal affairs.

In substantive policy terms, greens make some awfully radical demands – and furthermore, they make those demands on an all-or-nothing basis. Were those demands even partially satisfied, politics as we know it would be altogether altered. We would be living in a very different world of so very much smaller communities practising such very different policies that new rules, routines and programmes will have to be developed almost from scratch. Old ways, developed in and adapted to very different political settings, will simply no longer stand us in good stead.

Substantial though all those changes may be in principle (and, in the long term, perhaps even in actuality) in the shorter term green politics will inevitably have to be practised through the more established routines of politics-as-usual. To implement their substantive agenda, greens will have to form parties of an ordinary kind, fight elections in the usual way, and do parliamentary deals of the standard sort – at least for a while.[1] So, while the previous discussion has been largely couched in terms of green ideals and aspirations, in assessing the fate of green politics we are essentially asking embarrassing questions about how well

[1] And perhaps longer: in Macpherson's (1977b, pp. 112ff.) view, any credible model of direct, participatory democracy would inevitably be organized around a system of political parties.

greens can cope with the tricky problems of transition, of getting from here to there.

In parliamentary political terms, the crucial question is simply whether greens can see the way clear to compromising and forming coalitions with other parties. For surely it is clear that green parties are not now, and will not within the foreseeable future be, in a position to form a government – even a viable minority government – all on their own. The record of parties born *de novo* (rather than out of the ashes of some previous party) forming a government at any early date after their foundation is not good. The British Labour Party's record is probably among the best in that regard, and it took them a quarter of a century from foundation to MacDonald's first ministry. There is no reason to suppose the greens are likely to beat that record.

If green parties are going to make any practical difference to public policies in the short term, then, they are simply going to have to compromise and form coalitions. And if the issues that the greens have made their own really are as pressing as they say, it is the short term with which we must genuinely be concerned.

Greens have good reason to resist compromise. Intellectually, there is good reason (sketched in chapter 3 above) for supposing that they have a right – in a way that most parties do not – to insist on their policies being adopted on an all-or-nothing basis. Politically, blurring a party's image through too many messy compromises is always pragmatically dangerous. But as I hope to have shown (in chapter 3, section 6 above) it is intellectually permissible and morally defensible for greens to compromise, in a way that it is intellectually and hence morally impermissible for other parties to demand that they compromise.

The compromise reached would indeed be logically incoherent, if my arguments above are correct. But the blame for the logical incoherence would lie with the parties that insisted on adulterating the green programme, not with the greens who (let us presume) bargained as hard as they could and resisted as best they were able that adulteration.

It is morally defensible for greens themselves to make those compromises, if that is the only way in which they can get crucial parts of their programme implemented in time for them to do any practical good.[2] Indeed, if realizing the green theory of value takes priority over satisfying the demands of the green theory of agency – as I have argued it does, in chapter 4, section 1 above – then it would be morally mandatory for greens to enter into compromises and coalitions, on that

---

[2] That assumes, of course, that it is better to implement some of their programme than none at all: that will not always be true, but presumably it will at least sometimes be true.

assumption. There is simply no place for moral preciousness and keeping one's green credentials clean when the fate of the earth hangs in the balance. And if the arguments I have offered above are correct, that is a judgement in which green political theory itself must concur.

Whether or not green politics really take off is, in this sense, largely in the hands of green party activists themselves. If they are prepared to compromise and form coalitions, green parties might make a real difference to politics and policies. If greens are not prepared to play politics-as-usual, even in the interim, then green parties probably will not make any real impact. They will remain an amusing parliamentary sideshow, but little more.

In larger electoral terms, the issue is twofold. The first question is whether greens can find enough supporters to constitute a credible 'third force', over and above the traditional parties of the left and of the right. The second question – to be addressed shortly – is whether, having crossed that threshold, they can find some adequate basis for an electoral alliance with one of the other major parties that will carry them to power.

On the former issue, the news seems to be moderately good. There quite probably is an adequate popular basis for green parties to form at least a 'third force', if not to form a government all on their own. Clearly, the public at large cares deeply about many of issues which the greens have made their own. If there really is a serious prospect of catastrophic global warming or large holes in the ozone layer, then most people would probably be prepared to bear very considerable sacrifices in their standards of living to prevent those risks from becoming a reality. And if people can be persuaded that the green proposals for averting those catastrophes really are part of an all-or-nothing package, then many would quite probably be prepared to swallow hard and accept it all. Unpalatable though many people may find some of the green proposals, most of them would probably rather suffer it all than doing nothing efficacious to avert such global catastrophes.

Can people be persuaded that the green agenda forms an all-or-nothing programme, though? The essentially philosophical arguments deployed in chapters 3 and 4 above cannot be expected to grip many voters. They will be widely regarded as little more than logical niceties, no more. Inconsistency *per se* probably does not matter all that much to all that many voters.

Still, if the logic really is like that, then logical inconsistency will entail practical impossibility. If two things are logically incompatible, then any practical programme that attempts to put them together is bound to come to grief. What is impossible in logic is (if we are operating with the right logic, one which actually maps the real world) impossible in the real world, as well. The inevitable consequence of inconsistent promises is incompatible polices. So eventually the chickens are bound to come home to roost for any party or group of parties that tries to run a logically inconsistent political programme. That is as true for parties or coalitions of parties that try to pick and choose items off of a logically tightly integrated green agenda as it is for parties that simultaneously promise low inflation and low unemployment.[3]

That is just to say that there may be – and usually will be – a price that political parties will eventually have to pay for running on a logically incoherent political programme. But even if the chickens will eventually come home to roost sooner or later, that may well happen only very much later. Indeed, it might be expected to happen so much later that it is beyond the time horizon of the political parties we are hoping to influence with such arguments. For political parties, of course, are notoriously disinclined to look much beyond the next election – or, at most, the next beyond that.

Ultimately, then, the only remedy for this myopia of political parties is farsightedness among voters. Parties might only be looking to the next election; but if voters in that election are looking well into the next century, then parties hoping to win their votes must do so as well. How best to inculcate this attitude within voters is, of course, an open question. To a certain extent, it may come naturally to them.[4] To a certain extent, it might be further enhanced by political manipulation.[5] To a large extent, however, the only way really to achieve the goal is to do political philosophy in the public forum. People must be shown that it is a matter of high moral obligation to think ahead, not just for themselves but for their posterity.[6]

As it happens, the evidence suggests that people are indeed prepared to take just such a broader perspective when it comes to environmental issues. Narrowly self-interested voters concerned only with the quality of their own immediate environment would vote for whichever party they expect to best protect the local environment. As it happens, though, political scientists find that the strongest correlation is between

[3] Assuming the two really are, in the long run, mutually exclusive – which is of course increasingly being called into question.
[4] Notice, for example, how voters often support public works projects the benefits of which will not accrue until many years after they are themselves in their graves (Marglin 1963, p. 98).
[5] We can, for example, try putting options to voters one way rather than another so as to evoke more farsighted responses from them. But there are strict limits to the effectiveness of any such ploys (Goodin 1980b).
[6] I develop these themes elsewhere (Goodin 1992b).

people's voting intention and which party they expect to best protect the environment of the nation as a whole. On environmental questions like many others, people thus seem to vote on the basis of the common good rather than – and even in contradiction to – their narrow self-interest.[7]

Whether we can believe survey research – whether people really do what they say they would do, for the reasons they say they would do it – is an open question. But if they do, if there is any basis to contemporary political science built around those assumptions, then there would seem to be some real political point to the present exercise. On that evidence, it seems that people can, indeed, rise above narrow self interest and be moved by moral argumentation on questions of environmental policy and many others.

All that is by way of saying that there probably will be enough popular support for green causes – at least among the moderately well-off and well-educated 'new middle classes' – that green parties might reasonably hope to garner enough votes to become a credible 'third force' in electoral politics. But, realistically, it will be a long time before they can expect to form a government all on their own. If they are to influence policy in the short to medium term, they will have to do so in league with other, older parties of the right or (more likely) the left.

Green parliamentary parties will have to recognize that fact and form coalitions within parliament in consequence, as I have already argued. So too will green constituency parties have to recognize and adapt to the necessity of alliance politics. Certainly they will have to accept the necessity of defending electorally such formal or informal alliances that their parliamentary representatives might have had to strike to get green legislation enacted. Perhaps they ought also to accept the necessity (or perhaps just the convenience, given that other necessity) of forging formal 'electoral pacts' with those other parties to fight election campaigns on a common, agreed programme.

But in alliance politics, it takes two to tango. So the question is not just whether green parties can be persuaded to compromise; as importantly, there is the question of whether they can find anyone else to compromise with them. In the macrosociological terms of class fractions in which these matters are standardly cast – especially by Continental political sociologists – that resolves itself into further questions of class cleavages and the possibilities of cross-class alliances. The assumption, which I broadly share, is that only a green–social democratic alliance will be inclined to implement genuinely green policies. And given that assumption, the macrosociological question

[7] Rohrschneider (1988), adapting to voting on environmental issues a methodology first applied to voting on economic issues by Kiewiet (1983).

becomes one of whether the green 'new middle classes' can find a way of couching their case so as to appeal to the unionized working classes.[8]

That is traditionally regarded as, first and foremost, a question of empirical sociology. In the ponderous prose in which these matters are characteristically discussed, are there enough fractures in the class structure of postmodern, postindustrial societies to permit these re-alliances of traditional class fractions? But only those who very much believe that where you stand politically is determined in a strong sense by where you sit in the class structure can be wholly persuaded by that sort of analysis.

For my part, I would prefer to see this as being very largely a question of political argument rather than merely of social-structural determinism. Ideas as well as interests are capable of moving people to political action. So the question, as I see it, is how greens can phrase their case – how they can cast their appeal, how they can craft their programme – so as to appeal to the working-class constituencies which formed the basis of parties of the left.

It must be said, right from the outset, that this will not be easy. There is a certain sort of anti-capitalist rhetoric and a certain range of narrow, limited policy proposals on which green and workers' movements can easily enough agree.[9] But, basically, 'trade unions [are at present] locked into a "popular front for accumulation", dominated by their interests in industrial growth.' And it is perfectly understandable that that should be so. As an infamous slogan of US steel-workers would have it, 'We can't eat clean air.'[10]

Neither, though, should we underestimate the interests of the poor or the working classes in environmental quality. The poor, precisely because they are poor, enjoy a lower quality of life all around – lower environmental quality included. Blue-collar workers, participating most directly in dirty industrial processes, enjoy a lower quality of environment at work than do white-collar workers. Complain though American steel-

[8] Offe 1985, pp. 856–68.

[9] The 1983 manifesto of the German Greens, for example, maintains, 'The exploitative compulsions of growth arise from both the competitive economy and the concentration of economic power in state and private-capitalist monopolies, with consequences that threaten the utter pollution and destruction of the basis of human life. It is here that environmental protection and the ecology movement link up with the workers' movement and trade unions. We support a reduction in working time and humane working conditions' (Die Grünen 1983, sec. 1, p. 8). For practical political purposes, the relative modesty of the list of policy proposals upon which they can agree is far more worrying than is the relative grandeur of the rhetoric that they might share.

[10] Recalled by Offe (1983, p. 51). See further Goodin (1976, pp. 168–71).

workers may that they cannot eat clean air, they have nonetheless good grounds for complaint in the fact that they virtually can eat the unclean air that they have to breathe absent clean-air policies.[11]

So the first thing to say, in attempting to forge this cross-class alliance for environmental quality, is that those policies are in the interests of the poor and the working classes every bit as much as – and indeed more than – they are in the interests of the new middle classes. There is considerable survey evidence suggesting that the poor know that themselves. Of course in a list of 'most important problems' the poor do not rank environmental quality as highly as do the rich; but that is just because they have so many more problems, all around, than do the rich. Of course when asked how much they are willing to pay to secure environmental quality the poor are not willing to spend as much as the rich; but that is just because they do not have as much to spend, *tout court*. If we ask the question the right way – as 'what proportion of your income are you willing to spend on environmental quality?' – the poor prove far more concerned with the issue than are the rich. By one calculation, someone with an income just above the poverty level would be willing spend something like eight times as much (as a proportion of income) as someone with a middle-level income on controlling water pollution, for example.[12] In short, improved environmental quality benefits the poor as much as, if not more, than it does the new middle classes – even if the latter, being those for whom it is the 'next most important question' and hence the next political fight to be fought, will naturally form the vanguard on that issue.[13]

It is not enough just to say that, of course. Green parties must also find some credible scheme for 'immunizing the first victims of the capitalist system, the workers, [from the] consequences [of the greens'] policy of zero growth'.[14] Clearly, simply proposing to freeze everything at present levels for everyone will not be politically ·acceptable to the greens' necessary working-class allies in domestic politics, any more than it is internationally to their natural allies among the still-developing countries of the Third World. Domestically as well as internationally, greens will have to impose tougher restraints on the rich than on the poor; they will

[11] Pearce 1973; Goodin 1976, pp. 168–71.
[12] The calculation is from Goodin (1976, pp. 170–1), based on reanalysis of a survey by Frederickson and Magnas (1968).
[13] Stretton (1976) presents a particularly appealing case along those lines. Although his emphasis is more upon why greens should be socialists than on why socialists should be green, the practical political programme that he thinks the two sides should both be willing to agree upon comes to much the same from whichever end you approach it.
[14] Offe 1983, p. 51.

have to let the poor continue to damage the environment in ways that
they are prepared to prevent the rich from doing.

Beyond that, it will be politically crucial to the sort of alliance politics
that the greens must practise to come up with credible plans for
redistribution of income and wealth – and to show that those schemes
are genuinely central to the green agenda rather than merely tacked on
in a cynical attempt to attract coalition partners. Much work needs to be
done in outlining what a green economy would look like, not just at the
micro level (what sorts of work would be done in what sorts of
workshops) but also at the macro level (who would get how much of
what, as a result). Here, as elsewhere, what might seem to be purely
theoretical work might have considerable practical political pay-offs.

2   The Fate of the Earth

My conclusion that greens will not for the foreseeable future form a
government all on their own may seem discouraging to the point of
being downright damning of the the green political movement as such.
In a way, though, it might be just as well that green parties are unlikely
to get their way completely. Were they ever to be in a position to rule
without coalition and compromise – and especially were they in this
position worldwide – then the fate of the earth might be very perilous
indeed. For then they might actually implement their proposals for
radical decentralization, devolving all decision powers to very small
local units. And, as I have suggested in chapter 4, section 4, the greens
have no good account of how to achieve coordination (of a sort that
even they have to agree would be needed) among all these decentralized
units worldwide.

Happily, that is not the form in which greens are most likely to get
power. Instead, they are far more likely to get it locally rather than
globally. They are far more likely to get power in consort with other
parties rather than finding themselves in a position to govern all on their
own. And they are likely to find that those coalition partners resist,
tooth and nail, radical decentralization of any sort. So, realistically, the
question that we must contemplate is what would be the fate of the earth
assuming something very much like the present international structure
of independent nation-states but with strong green party influences
within and cutting across those states.

In that connection, green parties might have a particularly important
role to play. Precisely because they are so impervious to national

boundaries, green parties might actually facilitate coordination of international environmental policies which would otherwise fall between the stools of national self-interest. Not only are green parties inclined to press larger, transnational concerns on to the domestic agenda. They are also in a peculiarly good position, working in consort with sister parties in other nations, to frame some scheme for coordinated action towards shared ends worldwide. The activities of greens in the European parliament might serve as a model here.[15]

The fate of the earth, as I see it, depends in no small measure on how well this Green International succeeds in coordinating environmental policies worldwide. As I said at the outset of chapter 1, at the heart of the present environmental crisis lies a recognition of hazards – ozone depletion and climate change conspicuously among them – for which no purely local remedies would be reliably adequate. Those problems are shared internationally, not just in the weak sense that everyone suffers similarly but also in the strong sense that solving the problem requires concerted action by all the nations of the world.

Coming to grips with such problems will be no easy matter for an international system fundamentally structured around contrary premises.[16] Traditionally, international law has been premised on principles of national autonomy and noninterference with the domestic affairs of other nations; in order to complain about another's environmental misbehaviour under such a regime, a country would have to show that the other's activity actually produces spillovers that are damaging to someone or something within its own territory. More recently, international law has come to recognize certain duties (like the protection of human rights) that are shared by all nations alike; but, again, this is often seen as principally an injunction to 'do your own duty' (not to abuse your *own* citizens or your *own* environment) rather than as duties which any one nation may decently enforce on any other.

What we need, if the new environmental crisis characterized by problems like ozone depletion and climate change is to be met, is recognition within international law and practice of a new sort of *shared* responsibilities. The responsibilities in question are to produce certain sorts of *outcomes*, rather than merely to perform certain sorts of *actions*. And if it is clear that others are unwilling or unable to do their bit, then those who do acknowledge the responsibilities should be prepared, in a pinch, to do more than their bit.

[15] As represented in the European Greens' (1989) 'Common statement for the 1989 elections to the European parliament', for example.
[16] The following discussion summarizes arguments developed at length in Goodin (1990a).

This new principle of international morality is particularly useful in helping to block some of the most pernicious ripostes in international negotiations. Both are basically variations on the 'none of our business' theme. On the one side, environmental vandals appealing to those obsessed with the sovereignty of the nation-state say loudly and often that it is none of any other state's business what they do to their own environment. Notions of shared responsibilities would effectively block that reply. Not only are there environmental spillovers; there are also moral spillovers as well to block that claim, in so far as each state is obliged to pick up any slack left by the other's delict.

On the other side, there are the half-conscientious that are prepared to do their own duty but are reluctant to do *more* than their 'fair share'. The half-conscientious among us, too, take comfort in the thought that it is 'none of our business' whether or not other nations do their duty, so long as we do our own. Notions of internationally shared responsibilities would deprive the morally half-hearted of this comfortable middle ground. Under such a model, all nations would be jointly and separately responsible for producing certain outcomes (such as protecting the global environment), in the same way that both parents are jointly and separately responsible for the well-being of their children. And just as one parent is morally obliged to pick up the slack should the other default, so too are the other nations of the world morally responsible for picking up the slack should any one fail to do its fair share towards protection of the global environment.

Happily, these new and stronger notions of internationally shared responsibilities are coming increasingly to the fore, in both the theory and the practice of international relations, particularly as they touch on international environmental affairs. Contrast, in this connection, two international treaties on protection of the ozone layer concluded only two years apart, the 1985 Vienna Convention and the 1987 Montreal Protocol.[17] The former is very much in the spirit of traditional international law characterized by notions of strong state sovereignty. It requires states to make few sacrifices (a commitment to research and information-pooling apart); it is set to go into force whenever an arbitrary number of states, be they large polluters or small, happen to ratify it; it applies only to those who have ratified it, and does not license (much less require) those who have done so to take steps against those who have not.

Contrast that with the Montreal Protocol, just two years later. That protocol did not come into force until ratified by enough of the major

[17] Convention for the Protection of the Ozone Layer (Vienna Convention 1985), Protocol on Substances that Deplete the Ozone Layer (Montreal Protocol 1987).

polluters for the protocol to do some good. It required states to reduce their emissions substantially and at considerable cost. And it required them to try (through their import and export policies) to force non-signatory states to do likewise. In all those ways, the Montreal Protocol of 1987 is a harbinger of the new model of internationally shared responsibilities which seems so crucial for addressing the problems that characterize the second environmental crisis that is now on us.[18]

If that model is to be fully instantiated at the international level, though, there will have to be some strong mechanisms by which each state might tailor its activities to the activities of the other. This is in part a matter of bringing coordinated pressure to bear on recalcitrants who do not want to do their duty at all. Once it becomes clear that some recalcitrants really are (at least in the short term) incorrigible, it also becomes partly a matter of coordinating how all those who actually are prepared to shoulder their responsibilities should allocate among themselves the extra responsibilities involved in picking up that slack.

In the final analysis, all those negotiations will have to be inter-governmental ones, since it is nations that are bound by international treaties, and they can have effect only through influencing the actions of national governments. But in environmental as in so many other matters, most of the groundwork that lies behind intergovernmental agreements will perforce be done by both international agencies and nongovernmental organizations. Conspicuous among them will be organizations like the UN Environmental Programme and the World Meterological Organization, on the one hand, and the international scientific community and its constituent organizations on the other.[19]

Also conspicuous among those organizations so crucial for coordinating international responses to shared environmental responsibilities can and should be the green movement, in its international guise. It is paradoxical, perhaps, that a movement committed in principle to radical decentralization should – at least in the short term – make its greatest contribution by promoting such coordination (dare one say supercentral-ization?) at the highest levels of international organization.

Perhaps that is just the sort of paradox we ought really to learn to expect, when we are working in the murky world of second-best solutions. Where the ideal is unobtainable (at least for the moment), the next best can and usually probably will deviate systematically from the

[18] See further Goodin 1990a. Glennon (1990, esp. pp. 28–36) reaches similar conclusions on the parallel problem of international protection of endangered species.
[19] See more generally Young (1989) on international regimes, their underlying principles and governing institutions.

ideal end-state which our theory spends so much time describing.[20] Or perhaps this paradox is more peculiar to flaws in green political theory. Perhaps my fears (aired in chapter 4, section 4 above) are indeed well-grounded: greens have no coherent plan for coordinating the decentralized units that they advocate; the outcomes that they seek cannot be obtained without some such coordination; so the political structures that greens regard as ideal are not really to be desired at all. In that case, it might be best rather than merely second-best for a Green International to assist in the coordination of strong environmental protection policies worldwide.

Either way, though, that is the best greens can hope for in the short term. The good news for greens is that it may well be good enough – both good enough to halt the worst erosion in global environmental quality, and also good enough to give greens an important role to play in that process. Greens can indeed save the world environment, just not necessarily in the ways that they ordinarily envisage.

---

[20] Lipsey and Lancaster 1956.

Appendix:
The Green Political
Programme

---

1 Green Plans and Priorities

As was made plain in the preface, the aim of this book is not to survey particular green movements in particular countries. This is a book of political theory, not of political anthropology. Still, the theoretical propositions which I advance do nonetheless rely on some image of what green parties are and what they want.

The account that follows is a highly stylized model of the political programme of a composite green party. Stylized and selective though it may be, I trust that my account of the green agenda is nonetheless broadly accurate as a description of green parties in general – even if the level of generality means that it is necessarily slightly inaccurate as a description of any particular case.

The picture to be painted is a composite, in the sense that it will combine the political agenda of various different green parties worldwide rather than being a description of the proposals of any particular national green party or parties. Inevitably, I shall be drawing more heavily on some cases than others. I shall focus on the German, European, British and US cases, in particular. Skewed though this sample may be, I trust that the overall picture painted on the basis of it is broadly representative of the green movement worldwide.

Naturally, emphases vary (sometimes wildly) among green party programmes from locale to locale. Standing back a bit, though, we can see that there is enough commonality among them for a composite account genuinely to make sense. Where Scandinavians and Bavarians worry about acid rain destroying forests, Australians worry about wood-chipping of native rain forests; still, most greens worldwide worry about forests in general and about the destruction of the great tropical rain forests of the world in particular. Where British, French, German and US greens worry about the dangers of nuclear power plants, Norwegian greens worry about hydroelectric dams constricting all the nations' free-flowing rivers; still, most greens worldwide worry about the environmental impact of high-consumption, electricity-dependent lifestyles. Where greens in urban centres (Berlin, Hamburg) and on the Eastern seaboard of North America worry largely about the impact of contemporary lifestyles on social relations, greens in more sparsely populated areas (Scandinavia, Australia, the American West) worry more about their impact on nature; still, most greens worldwide would agree that getting social relations right would be both the cause and the consequence of our achieving the right relations between humanity and nature.

The picture to be painted is not only a composite but is, furthermore, a highly stylized one. It abstracts from the details of particular policy proposals made by particular green parties, indicating instead merely the sorts of issues that worry greens and the flavour of the characteristically green response to them. To a certain extent, such stylization is inevitable whenever trying to present a composite account that straddles various different places and various different periods. Here it also serves a further function. It conveniently buffers my analysis from the effects of larger sociopolitical changes which will inevitably impact on green parties, along with all others.

Some new items are always coming on to the national political agenda, others are always passing off it. A detailed list of a party's present policy proposals will therefore quickly become dated. Much of what greens used to say about the stationing of nuclear-armed NATO troops in central Europe, for example, may soon happily have ceased to be relevant.[1] If we are looking at the general style of a party's response rather than at its particular details, however, we might glean important clues as to how it would react to other, related issues in the future.

It is important, also, to say something about the green political package as a whole. It is not enough to ask what a party would do about each issue, one by one. We also have to look at the connections between a party's responses to related issues. We have to ask what lies at the core of their programme and what lies at its periphery. Where is the intellectual centre of gravity in their programme?

In conventional political discourse – in debates between Labour and Tories in Britain, Social Democrats and Christian Democrats across Europe, Democrats and Republicans in the US, Labor and Liberals in

---

[1] Die Grünen 1983, sec. III, pp. 26–7.

Australia – debates are usually organized around distributional issues. The defining question of politics is then seen to be 'who gets what, when and how?' Parties are defined by their response to that question. Of course, they say much about other questions as well; sometimes those other responses are derived from their stance on the distributional question, sometimes not. But whatever they say about those other issues is somehow peripheral to their main, defining position – their position on questions of distribution.

That is not the only possible way to organize political discourse, though. Consider the contrast with, for example, religious parties – the Christian People's Party in Norway, say. Such parties also take stands on a wide variety of issues. Among them are issues of distribution. But from the perspective of parties such as these, it is the distributional planks in their platform which are peripheral and some other (religious or cultural) planks which are central. That does not make them single-issue parties, any more than the centrality of distributional concerns in the programmes of Tories or Labour makes them single-issue parties. It is just that the intellectual centre of gravity in their programme is located elsewhere than in the debate between 'mainstream' parties.

The position of green parties is rather like that. They take stands on a whole panoply of political issues, as we shall see. They can credibly claim, by virtue of that, to be full-service political parties rather than single-issue movements. But while they take a stand on distributional issues, that is not what lies at the core of their programme. Rather, it is ecological values that form the focus of the green programme. Their stands on other issues are either derived from or peripheral to their stands on the questions of ecology, which they see as central.

The strategy of the greens is, in this regard, undeniably radical. Essentially, they are trying to shift the focus of discourse in the political community as a whole. Instead of centring on questions of where parties stand on the issue of how to cut the economic pie, green parties want to make the litmus test where parties stand on saving the planet.

It is a high-risk gambit, but one which – if successful – might prove politically devastating to traditional parties. For there is an impressive body of empirical research suggesting that elections are not won or lost by persuading voters that your party's solutions to any given problem are right and those of other parties wrong. Instead, parties 'own' particular issues, and elections are won or lost by persuading voters that 'the' issue on which this election ought be decided is one of those which your party happens to own. If, for example, a British election is fought on the issue of economic management, the Tories will almost inevitably win; if the election is fought on the issue of unemployment, Labour will almost inevitably win.[2]

There are, then, two ways of viewing the fact that the focus of the green programme is orthogonal to the distributional cleavage dominating ordinary political debates. One is to say that green parties (as we would presumably want to say of religious parties, in most countries of the world) are simply out of touch with the electorate at large and are deliberately marginalizing themselves. The other is to say that green parties are playing a very smart political game, indeed, in trying to move the debate on to issues of environmental integrity which they have made their own. Therein, political scientists tell us, may actually lie their best chance of major and long-term political success.

Finally, a note on sources. For the composite picture of a stylized 'green party programme' which I am about to concoct, I shall focus on three documents which I take to be foundational for green politics. They are:

- the 1983 *Bundesprogramm* of Die Grünen in Germany – the manifesto underpinning the greens' first real electoral breakthrough, which remains canonical for the green movement worldwide (even though German politics have since moved on);[3]
- the *Common Statement of the European Greens for the 1989 Elections to the European Parliament* – substantively derivative, in many ways, but representing a consensus position which makes it arguably the most authoritative single statement of 'the' green position across Europe;[4]
- the *Ten Key Values* adopted by the umbrella organization for US greens, the Green Committees of Correspondence.[5]

These seem to me to be the seminal statements of the green position.[6] Convergence among them, where it exists, can safely be taken to represent an almost-defining feature of a genuinely green political programme.

[2] Budge and Farlie 1983; Budge, Robertson and Hearl 1987.
[3] Die Grünen 1983.
[4] European Greens 1989.
[5] Green CoC 1986.
[6] These will be supplemented by reference to Bahro 1986; Daly and Cobb 1989, pt 3; Dobson 1990, 1991; Frankel 1987; Gorz 1987; Irvine and Ponton 1988; Kemp and Wall 1990; Naess 1989, esp. ch. 6; New Hampshire and Vermont Greens (n.d.); Porritt 1984, 1987; Porritt and Winner 1988; Sale 1980, 1985; Spretnak and Capra 1986; and Tokar 1987.

2 Ecology

Principles of 'ecological wisdom' are preeminent among the 'key values' contained in green political programmes worldwide.[7] Green politics, thus understood, is first and foremost a matter of finding answers to questions like, 'How can we operate human societies with the understanding that we are part of nature, not on top of it? How can we live within the ecological and resource limits of the planet . . .? . . . How can we further biocentric wisdom in all spheres of life?'[8]

The diagnosis of the central problem that we find contained in the German Greens' 1983 election manifesto would be common currency among greens worldwide. There they say,

> The global ecological crisis is becoming daily more acute: raw materials are getting scarce, one poison scandal follows another, animal species are being exterminated, plant species becoming extinct. Rivers and oceans are turned into sewers, human beings are threatened with mental and spiritual atrophy in the midst of a late-industrial and consumer society, and we are burdening future generations with a deadly inheritance. The destruction of the very basis of life and work, and the demolition of democratic rights, have reached such a threatening scale as to make necessary a fundamental alternative in economics, politics and society.[9]

Even if only as a matter of purely self-interested prudence, humanity must learn nature's lessons, for 'human life . . . is enmeshed in the circuits of the ecosystem: we intervene in it by our actions and this reacts back on us. We must not destroy the stability of the ecosystem. . . . [U]nlimited growth is [simply] impossible in a limited system.'[10]

The general terms of the prescribed cure follow fairly straightforwardly from that diagnosis of the problem. 'Proceeding from the laws of nature . . . an ecological policy means understanding ourselves and our environment as part of nature. . . . Our policy is a policy of active partnership [between] nature and human beings. . . . The supreme commandment must be the smallest possible change in natural processes.'[11]

Somewhat more concretely, 'an ecological policy implies all-round

---

[7] Green Committees of Correspondence 1986, item 1; Die Grünen 1983, sec. I, p. 7; European Greens 1989, preamble and sec. 3; Tokar 1987, ch. 3.
[8] Green Committees of Correspondence 1986, item 1.
[9] Die Grünen 1983, sec. I, p. 6. See similarly European Greens 1989, preface and sec. 3.
[10] Die Grünen 1983, sec. I, p. 7.
[11] Ibid. and sec. IV.1, p. 30.

rejection of an economy based on exploitation and the uncontrolled pillage of natural wealth and raw materials, as well as refraining from destructive intervention in the circuits of the natural ecosystem.' Greens say that 'we stand for an economic system oriented to the necessities of human life today and for future generations, to the preservation of nature and a careful management of natural resources.'[12]

More concretely still, there are certain things that greens say that they simply 'will not accept'. Included among those intolerable outcomes are: 'the irresponsible treatment of soil, water and air like a disposable consumer good'; 'the ever increasing number of animal and plant species that are exterminated . . . due to the destruction of their habitats'; and 'the occurrence of climatic deterioration, soil erosion and . . . deforestation. . .'[13]

The policy measures that greens propose along these lines are fairly unsurprising. They include:

- The immediate application of the principle that the causer of pollution must pay its costs.
- The maintenance and extension of forests, especially for the biological cleaning of air, the safety of water supply and for recreation.
- Production processes which do not produce toxic refuse.
- In principle, all 'waste' should be discharged in such a way that it is reusable as raw material.
- The quantity of refuse should be reduced by replacing one-way packaging and short-lived consumer goods by standardized packaging and durable products.[14]

In the area of air and water quality greens recommend that 'production processes and products should . . . produce only a minimum of ecologically bearable effluents.' They envisage that being done through 'closed circuit water systems in industry' and through reducing airborne emissions from industry, power stations, public and private heating equipment and refuse incinerators and, most especially, motor vehicles. Greens insist that reduced limits on air and waterborne emissions should be strictly enforced, and charges should be levied on those that are still permitted. They say that certain emissions should be

[12] Ibid., sec. I, p. 7.

[13] Ibid., sec. IV.1, p. 30. See similarly European Greens 1989, secs 6 and 7.

[14] Die Grünen 1983, sec. IV.1, p. 30; see similarly European Greens 1989, secs 1, 3 and 7. In all this, greens are alluding to principles familiar in environmental economics for over two decades – principles of pollution taxes (Kneese and Schultze 1975; Pearce, Markandya and Barbier 1989) and a 'materials balance' approach to environmental management (Kneese, Ayres and D'Arge 1970; see further Freeman, Haveman and Kneese 1973, esp. chs 2 and 5). All this echoes more popular critiques of 'the waste makers' and the throw-away society (Packard 1960).

banned altogether on account of the environmental damage that they do; among these are phosphates in washing powder, phosphates in fertilizers, carcinogens of all sorts, and fluorohydrocarbons as propellants in aerosols.[15] As the threat of ozone depletion has come to loom ever larger, the latter sort of proposal has come to occupy an increasingly central role in green policy discussions – just as the increasing threat of climate change has moved proposals for a certain sort of pollution tax (the carbon tax) to the forefront of green policy thinking.

Greens urge protection of the countryside and town planning based on open spaces, public transport and reduction of private automobile traffic.[16] They inveigh against agricultural policies based on artificial fertilizers and pesticides, and they commend instead organic farming ('healthy foodstuffs can only be produced on healthy soil') and mixed farming.[17] They commend a forestry policy based on 'mixed foliage, mainly with native types of wood' and 'individual selective felling' instead of complete deforestation of particular areas.[18] While greens are often prepared to tolerate the raising of farm animals for human consumption, they say that animals nonetheless have rights and they urge protection of animals from cruelty both on the farm and in research laboratories.[19]

What especially worries greens, though, is the survival of nonhuman species threatened with extinction. The burning question is not so much 'how can we ensure the rights of individual animals?' but, rather, 'how can we guarantee rights of nonhuman species' as a whole?[20] Towards that end, greens commend a fishery policy based on the 'immediate reduction of catch quotas of endangered species to allow stocks to recover' and 'an immediate ban on catching and hunting of any species of whale' in particular.[21] Greens oppose the 'industrialization of agriculture', precisely because it is 'one of the main reasons for the disappearing of more and more plant species'.[22] And they urge

[15] Die Grünen 1983, sec. IV.3, p. 32, and sec. IV.4, p. 33. See similarly European Greens 1989, secs 3 and 7.
[16] Die Grünen 1983, sec. IV.2, pp. 31, and sec. II.8, pp. 20–3; European Greens 1989, sec. 5.
[17] Die Grünen 1983, sec. II.7.1, pp. 17–18; European Greens 1989, sec. 7.
[18] Die Grünen 1983, sec. II.7.2, p. 19.
[19] Ibid., sec. IV.7, p. 35; European Greens 1989, sec. 7.
[20] The latter, anyway, is the form in which the question is posed in the carefully worded statement of the Green Committees of Correspondence in the US (1986, item 1).
[21] Die Grünen 1983, sec. II.7.3, p. 20.
[22] European Greens 1989, sec. 7; note that they are even more implacably opposed to biotechnology (sec. 6) on similar grounds.

measures to protect plant and animal species under threat of extinction, more generally.[23]

There are many legitimate reasons we might worry about the preservation of species. Some are purely pragmatic. Having a great deal of variety in nature (especially in the gene pool) is instrumental in various ways for various human purposes. Others are essentially aesthetic. We enjoy looking at more complex and variable scenes. Still others point to the intrinsic (non-anthropocentric) value of the species which are being destroyed.[24]

It is admittedly anomalous that greens should be so little concerned about the demise of any particular animal and so disproportionately more concerned about the demise of the species as a whole. What is it about a species as such that makes the whole so much more valuable than the sum of its parts?[25] The green response is, I think, best seen as being rooted in their respect for nature as such – combined with the fact that destroying a whole 'type' (a whole species) constitutes so much more of a violation of the natural order than does destroying a mere 'token' (a particular animal of that species).

3 Technology

It follows from much of what greens say about environmental despoliation that they regard modern technology as very much a mixed blessing. They regard chemical fertilizers and pesticides as 'agricultural poisons';[26] and they are particularly wary of biotechnology and of 'genetically manipulated organisms', whose 'ecological risks are unknown'.[27] They bemoan the way in which 'monotony, mental stress and

[23] Die Grünen 1983, sec. IV.6, p. 34.

[24] Norton 1986; 1987.

[25] Indeed, Feinberg (1974 in Feinberg 1980, pp. 171–3) rightly remarks that if our concern is with the 'rights' of animals, it is only individual animals and not species as such which could possibly be said to possess rights. Any case we want to make for species preservation in those terms would have to be parasitic either upon the rights of particular animals constituting the species not to be destroyed or upon interests that others (humans, particularly) might have in the preservation of the species as such.

[26] Die Grünen 1983, sec. II.2, p. 11. Elsewhere they say that their 'intensive use permanently destroys the natural fertility of the soil. Leached-out phosphates endanger the water balance, nitrates in drinking water increase deaths from cancer. Non-degradable pesticides attach themselves to the food chain right through to human milk, where the maximum safety level is already considerably exceeded' (sec. II.7.1, pp. 17–18). See similarly European Greens 1989, sec. 7.

[27] European Greens 1989, sec. 6.

lack of communication have all become worse due to the introduction of new technologies' into the workplace.[28] They complain about the way in which the pharmaceutical industry 'constantly throw[s] new medicines onto the market, with negative side-effects which frequently outweigh their healing powers'.[29] Greens save their very special anger, though, for one particular modern technology: nuclear-powered electricity generating plants. 'Nuclear power is', quite simply, 'not safe': 'the operation of nuclear plants leads to creeping contamination by radioactivity, the potential for catastrophe presents an irresponsible risk, and nuclear waste still cannot be got rid of.'[30]

It would be a mistake to infer from all that rhetoric that greens are unqualified Luddites, though. Sensitive though they are to all the various ways in which modern technology has made life worse, they are also alive to the possibility that it might also make life better. In particular, they welcome the fact that, 'with the use of modern technologies, productivity has in many cases reached a level which would . . . make it possible to reduce the working week while maintaining full pay.'[31]

The issue, then, is not how to do away with modern technologies altogether but is rather one of how to choose in a discriminating way between them. 'How can we judge whether new technologies are socially useful – and use those judgments to shape our society? . . . How can we develop new economic activities and institutions that will allow us to use our new technologies in ways that are humane, freeing, ecological, and accountable and responsive to communities?'[32]

As that latter reference suggests, notions of community control – here, control of technology policy – are once again, here as in chapter 4 above, found to lie at the core of green policy proposals. But, again, greens have clear views as to the directions in which those communities ought be trying to exercise their control. They have clear ideas about which sorts of technology are desirable and (more especially) which are not.

Greens are opposed, most of all, to the use of nuclear technology for

[28] Die Grünen 1983, sec. II.4, p. 13.
[29] Ibid., sec. V.9.3, pp. 53–4.
[30] Ibid., sec. II.6, pp. 15–16.
[31] Ibid., sec. II.4, p. 12.
[32] Green CoC 1986, items 10 and 6 respectively. The German Greens similarly suggest that 'before new technologies are introduced, an evaluation stage should be allowed for in which these technologies are examined for environmental compatibility, economic use of energy and humane design at work. An overall social cost–benefit analysis must be carried out, in which all subsequent costs are taken into account' (Die Grünen 1983, sec. II.3, p. 12).

generating electricity.[33] They demand the 'immediate halt' to the building of new nuclear power plants and to the operation of all existing ones, and they insist on the 'dismantling of [all] existing nuclear installations'.[34] Greens say that they 'unequivocally oppose the use of . . . nuclear technology as an outdated, expensive, inhuman and extremely dangerous technology that creates environmental problems persisting for thousands of years'.[35] Greens say that, 'in the long term, the entire energy supply must come from . . . environmentally benign and renewable energy sources such as sun, wind and water,' and they urge that 'available technical and scientific resources must be used for the development of soft energy' sources of that sort.[36]

Of course, that target is not so high as it might seem. The energy levels that greens think ought eventually to be required will be considerably less than those presently being supplied. Green policy calls for 'a serious programme of efficient energy production' to be conjoined with 'an overall reduction of energy consumption'.[37] Greens encourage us to renounce our quest for 'economic growth' without end and to moderate our demand for constantly increasing energy supplies in consequence.[38] And they emphasize that a substantial portion of our present energy requirements could in principle be met through energy conservation (better insulation, reusing waste heat, and so on).[39]

Greens recognize that reducing energy requirements to levels that can be met by renewable sources alone is a pretty long-term goal, though. 'In the short and medium term', the most that they insist on is 'careful management of existing energy resources, improved efficiency in the combustion of fossil fuels, conversion to different forms of energy, and decentralized energy generation adapted to [the end] use' to which that energy will be put.[40]

Note the important concession contained in that statement. Greens are prepared to tolerate, at least for a little longer, the continued burning of fossil fuels. Of course, they demand 'increased efficiency in . . . [their] combustion'. But that still stops well short of the 'clean burning of fossil fuels'.[41] For even with more complete combustion, and even with

---

[33] For my own arguments along those lines, see Goodin (1982b, pp. 187–219).
[34] 'Under the most rigorous safety precautions', of course (Die Grünen 1983, sec. II.6, p. 16).
[35] European Greens 1989, sec. 4.
[36] Die Grünen 1983, sec. II.6, p. 16. See similarly European Greens 1989, sec. 4.
[37] European Greens 1989, sec. 3.
[38] Die Grünen 1983, sec. II.6, p. 14.
[39] Ibid., p. 17; Lovins 1977.
[40] Die Grünen 1983, sec. II.6, p. 16.
[41] European Greens 1989, sec. 4.

scrubbers in the smokestacks, a certain amount of 'damaging substances such as sulphur and nitrous oxides' will inevitably still be emitted into the environment. So while greens are inclined to demand an immediate halt to nuclear power and its risk of radioactive contamination of the planet, they are prepared to tolerate (at least for a while longer) a certain amount of air pollution, acid rain and climate change. That greens are prepared to be so much more adamant on the one subject than the other is, perhaps, the best measure of the depth of their hostility to high-risk, high-technology solutions like nuclear power.[42]

Green technology policy calls for the use of 'appropriate technology' to use in guiding our communities' more generally.[43] 'Appropriate' here runs the risk of serving as an all-purpose term of approbation, devoid of any particular meaning.[44] But it is best understood as referring, in this context, to the fit between the technology and the end-uses to which it will be put, the purposes for which it will be employed, the goals we are trying to achieve through its use. The best example, perhaps, comes once again in connection with discussions of energy policy. In the masterly study of 'soft energy paths' to which the 1983 German Green manifesto refers, Amory Lovins stresses that such schemes are more appropriate forms of technology because they are better matched (both in terms of scale and geographical distribution and in terms of energy quality) to 'end-use needs'.[45]

The latter is a particularly telling point. Electricity, in particular, is an especially 'high-quality' form of energy. There are certain purposes for which electricity, and electricity alone, will suffice. Among them are 'lighting, electronics, telecommunications, electrometallurgy, electrochemistry, arc welding, [and running] electric motors'. But those applications account for only about 8 per cent of all US energy use. Mostly, energy requirements – in the US and elsewhere in the First World – are for home heating and cooking and driving mechanical

[42] The green objection is to high risks, as much as to high technology. Their objection is all the more apt – and all the more aptly couched in terms of democratic community control, understood in a broadly consensual fashion – where 'collective risks' are concerned. If the neighbouring reactor melts down, everyone nearby goes with it; and in those circumstances it is only right to give the most risk-averse member of the community an effective veto over the life-threatening gambles (Goodin 1980a; 1982b, pp. 158–61; cf. Wildavsky 1988, ch. 1).

[43] Schumacher 1973, pt 2, ch. 5, and pt 3, ch. 2; Tribe 1973; Winner 1978; Sale 1980, pp. 156–65.

[44] The 1987 *British Green Party Manifesto*, for example, says, 'We favour appropriate technology: technology that is good and satisfying to work with, produces useful and results, and is kind to the environment. Many such technologies will be "high-tech"' (quote in Dobson 1990, p. 101).

[45] Lovins 1977, p. 39.

motors, and for those purposes forms of energy of much lower quality would suffice. As Lovins puts it,

> Plainly we are using premium fuels and electricity for many tasks for which their high energy quality is superfluous, wasteful and expensive. . . . Where we want only to create temperature differences of tens of degrees, we should meet the need with sources whose potential is tens or hundreds of degrees, not with a flame temperature of thousands or a nuclear reaction temperature equivalent to trillions. . .

That, in Lovins's telling phrase, is rather like 'cutting butter with a chainsaw'.[46]

That is just one particularly telling example, though. Notions of appropriate technology have application in organizing social production more generally. Taking a leaf from Gandhi, E. F. Schumacher insists that 'the poor of the world cannot be helped by mass production' but 'only by production by the masses'. Elaborating on that theme, he writes,

> The system of *mass production*, based on sophisticated, highly capital-intensive, high energy-input dependent, and human labour-saving technology, presupposes that you are already rich, for a great deal of capital investment is needed to establish one single workplace. . . . [It] is inherently violent, ecologically damaging, self-defeating in terms of non-renewable resources, and stultifying for the human person. The technology of *production by the masses* . . . is conducive to decentralization, compatible with the laws of ecology, gentle in its use of scarce resources, and designed to serve the human person instead of making him the servant of machines.

Schumacher suggests that this technology might, equally well, be called 'intermediate technology', on the grounds that it is 'vastly superior to the primitive technology of bygone ages but . . . much simpler, cheaper and freer than the super-technology of the rich'. It could also be called a 'self-help . . . democratic . . . people's technology', on the grounds that it 'is not reserved to those already rich and powerful'.[47]

That is the sort of technology that greens would favour. Instead of tyrannizing over humanity and over nature, such technology harmonizes with them. It puts people more in control of their own lives. It permits people to live and work in more human-sized communities. It is more in tune with both human purposes and the natural order.

[46] Ibid., pp. 39–40.
[47] Schumacher 1973, pp. 153–4.

4 The Economy

The green environmental programme depends on a reorientation of the present economic system every bit as much as on a renunciation of high technology.[48] As the German Greens put it in the preamble to their 1983 election manifesto, 'We do not accept that the present economy of waste promotes happiness or a fulfilling life. On the contrary.' It leads to 'a real impoverishment, in spite of increased incomes. . . . Only if we free ourselves from over-valuing the material standard of living . . . will our creative forces also be freed for reshaping life on an ecological basis.'[49]

'A radical reorganization of our short-sighted economic rationality is', greens say, 'essential.'[50] They call for 'shifting economic priorities [away] from consumption [and] to conservation'. And part and parcel of that is shifting 'away from . . . self-defeating economic growth . . . and towards sustainable regional economies'.[51]

The central question for greens is 'how can we make the quality of life, rather than open-ended economic growth, the focus of future thinking?'[52] Green economic policy 'thoroughly repudiates a way of thinking oriented to output and hierarchy and governed by lethal competition'.[53] It would involve an 'all-round rejection of an economy based on exploitation and the uncontrolled pillage of natural wealth and raw materials'. In its place, greens would advocate 'an economic system oriented to the necessities of human life today and for future generations, to the preservation of nature and a careful management of natural resources'.[54]

Accordingly, greens place heavy emphasis in their political programmes on their vision of a green economy. In so doing, they are in many respects merely picking up on some by now fairly well-established critiques of economic theory. Economists themselves are the first to

[48] See in general: Frankel 1987, pp. 22–63; Gorz 1987, pp. 40–2; Pearce, Markandya and Barbier 1989; Pearce 1991; Kemball-Cook, Baker and Mattingly 1991; and Kemp and Wall 1990, chs 4–5.
[49] Die Grünen 1983, sec. I, pp. 6–7. See similarly European Greens 1989, sec. 1. Such statements, of course, merely echo earlier critiques of capitalists as 'waste makers' (Packard 1960) and socialist ideals of 'artisanship' (Lee 1989, ch. 8).
[50] Die Grünen 1983, sec. I, p. 6.
[51] European Greens 1989, sec. 1.
[52] Green CoC 1986, item 10.
[53] Die Grünen 1983, sec. I, p. 7.
[54] Ibid. See similarly: Ekins, 1986, pp. 49–55; Porritt 1988, p. 196; Dobson 1990, p. 92; Meadows 1991.

acknowledge the uncounted 'costs of economic growth', in the sense of 'external costs' that have not been properly captured in ordinary growth statistics.[55] Making producers bear the full costs of their activities, through for example pollution taxes of the sort that greens recommend, would be required if we are to maximize growth in *real* economic well-being, properly calculated. And at least some economists are sensitive to the need, keenly felt among greens, for 'sustainable' development – for a steady-state economy reliably yielding a tolerable standard of living rather than a boom–bust economy whose highs (and even average yield) might be higher but whose lows are much lower as well.[56]

Beyond picking up on those familiar points within established and semi-established economic theory, greens also take on board some more radical critiques of neoclassical economics. Greens would have the economy produce what people really need rather than what, through advertising, they have been artificially made to desire; and, indeed, they would radically restrict the sort of advertising that would be allowed at all.[57] Greens are sensitive to the ways in which 'instruments' shape rather than just serve our desires;[58] they would take advantage of that fact, reshaping our desires in more modest directions. They would restrict counterproductive competition in 'status goods', which lose their value to you once everyone else has them as well.[59] There are, furthermore, more radical possibilities – so far largely unexplored among greens – within Georgescu-Roegen's reformulation of economic theory around the Second Law of Thermodynamics.[60] That, properly understood, might provide the strongest theoretical warrant yet for the greens' natural inclination towards keeping our interventions into the natural order as modest as possible.

[55] Mishan 1967.

[56] Boulding 1966; Daly 1974a, 1974b; Page 1977; Sale 1980, pp. 329–42; World Commission on Environment and Development 1987; Redclift 1987; Pearce, Markandya and Barbier 1989, chs 1 and 2; Pearce 1991; Australia, Department of Prime Minister and Cabinet 1990; Kemball-Cook, Bauer and Mattingly 1991.

[57] For a reformulation of welfare economics in this light, see Gintis (1972). German Greens regard 'as essential': the 'replacement of private advertising geared to manipulating and increasing consumption by objective consumer information relayed through the media by independent institutions (e.g. a consumer-goods testing foundation)'; the immediate 'prohibition of TV and radio advertising'; and 'the prohibition of . . . all advertising for . . . cigarettes, sweets, spirits, pharmaceutical products for farm animals . . . agricultural poisons . . . and artificial fertilizers' (Die Grünen 1983, sec. II.2, p. 11).

[58] Tribe 1973.

[59] Hirsch 1976; Goodin 1990c.

[60] Georgescu-Roegen 1971; 1972, Lee (1989, ch. 2) bases the green social philosophy more generally on the conjunction of the First and Second Laws of Thermodynamics.

All of that operates on the plane of high theory, though. In more concrete terms, green economic proposals essentially revolve around notions of localism. The goal is production for use, rather than production for profit.[61] The aim is to produce for own consumption rather than for gains from trade. The green economy 'would be based, above all, on the most elemental and most elegant principle of the natural world, that of self-sufficiency. Just as Nature does not depend on trade, so the bioregion would find all its needed resources – for energy, food, shelter, clothing, craft, manufacture, luxury – within its own environment.'[62]

Of course, much turns on what one supposes is 'needed'. The more narrowly needs are defined, the more possible it is to satisfy them all purely locally.[63] But greens advocating economic decentralization are anxious to insist that, while small communities 'cannot possibly supply all the gadgets and geegaws and gimcrackery that is to be found in our stores today', neither would life in such communities be at a bare subsistence standard either.[64] 'Using current standards', it is observed, a community of one 'thousand people could operate one plant in each of the thirteen basic manufacturing categories.'[65]

So, arguably, 'a small town can without much difficulty provide for virtually *all* material needs on a household or community level – and make the goods more affordable, more durable, more aesthetic, more repairable, and more harmless, too.' It can do this, greens would say, in various ways:

- by sharing, . . .
- by recycling and repairing, . . .
- by depending on handicrafts rather than manufactures, . . .
- by developing and using local products and raw materials instead of depending on imported ones, . . .
- by local ingenuity, . . .
- by using general instead of specialized machines, . . .
- by . . . use of multipurpose factories, . . .
- by adapting plants to the community level, . . .

[61] As the German Greens' 1983 manifesto puts it, in the present economy 'production is not governed by the needs of people but by the interests of big capital' (Die Grünen 1983, sec. II.1, p. 10).

[62] Sale (1984, p. 169), elaborated in Sale (1985, ch. 6); cf. criticisms in Frankel (1987, pp. 55–63, 87–91).

[63] Lee (1989, ch. 10) tries to pare down needs in this way.

[64] 'An ecologically based economy does not mean any reduction in the quality of life,' the German Greens insist; it merely 'means that people use products which correspond to their needs and are compatible with the natural environment' (Die Grünen 1983, sec. II.2, p. 10).

[65] Sale 1980, pp. 404, 398.

- by networking, where necessary, with other communities, . . .and
- finally, and simplest, by doing without what is not needed.[66]

That emphasis on local, community-based production entails restricting 'the size and concentrated power of [distant] corporations'.[67] Greens 'oppose an economy in which the economically powerful decide on work processes, products and the conditions of life of the great majority of the population'.[68] They insist that 'the key premise is that those people affected by any decision should make that decision themselves.' They must decide for themselves '*what* is produced, *how*, and *where*'.[69]

This means, in part, ensuring that production decisions be made in ways that are 'accountable and responsive' to the wishes of local communities, rather than being dictated from afar by corporate heads insensitive to local needs.[70] 'The population involved must have the political authority' through economic and social councils 'needed to control business activities and subject them to ecological and social obligations.'[71]

Equally importantly – though perhaps not altogether consistently – greens also insist that production decisions be made by workers themselves. 'Large combines', they say, 'are to be broken down into surveyable units which can be run democratically by those working in them.'[72] They oppose economic organizations based on 'hierarchy' and 'lethal competition'.[73] They prefer instead to 'redesign our work structures to encourage employee ownership and workplace democracy'.[74]

Shifting ownership and control to workers themselves has the further advantage, much valued from a green perspective, of reducing the distributional imbalances found in present society. The German Greens complain that 'income and wealth differentials between rich and poor are being sharpened still further' by the inexorable effects of the capitalist mode of production and its inevitable consumerism.[75] Production

[66] Ibid., pp. 405–11.

[67] Green CoC 1986, item 6.

[68] Die Grünen 1983, sec. II.3, p. 11; see similarly sec. 1, p. 7.

[69] Ibid., sec. II.2, p. 10.

[70] Green CoC 1986, item 6.

[71] Die Grünen 1983, sec. II.3, p. 11. European Greens (1989, sec. 1) similarly called for a shift away from the 'Single Market' of the European Economic Community as a whole and 'towards sustainable regional economies' – regions which we can safely infer, from context, will be substantially smaller than Europe as a whole.

[72] Die Grünen 1983, sec. II.3, p. 11.

[73] Ibid., sec. 1, p. 7.

[74] Green CoC 1986, item 6. See similarly strong praise for workplace democracy in Roszak (1978, ch. 8), Sale (1980, pp. 352–91) and Tokar (1987, ch. 5).

[75] Die Grünen 1983, sec. I, p. 7.

for use rather than for profit, organized around small-scale local producers' and consumers' cooperatives, would in their view go far towards alleviating the distributional inequities found in present society.

Greens are, at root, egalitarian. They are greatly exercised by the gross imbalances in the distribution of income and wealth, both within societies and across the world. They 'are committed to a radical sharing of wealth – between continents and between generations, not only between classes'.[76] This egalitarianism manifests itself, internationally, as a concern that peoples of the Third World should 'receive a fair price for their work and products'.[77] It manifests itself, in domestic economic policy, primarily as a concern to miminize unemployment through a variety of measures (ranging from job retraining to early retirement and shorter work weeks).[78]

Anxious though they are that people not be involuntarily excluded from the labour market, the greens are equally anxious to emphasize that participation in the paid labour force is not the be-all and end-all of human existence. It is important to them that 'people must be able to freely develop their various abilities', both 'at work and at leisure'.[79] And it is particularly important to them that the productive contributions which people make outside of the formal, paid workforce be socially recognized and rewarded. Towards that end, greens want to 'restructure our patterns of income distribution to reflect the wealth created by those outside the formal, monetary economy: those who take responsibility for parenting, housekeeping, home gardens, community volunteer work' and so on.[80]

That way of putting the proposition might seem to suggest that what the greens want to ensure is merely that everyone should have an opportunity to perform productive labour of one sort or the other, and that everyone should be properly rewarded when they do so. But that would be to suggest, falsely, that greens propose that distributive shares in general (and social benefits in particular) ought be subject to something like a 'work test'. On the contrary, greens hope to 'establish some form of basic economic security, open to all', whether or not they

---

[76] European Greens 1989, sec. 1. See further Lee (1989, ch. 9) and Meadows (1991). Douglas and Wildavsky (1982) purport, more than a little tendentiously, to trace environmentalists' egalitarianism and opposition to social risk-taking to a common cultural cause.

[77] Die Grünen 1983, sec. II.9, p. 24. See similarly Kemp and Wall 1990, ch. 7; Pearce 1991.

[78] Die Grünen 1983, sec. II.4, p. 12–13; European Greens 1989, sec. 9. See similarly Kemp and Wall 1990, ch. 6.

[79] Die Grünen 1983, sec. II.2, p. 10.

[80] Green CoC 1986, item 6.

work.[81] Towards that end, many greens favour a scheme paying everyone in society an unconditional 'basic income', regardless of any tests of their assets, their work history, their household status or whatever.[82] Not all greens would necessarily go quite that far. But absolutely unconditional social benefits of that sort would capture most completely the egalitarianism underlying the green ethos.

5   Social relations

Greens are egalitarian not only on distributional questions but on social issues more generally. They strive for a society in which 'the oppression of one person by another is abolished.'[83] They oppose discrimination in all its forms – against women, the old, immigrants, Romanies and 'sexual outsiders'.[84] The 'solidarity' the greens propose is, at one and the same time, 'with the earth, with the poor and with . . . future generations'.[85] They do so primarily on the grounds, often regarded as too obvious to be stated, that any such social divisions are 'unnatural'. Social discrimination is an artificial artefact of deformed human culture, and it is opposed by greens for precisely that reason.

The policies which greens propose to remedy discrimination against the presently disadvantaged may not seem particularly radical. They are familiar enough from the academic literature, it is true. Still, they are rare indeed on the statute books. In that sense, they would mark a genuinely radical change from present policies.[86]

Putting the point in terms of non-discrimination might seem to

[81] Ibid.

[82] The 1987 *British Green Party Manifesto*, for example, advocates 'an automatic weekly payment to everybody throughout life, regardless of sex or marital status, non-means tested and tax free, at different rates for different age-groups'; and it adds that this payment would be 'higher than current welfare benefits' (quoted in Dobson 1990, pp. 112–3; on the basic income more generally, see van der Veen and Van Parijs 1987 and Van Parijs 1990; 1991a, 1991b). There are, of course, embarrassing questions both as to where the money is going to come from to fund this scheme and, in a decentralized society of the sort greens advocate, where the administrative apparatus will come from to implement it (Dobson 1990, pp. 114–6; Frankel 1987, pp. 73–86).

[83] Die Grünen 1983, sec. I, p. 8.

[84] Ibid., sec. V.2, pp. 39–43, sec. V.4, p. 43, and sec. V.5, pp. 44–6, respectively. See similarly European Greens 1989, sec. 8 (women) and sec. 10 (immigrants and racial minorities).

[85] European Greens 1989, sec. 12.

[86] This is particularly true of their policies on women, children and the family, for example. A wide range of proposed reforms is surveyed in Frankel (1987, pp. 146–96).

suggest that greens are simply advocating tolerance of deviant minorities. That would give a completely false impression of their programme. In truth, they positively embrace pluralism. They count 'respect for diversity' as one of their 'key values', and they cherish diversity in its social every bit as much as in its biological form.[87] They bemoan the effects of the 'dominant monoculture' and want to encourage instead the flourishing of a multiplicity of cultures, both within a single region and especially across regions.[88]

Greens suppose that discrimination and social oppression are largely responsible for the 'instabilities' of existing society. Merely eliminating it would, they say, do much to alleviate problems of 'crime, higher suicide rates, drug consumption and alcoholism'.[89] But greens would not stop at eliminating those evils. They would also strive, more positively, for a 'nonviolent' society. They want to find ways to 'resolve interpersonal and intergroup conflicts without just turning them over to lawyers and judges'. They seek to 'use nonviolent methods to oppose practices and policies with which we disagree and in the process reduce the atmosphere of polarization and selfishness that is itself a source of violence'.[90]

6 Foreign Relations

Many of the most central environmentalist planks in the green platform have an important international dimension, of course. Protection of the global environment – natural resources, the oceans and the upper atmosphere, especially – require international rather than merely national efforts. And it was concern with those genuinely international aspects of the environmental crisis which, as I said at the outset, has given rise to the new and distinctively green wave of environmentalist concern.[91] As regards more traditionally 'foreign affairs' aspects of the green agenda, however, broadly the same principles guide green policy internationally as domestically. These are principles of egalitarianism, of respect for diversity and of nonviolence.

[87] Green CoC 1986, item 8.
[88] Ibid., item 5; Die Grünen 1983, sec. V.7, pp. 48–9; Sale 1980, 1984, 1985. In the flat prose of the European Greens (1989, preamble), they seek 'as many reciprocal cultural contacts as possible'.
[89] Die Grünen 1983, sec. 1, p. 8.
[90] Green CoC 1986, items 3 and 4.
[91] See chapter 1, section 1 above.

As a manifestation of their egalitarianism internationally, First World greens advocate 'international solidarity', in the form of a 'partnership with Third World countries'.[92] They aim at 'the increased emancipation for the peoples of the Third World' from their 'double dependency on the industrialized countries and also on the upper classes in their own countries'; they demand an end to the 'domination of the world market by giant corporations', which 'leads to an increasing impoverishment of the Third World countries'; they demand that countries of the Third World be given increased control over raw materials and means of production.[93] They insist on an end to trade preferences which merely 'solidify . . . neo-colonial trade patterns' and are keenly aware of 'the oppression of the majority of Third World peoples by the debt crisis and the "structural adjustment" measures of the IMF and the World Bank'.[94] They insist on increased development aid, with no expectation of repayment and oriented towards small-scale projects designed to increase the welfare of the local population rather than towards export industries. All these proposals are aimed, ultimately, at the goal of combining 'self-sufficiency' and 'a sensible global division of labour . . . in such a way as to meet the interests of the poor and poorest countries'.[95]

As a manifestation of their respect for diversity cross-nationally, greens insist that 'each nation and each population group must . . . be in a position to preserve its own particular culture. We condemn the presumption of the industrialized countries in seeking to force on all other countries . . . their uniform technical and materialistic civilization.' This respect for diversity even extends to the ecological issues nearest green hearts. Greens say that 'it would be quite contrary to [our] principles . . . if we were to try and solve all problems uniformly and centralistically . . . Each nation . . . must develop an ecologically appropriate economy' for itself.[96] Diversity in almost all respects is to be the rule, across nations as well as within them.

Finally, greens insist that 'ecological foreign policy is a policy of nonviolence.'[97] The root intuition behind green thinking on defence and

[92] The quotations are from the European Greens (1989, sec. 2) and Die Grünen (1983, sec. III.3, pp. 27) respectively. See also Green CoC 1986, item 9.
[93] Die Grünen 1983, sec. III.3, pp. 27–9.
[94] European Greens 1989, sec. 2.
[95] Die Grünen 1983, sec. III.3, pp. 27–9; see similarly European Greens 1989, sec. 2. There is of course another version of 'self-sufficiency' promoted by the World Bank, for example, that has less happy consequences; see George (1976) and Frankel (1987, pp. 134–45).
[96] Die Grünen 1983, sec. III.1, p. 25.
[97] Ibid., sec. III.2, p. 26.

foreign policy is that the real threats to human existence come, first of all, from threats to the physical basis of life on earth and, second, from the weapons of mass destruction designed to protect us from one another. A foreign policy designed to protect us against the first sort of threat is a policy of international cooperation in environmental protection: 'security' is redefined to include, above all, threats to and from the natural environment.[98]

That, however, is largely a rhetorical ploy, an attempt at appropriating one of the militarists' most cherished terms and redeploying it for green purposes. In the short term, at least, the principal concern of green foreign and defence policy must be with threats of the second sort, from weapons of mass destruction. They are committed to the ultimate abolition of such weapons.[99] In the meanwhile, they suggest ingenious strategies for ensuring that those weapons are never used.[100]

All that said, greens are often really rather ambivalent about lesser instruments of political violence. European Greens, for example, are opposed to 'military alliances' and a 'bloc-divided Europe'.[101] But that does not mean that they are opposed to military hardware, necessarily.[102] Nor does it necessarily mean that they are against groupings of nations that are the functional equivalents of alliances.[103] Greens are themselves quick to add that, while they are committed to nonviolence, that 'does

---

[98] Mathews 1989; Myers 1989.

[99] 'Ultimately', but not necessarily unilaterally: The Green Committees of Correspondence in the US (1986, item 4) want to ensure that they are not 'being naive about the intentions of other governments' in suggesting the 'eliminat[ion of] nuclear weapons from the face of the earth'.

[100] Lovins and Lovins (1987, pp. 18–19), for example, made the suggestion – still highly relevant at the time it was made – of 'a formal revival of the mediaeval concept of mutual hostages', in the form of 'members of the Congress and of the Politburo . . . send[ing] their children to live and study in the other country's main cities' and 'large numbers of US and Soviet troops be[ing] given tickets to ride around all the time on each others' railway systems'.

[101] European Greens 1989, preamble; see also sec. 11. But there is no absolute consensus, even among indisputably green thinkers, on that point; see e.g. the exchange between Rudolf Bahro and André Gorz in *Telos*, no. 51 (Spring 1982), pp. 117–28. Proto-green 'postindustrial utopian' writers more generally, such as Alvin Toffler and Barry Jones, particularly tend to shy away from it (as discussed in Frankel 1987, pp. 104–24).

[102] North American greens display similar ambivalence in asking, 'how can we cut our defense budget while maintaining an adequate defense?' (Green CoC 1986, item 9).

[103] While campaigning 'for one Europe . . . without military alliances', the European Greens (1989, preamble) nonetheless endorse the idea that "the neutral and non-aligned states, together with the countries of the EFTA . . . develop a new dynamic in the balance of power within today's divided Europe'.

not mean passivity'. Specifically, it 'does not exclude active social resistance'.[104]

Such resistance usually 'can be carried out most effectively in a social manner' through, 'for example, sit-ins, blocking of roads, obstruction of vehicles'.[105] Things might well get a little bit bloody, as the invoking of notions of 'civil courage' at this point rather seems to suggest.[106] But basically 'social defence means organising and reorienting our society in such a way' – 'in the direction of . . . alternative and decentralized structures', most especially – 'as to make immediately clear to an aggressive foreign power that attempted occupation and domination would entail more difficulties and a greater burden than the increase in power and profit it might bring'.[107]

Greens are anxious to emphasize that their advocacy of a policy of nonviolence 'does not affect the fundamental right of self-defence'. They insist 'that resistance against government measures is not only legitimate in certain circumstances [but] . . . may even be essential for people to defend their vital interests against an authority which escapes their control'. Greens boast that 'we therefore put forward an active peace policy in international relations. This means that we oppose the occupation of countries and the oppression of national groups, and support the independence and autonomy of national groups in all countries. Peace is inseparably linked with the independence of countries and the existence of democratic rights.'[108]

It is not altogether clear exactly what levels and what kinds of armaments might be required to conduct active social resistance of the sort greens recommend.[109] But what is clear is the fact that there are certain sorts of weapons that they are simply not prepared to tolerate. When saying that 'worldwide disarmament is a must,' greens mean specifically that 'nuclear, biological and chemical weapons must be destroyed on a world scale.'[110] They insist on 'eliminat[ing] nuclear weapons from the face of the Earth'.[111]

[104] Die Grünen 1983, sec. I, p. 9.
[105] Ibid.
[106] Ibid., sec. III.2, p. 26.
[107] Ibid. See similarly Roberts (1967), Alternative Defence Commission (1983), Galtung (1984) and Kemp and Wall (1990, ch. 9); in Sweden, an official Commission on Resistance (Bergfeldt 1985) has endorsed such schemes, at least in broad outline. Frankel (1987, pp. 124–33) provides a useful overview and critique of the various different scenarios in view here.
[108] Die Grünen 1983, sec. I, p. 9.
[109] Contrast, for example, the proposals of the Alternative Defence Commission (1983) with those of Galtung (1984).
[110] Die Grünen 1983, sec. I, p. 9.
[111] Green CoC 1986, item 4. See similarly European Greens 1989, secs 4 and 11.

The official green rationale for this absolute intolerance of nuclear and chemical weapons is straightforward, and wholly in keeping with the emphasis on respect for nature and life as such found at the core of their theory of value.[112] 'With the introduction of nuclear weapons, war has reached completely new dimensions. The possibility of destroying the whole Earth several times over has turned war into . . . a crime against life in general.'[113]

7 Conclusion

All this is no more than the briefest indication of how greens see the main issues of our day. Still, even this brief sketch should be enough to show (or if not to show, anyway to suggest) several things.

• One is that the greens are no single-issue movement. They take stands on a wide range of contemporary social and political problems.

• A second is that there is an interestingly different intellectual centre of gravity in the green political programme, as compared to that of the programmes of other more mainstream parties.

• A third is that the green agenda is organized around, and justified by, the distinctively 'green theory of value' (explicated in chapter 2 above); and that the green theory of value both underpins and bolsters the green cause, politically (as has been demonstrated in chapter 3 above).

[112] I have myself offered arguments for unilateral nuclear disarmament on the part of either of the superpowers which, while really rather different, could easily enough be linked to this proposition. From that perspective, the crucial thing to be said in favour of such a policy is that it produces modal changes in the possibility of destroying life on earth. See Goodin 1985a, 1985b.

[113] Die Grünen 1983, sec. II.2, p. 28.

References

Achterberg, Wouter 1991: Can liberal democracy survive the environmental crisis? Paper presented to the Workshop on Green Political Theory, ECPR Joint Sessions, Colchester UK, March 1991.

Ackerman, Bruce A. and Hassler, William T. 1981: *Clean Coal, Dirty Air*. New Haven, Conn.: Yale University Press.

Alternative Defence Commission 1983: *Defence without the Bomb*. London: Taylor and Francis.

American Political Science Association (APSA) 1950: Toward a more responsible two-party system: a report of the committee on political parties. *American Political Science Review* 44 (supplement).

Arrow, Kenneth J. and Fisher, Anthony C. 1974: Environmental preservation, uncertainty and irreversibility. *Quarterly Journal of Economics* 88: 312–9.

Attfield, Robin 1983: *The Ethics of Environmental Concern*. New York: Columbia University Press.

Australia. Department of Prime Minister and Cabinet 1990: *Ecologically Sustainable Development*. A Commonwealth discussion paper, June 1990. Canberra: Australian Government Publishing Service.

Axelrod, Robert 1984: *The Evolution of Cooperation*. New York: Basic Books.

Bachrach, Peter 1967: *The Theory of Democratic Elitism*. Boston: Little, Brown.

Bahro, Rudolf 1986: *Building the Green Movement*, trans. Mary Tyler. London: Heretic Books.

Barber, Benjamin 1984: *Strong Democracy: Participatory Politics for a New Age*. Berkeley: University of California Press.

Barry, Brian 1965: *Political Argument*. London: Routledge and Kegan Paul.

—— 1977: Justice between generations. In P. M. S. Hacker and J. Raz (eds), *Law, Morality and Society*, Oxford: Clarendon Press, 268–84. Reprinted in Barry 1989.

—— 1978: Circumstances of justice and future generations. In R. I. Sikora, and Barry, Brian (eds), *Obligations to Future Generations*, Philadelphia, Pa.: Temple University Press, 204–48.

—— 1983: Intergenerational justice in energy policy. In Douglas MacLean and Peter G. Brown (eds), *Energy and the Future*, Totowa, NJ: Rowman and Littlefield, 15–30. Reprinted in Barry 1989.

—— 1989: *Democracy, Power and Justice: Essays in Political Theory*. Oxford: Clarendon Press.

Baumol, William J. 1986: On the possibility of continuing expansion of finite resources. *Kyklos* 39: 167–79.

Becker, Lawrence C. 1977: *Property Rights: Philosophic Foundations*. London: Routledge and Kegan Paul.

Beitz, Charles, Cohen, Marshall, Scanlon, Thomas and Simmons, A. John (eds) 1985: *International Ethics*. Princeton, NJ: Princeton University Press.

Benn, Stanley I. 1988: *A Theory of Freedom*. Cambridge: Cambridge University Press.

Bennett, Jonathan 1966: Whatever the consequences. *Analysis* 26: 83–102.

—— 1983: Positive and negative relevance. *American Philosophical Quarterly* 20: 185–94.

Benton, Ted 1989: Marxism and natural limits: an ecological critique and reconstruction. *New Left Review* 178: 51–86.

Berg, Elias 1978: Democracy and self–determination. In Pierre Birnbaum, Jack Lively and Geraint Parry (eds), *Democracy, Consensus and Social Contract*, London: Sage, 149–72.

Bergfeldt, Lennart 1985: Complementary forms of defence: Report of the Swedish Commission on Resistance. *Bulletin of Peace Proposals* 16: 21–32.

Berry, Jeffrey M. 1984: *The Interest Group Society*. Boston: Little, Brown.

Blackstone, William 1765: *Commentaries on the Laws of England*. Oxford: Clarendon Press.

Bookchin, Murray 1971: *Post-scarcity Anarchism*. Berkeley, Calif.: Ramparts Press.

—— 1982: *The Ecology of Freedom: The Emergence and Dissolution of Hierarchy*. Palo Alto, Calif.: Cheshire Books.

—— 1990: *Remaking Society: Pathways to a Green Future*. Boston: South End Press.

Boulding, Kenneth 1966: The economics of the coming spaceship earth. In Henry Jarrett, (ed), *Environmental Quality in a Growing Economy*,

Baltimore, Md: Johns Hopkins University Press (for Resources for the Future), 3–14.

—— 1973: The shadow of the stationary state. *Daedalus* 102. 4: 89–101.

Boyle, Stewart and John Ardill 1989: *The Greenhouse Effect: A Practical Guide to the World's Changing Climate*. London: New English Library, Hodder and Stoughton.

Bramwell, Anna 1989: *Ecology in the 20th Century: A History*. New Haven, Conn.: Yale University Press.

Brandt, Richard B. 1979: *Theory of the Good and the Right*. Oxford: Clarendon Press.

Brittan, Samuel 1988: *A Restatement of Economic Liberalism*, 2nd edn. London: Macmillan.

Brundtland Commission. *See* World Commission on Environment and Development.

Buchanan, James M. 1975: The Samaritan's dilemma. In Edmund S. Phelps (ed), *Altruism and Economic Theory*, New York: Russell Sage Foundation, 71–85.

Budge, Ian and Farlie, Dennis J. 1983: *Explaining and Predicting Elections*. London: Allen and Unwin.

Budge, Ian; Robertson, David and Hearl, Derek (eds) 1987: *Ideology, Strategy and Party Change*. Cambridge: Cambridge University Press.

Caldwell, Lynton Keith 1971: *Environment, A Challenge to Modern Society*. New York: Anchor Books, Doubleday.

—— 1990: *Between Two Worlds: Science, the Environmental Movement and Policy Choice*. Cambridge: Cambridge University Press.

Caplan, Ruth and staff of Environmental Action 1990: *Our Earth, Ourselves*. New York: Bantam.

Capra, Fritjof 1975: *The Tao of Physics*. London: Wildwood House.

—— 1982: *The Turning Point*. New York: Simon and Schuster.

Carson, Rachel 1962: *Silent Spring*. Boston: Houghton Mifflin.

Chase, Alston 1987: How to save our national parks. *Atlantic Monthly* 260. 1: 35–44.

Chenery, Hollis, Ahluwalia, Montek S., Bell, C. L. G., Duloy, John H. and Jolly, Richard 1974: *Redistribution with Growth*. London: Oxford University Press.

Club of Rome. See Meadows et al. 1972.

Coase, R.H. 1960: The problem of social cost. *Journal of Law and Economics* 3: 1–44.

Cohen, Jean L. and Arato, Andrew 1984: The German Green party. *Dissent* 31: 327–32.

Cohen, Marshall, Nagel, Thomas and Scanlon, Thomas (eds) 1980: *Marx, Justice and History*. Princeton, NJ: Princeton University Press.

Cohen, Nick 1991: Bouncing Icke reveals cosmic mission to save the world from Lucifer. *Independent* (London), 28 March, p. 5.

Cole, H. S. D., Freeman, Christopher, Jahoda, Marie and Pavitt, K. L. R. (eds) 1973: *Thinking About the Future*. London: Sussex University Press.

Commoner, Barry 1971: *The Closing Circle: Nature, Man, Technology*. New York: Knopf.

—— 1990: *Making Peace with the Planet*. London: Gollancz.

Cook, Philip J. and Graham, Daniel A. 1977: The demand for insurance and protection: the case of irreplaceable commodities. *Quarterly Journal of Economics* 91: 143–56.

Cotgrove, Stephen 1976: Environmentalism and utopia. *Sociological Review* 24: 23–42.

—— 1982: *Catastrophe or Cornucopia*. Chichester: John Wiley.

Cotgrove, Stephen and Duff, Andrew 1980: Environmentalism, middle-class radicalism and politics. *Sociological Review* 28: 333–51.

Cyert, Richard M. and March, James G. 1963: *A Behavioral Theory of the Firm*. Englewood Cliffs, NJ: Prentice–Hall.

Dahl, Robert A. 1956: *A Preface to Democratic Theory*. Chicago: University of Chicago Press.

—— 1970: *After the Revolution?* New Haven, Conn.: Yale University Press.

—— 1985: *A Preface to Economic Democracy*. Berkeley: University of California Press.

Dahl, Robert A. and Tufte, Edward R. 1973: *Size and Democracy*. Stanford, Calif.: Stanford University Press.

Daly, Herman E. 1972: The stationary-state economy. *The Ecologist* 2. 7: 4–13.

—— 1974a: Steady-state economics vs. growthmania: a critique of the orthodox conceptions of growth, wants, scarcity and efficiency. *Policy Sciences* 5: 149–67.

—— 1974b: The economics of the steady state. *American Economic Review (Papers and Proceedings)* 64: 15–21.

Daly, Herman E. and Cobb, John B. Jr 1989: *For the Common Good: Redirecting the Economy towards Community, the Environment and a Sustainable Future*. Boston: Beacon Press.

D'Arge, Ralph C., Schultze, William D. and Brookshire, David S. 1982: Carbon dioxide and intergenerational choice. *American Economic Review (Papers and Proceedings)* 72: 251–6.

Dasgupta, P. S. and Heal, G. M. 1979: *Economic Theory and Exhaustible Resources*. Cambridge: Cambridge University Press.

Davidson, Donald 1980: *Essays on Actions and Events*. Oxford: Clarendon Press.

Davis, Donald Edward 1989: *Ecophilosophy: A Field Guide to the Literature*. San Pedro, Calif.: R. and E. Miles

Demsetz, Harold 1967: Towards a theory of property rights. *American Economic Review (Papers and Proceedings)* 57: 347–73.

Devall, Bill and Sessions, George 1985: *Deep Ecology*. Salt Lake City, Utah: Peregrine Smith Books.

Die Grünen (German Greens) 1983: *Programme of the German Green Party*, trans. Hans Fernbach. London: Heretic Books.

Dobson, Andrew 1990: *Green Political Thought*. London: Unwin Hyman.

—— (ed.) 1991: *The Green Reader*. London: André Deutsch.

Dodd, Lawrence C. and Oppenhiemer, Bruce I. (eds) 1981: *Congress Reconsidered*, 2nd edn. Washington, DC: Congressional Quarterly Press.

Dodds, Felix (ed.) 1988: *Into the 21st Century: An Agenda for Political Realignment*. Basingstoke, Hants: Green Print.

Douglas, Mary and Wildavsky, Aaron 1982: *Risk and Culture*. Berkeley: University of California Press.

Downing, Thomas E. and Kates, Robert W. 1982: The international response to the threat of chlorofluorocarbons to atmospheric ozone. *American Economic Review (Papers and Proceedings)* 72: 267–72.

Dryzek, John S. 1987: *Rational Ecology*. Oxford: Blackwell.

—— 1990a: *Discursive Democracy*. Cambridge: Cambridge University Press.

—— 1990b: Green Reason: Communicative Ethics for the Biosphere. *Environmental Ethics* 12: 195–210.

Dunlap, Thomas R. 1981: *DDT: Scientists, Citizens and Public Policy*. Princeton, NJ: Princeton University Press.

Dutton, Denis (ed.) 1983: *The Forger's Art*. Berkeley: University of California Press.

Dworkin, Gerald 1988: *The Theory and Practice of Autonomy*. Cambridge: Cambridge University Press.

Eckersley, Robyn 1991: Habermas and green political theory. *Theory and Society* 19: 739–76.

Ecology Party (UK) 1980: *Working for a Future*. London: Ecology Party.

Ekins, Paul (ed.) 1986: *The Living Economy*. London: Routledge and Kegan Paul.

Elgin, Duane 1982: *Voluntary Simplicity: An Ecological Lifestyle that Promotes Personal and Social Renewal*. New York: Bantam.

Elkins, Stephan 1989–90: The politics of mystical ecology. *Telos*, no. 82: 52–70.

Elliot, Robert 1982: Faking nature. *Inquiry* 25: 81–93.

—— 1989: Environmental degradation, vandalism and the aesthetic objection. *Australasian Journal of Philosophy* 67: 191–204.

Elster, Jon 1983: *Explaining Technical Change*. Cambridge: Cambridge University Press.

—— 1985: *Making Sense of Marx*. Cambridge: Cambridge University Press.

—— 1986: The market and the forum. In Jon Elster and Aanund Hylland (eds), *Foundations of Social Choice Theory*, Cambridge: Cambridge University Press, 103–32.

Engelberg, J. and Boyarsky, L.L. 1979: The noncybernetic nature of ecosystems. *American Naturalist* 114: 317–24.

Epstein, Joshua M. and Gupta, Raj 1990: *Controlling the Greenhouse Effect: Five Global Regimes Compared*. Brookings Occasional Paper. Washington, DC: Brookings Institution.

Epstein, Richard 1985: *Takings: Private Property and the Power of Eminent Domain*. Cambridge, Mass.: Harvard University Press.

European Greens 1989: *Common Statement of the European Greens for the 1989 Elections to the European Parliament*. Brussels: European Greens.

Evelyn, John 1661: *Fumifugium: or The Inconveniencie of the Aer and Smoak of London Dissipated*. London: Gabriel Bedel and Thomas Collins.

Falk, Richard A. 1971: *This Endangered Planet: Prospects and Proposals for Human Survival*. New York: Random House.

Feinberg, Joel 1974: The rights of animals and unborn generations. In William T. Blackstone (ed.), *Philosophy and Environmental Crisis*, Athens: University of Georgia Press, 43–68. Reprinted in Feinberg 1980.

—— 1980: *Rights, Justice and the Bounds of Liberty*. Princeton, NJ: Princeton University Press.

Fisher, Anthony C. 1981: *Resource and Environmental Economics*. Cambridge: Cambridge University Press.

Foreman, Dave and Haywood, Bill (eds) 1987: *Ecodefense: A Field Guide to Monkeywrenching*, 2nd edn. Tucson, Az.: New Ludd Books.

Forrester, Jay 1971: *World Dynamics*. Cambridge, Mass.: Wright-Allen Press.

Fox, Warwick 1989: The deep ecology-ecofeminism debate and its parallels. *Environmental Ethics* 11: 5–26.

Frankel, Boris 1987: *The Post-industrial Utopians*. Cambridge: Polity Press.

Frankel, Charles 1976: The rights of nature. In L. H. Tribe, C. S. Schelling and J. Voss (eds), *When Values Conflict*, Cambridge, Mass.: Ballinger, 93–113.

Frederickson, H. George and Magnas, Howard 1968: Comparing attitudes towards water pollution in Syracuse. *Water Resources Research* 4: 877–89.

Freeman, Christopher 1973: Malthus with a computer. In H. S. D. Cole, C. Freeman, M. Jahoda and K. L. R. Pavitt (eds), *Thinking about the Future*, London: Chatto and Windus for Sussex University Press, 5–13.

Freeman, A. Myrick III, Haveman, Robert H. and Kneese, Allen V. 1973: *The Economics of Environmental Policy*. New York: Wiley.

French, Peter A. 1984: *Collective and Corporate Responsibility*. New York: Columbia University Press.

Friedman, Milton and Friedman, Rose 1980: *Free to Choose*. Harmondsworth, Mddx: Penguin.

Frohock, Fred M. and Sylvan, David J. 1983: Liberty, economics and evidence. *Political Studies* 31: 541–55.

Galtung, Johan 1969: Violence, peace and peace research. *Journal of Peace Research* 6: 167–91.

—— 1984: Transarmament: from offensive to defensive defence. *Journal of Peace Research* 21: 127–39.

George, Susan 1976: *How the Other Half Dies*. Harmondsworth, Mddx: Penguin.

Georgescu-Roegen, Nicholas 1954: Choice, expectations and measurability. *Quarterly Journal of Economics* 69: 503–34.

—— 1971: *The Entropy Law and the Economic Process*. Cambridge, Mass.: Harvard University Press.

—— 1972: Economics and entropy. *The Ecologist* 2. 7: 13–18.

Gintis, Herbert 1972: A radical analysis of welfare economics and individual development. *Quarterly Journal of Economics* 68: 572–99.

Glennon, Michael J. 1990: Has international law failed the elephant? *American Journal of International Law* 84: 1–43.

Glover, Jonathan 1977: *Causing Death and Saving Lives*. Harmondsworth, Mddx: Penguin.

Golding, M. P. and Golding, N. H. 1979: Why preserve landmarks? a preliminary inquiry. In K. E. Goodpaster and K. M. Sayre (eds), *Ethics and Problems of the 21st Century*, Notre Dame, Ind.: University of Notre Dame Press, 175–90.

Goldman, Alvin I. 1970: *A Theory of Human Action*. Princeton, NJ: Princeton University Press.

Goldman, Marshall I. 1972: *The Spoils of Progress: Environmental Pollution in the Soviet Union*. Cambridge: Cambridge University Press.

Goldsmith, Edward et al. 1972: A blueprint for survival. *The Ecologist* 2. 1: 1–44.

Goodin, Robert E. 1976: *The Politics of Rational Man*. London: Wiley.

—— 1979: The development–rights tradeoff: some unwarranted economic and political assumptions. *Universal Human Rights* (now *Human Rights Quarterly*) 1: 31–42.

—— 1980a: The ethics of social risks. *Science and Public Policy* 131–45.

—— 1980b: *Manipulatory Politics*. New Haven, Conn.: Yale University Press.

—— 1982a: Discounting discounting. *Journal of Public Policy* 2: 53–72.

—— 1982b: *Political Theory and Public Policy*. Chicago: University of Chicago Press.

—— 1983: The ethics of destroying irreplaceable assets. *International Journal of Environmental Studies* 21: 55–66.

—— 1985a: Disarming nuclear apologists. *Inquiry* 28: 153–76.

—— 1985b: Nuclear disarmament as a moral certainty. *Ethics* 95: 641–58.

—— 1985c: *Protecting the Vulnerable*. Chicago: University of Chicago Press.

—— 1987: Civil disobedience and nuclear protest. *Political Studies* 35: 461–6.

—— 1988: *Reasons for Welfare*. Princeton, NJ: Princeton University Press.

—— 1989: Theories of compensation. *Oxford Journal of Legal Studies* 9: 56–75.

—— 1990a: International ethics and the environmental crisis. *Ethics and International Affairs* 4: 91–105.

—— 1990b: Property rights and preservationist duties. *Inquiry* 33: 401–32.

—— 1990c: Relative needs. In Alan Ware and Robert E. Goodin (eds), *Needs and Welfare*, London: Sage, 12–33.

—— 1990d: Stabilizing expectations: the role of earnings-related benefits in social welfare policy. *Ethics* 100: 530–53.

—— 1992a: The high ground is green. *Environmental Politics* 1: 1–18.

—— 1992b: *Motivating Political Morality*. Oxford: Blackwell.

Goodin, Robert E. and Dryzek, John 1980: Rational participation: the politics of relative power. *British Journal of Political Science* 10: 273–92.

Goodman, Nelson 1968: *Languages of Art*. Indianapolis, Ind.: Bobbs-Merrill.

—— 1983: Art and authenticity. In Dennis Dutton (ed.) *The Forger's Art*, Berkeley: University of California Press, 93–114.

Gordon, H. Scott 1954: The economic theory of a common-property resource: the fishery. *Journal of Political Economy* 62: 124–42.

Gorz, André 1987: *Ecology as Politics*, trans. P. Vigderman and J. Cloud. London: Pluto Press.

Green Committees of Correspondence (Green CoC) (US) 1986: *Ten Key Values*. Kansas City, Mo.: CoC. Reprinted in Spretnak and Capra 1986.

Greenberg, Edward S. 1986: *Workplace Democracy*. Ithaca, NY: Cornell University Press.

Griffin, James 1986: *Well-being*. Oxford: Clarendon Press.

Griffiths, T.R 1991: History and natural history: conservation movements in conflict? In D. J. Mulvaney (ed.), *The Humanities and the Australian Environment*. Canberra: Australian Academy of the Humanities, 87–110.

Grubb, Michael 1990: What to do about global warming. *International Affairs* 66: 67–90.

Habermas, Jürgen 1976: *Legitimation crisis*, trans. Thomas McCarthy. London: Heinemann.

—— 1981: New social movements. *Telos*, no. 49: 33–7.

Haefele, Edwin T 1973: *Representative Government and Environmental Management*. Baltimore, Md: Johns Hopkins University Press (for Resources for the Future).

Hands, Gordon 1971: Roberto Michels and the study of political parties. *British Journal of Political Science* 1: 155–72.

Hardin, Garrett 1968: The tragedy of the commons. *Science* 162: 1243–8.

Hardin, Russell 1982: *Collective Action*. Baltimore, Md: Johns Hopkins University Press (for Resources for the Future).

Hayek, Friedrich A 1960: *The Constitution of Liberty*. London: Routledge and Kegan Paul.

—— 1973–9: *Law, Legislation and Liberty*. Chicago: University of Chicago Press.

Hays, Samuel P. 1987: *Beauty, Health and Permanence: Environmental Politics in the United States, 1955–1985*. Cambridge: Cambridge University Press.

Hayward, Tim 1990: Ecosocialism – utopian and scientific. *Radical Philosophy* 56: 2–14.

Herring, Ronald J. 1990: Resurrecting the commons: collective action and ecology. *Items* 44. 4: 64–8.

Hill, Thomas Jr 1983: Ideals of human excellence and preserving the natural environment. *Environmental Ethics* 5: 211–24.

Hilton, Tim 1991: Game show for androids. *Guardian Weekly*, 29 September, p. 23.

Hinckley, Barbara 1971: *The Seniority System in Congress*. Bloomington: Indiana University Press.

Hirsch, Fred 1976: *Social Limits to Growth*. London: Routledge and Kegan Paul.

Honderich, Ted 1980: *Violence for Equality*. Harmondsworth, Mddx: Penguin.

Honoré, A. M. 1961: Ownership. In A. G. Guest (ed.), *Oxford Essays in Jurisprudence*, Oxford: Clarendon Press, 107–47.

Horkheimer, Max and Adorno, Theodor W. 1972: *Dialectic of Enlightenment*. New York: Seabury.

Hornsby, Jennifer 1980: *Actions*. London: Routledge and Kegan Paul.

Hotelling, Harold 1931: The economics of exhaustible resources. *Journal of Political Economy* 39: 137–75.

Hülsberg, Werner 1985: The greens at the cross-roads. *New Left Review* 152: 5–29.

—— 1988: *The German Greens*. London: Verso.

Inglehart, Ronald 1977: *The Silent Revolution*. Princeton, NJ: Princeton University Press.

Irvine, Sandy and Ponton, Alec 1988: *A Green Manifesto*. London: Optima.

Jamieson, Dale 1984: The city around us. In Tom Regan (ed.), *Earthbound*, Philadelphia, Pa.: Temple University Press, 38–73.

Jarrett, Henry (ed.) 1966: *Environmental Quality in a Growing Economy*. Baltimore, Md: Johns Hopkins University Press (for Resources for the Future).

Jevons, W. Stanley 1906: *The Coal Question: An Inquiry Concerning the Progress of the Nation and the Probable Exhaustion of our Coal-mines*, 3rd edn, ed. A. W. Flux. London: Macmillan.

Jones, R. M. 1991: Landscapes of the mind: aboriginal perceptions of the environment. In D.J. Mulvaney (ed.), *The Humanities and the Australian Environment*. Canberra: Australian Academy of the Humanities, 21–48.

Kant, Immanuel 1785: *Foundations of the Metaphysics of Morals*. Trans. L. W. Beck. Chicago: University of Chicago Press, 1949.

Kaplan, Rachel and Kaplan, Stephen 1989: *The Experience of Nature: A Psychological Perspective*. Cambridge: Cambridge University Press.

Kelly, Petra 1987: The green movement. In Tim Woodhouse (ed.), *People and Planet: Alternative Nobel Prize Speeches*. Hartland, Devon: Green Books, 22–32.

—— 1988: Towards a green Europe and a green world. In Felix Dodds (ed.), *Into the 21st Century: An Agenda for Political Realignment*, Basingstoke, Hants: Green Print, 107–18.

—— 1989: German Greens in crisis: the trials of Petra Kelly (interview). *Living Marxism* 4 (Feb.): 24–9.

Kemball-Cook, David; Baker, Mallen and Mattingly, Chris (eds) 1991: *The Green Budget*. London: Green Print.

Kemp, Penny and Wall, Derek 1990: *A Green Manifesto for the 1990s*. Harmondsworth: Penguin.

Kennan, George F. 1970: To prevent a world wasteland. *Foreign Affairs* 48: 401–13.

Kiewiet, D. Roderick 1983: *Macroeconomics and Micropolitics*. Chicago: University of Chicago Press.

Kirchheimer, Otto 1966: The transformation of the Western European party system. In Joseph LaPalombara and Myron Wiener (eds), *Political Parties and Political Development*. Princeton, NJ: Princeton University Press, 177–200.

Kneese, Allen V. and Schultze, Charles L. 1975: *Pollution, Prices and Public Policy*. Washington, DC: Brookings Institution.

Kneese, Allen V., Ayres, Robert U. and D'Arge, Ralph C. 1970: *Economics and the Environment*. Baltimore, Md: Johns Hopkins Press.

Knight, Frank H. 1922: Ethics and the economic interpretation. *Quarterly Journal of Economics* 36: 454–81.

—— 1935a: *The Ethics of Competition*. New York: Harper and Row.

—— 1935b: Value and price. In E. R. A. Seligman (ed.), *Encyclopedia of the Social Sciences*, vol. 15, New York: Macmillan, 218–25.

Kolinsky, Eva 1984: The greens in Germany: prospects of a small party. *Parliamentary Affairs* 37: 434–47.

Kriger, Martin H. 1973: What's wrong with plastic trees? *Science* 179: 446–55.

Krutilla, John V. 1967: Conservation reconsidered. *American Economic Review* 57: 777–86.

Kurz, Otto 1967: *Fakes*, 2nd edn. New York: Dover.

Lancaster, Kelvin J. 1967: A new approach to consumer theory. *Journal of Political Economy* 75: 132–57.

—— 1971: *Consumer Demand*. New York: Columbia University Press.

Laslett, Peter 1956: The face to face society. In Peter Laslett (ed.), *Philosophy, Politics and Society*, first series, Oxford: Blackwell, 157–84.

Lave, Lester B. 1981: *The Strategy of Social Regulation*. Washington, DC: Brookings Institution.

Lee, Keekok 1989: *Social Philosophy and Ecological Scarcity*. London: Routledge.

Leiss, William 1972: *The Domination of Nature*. New York: G. Braziller.

Leopold, Aldo 1949: *A Sand County Almanac*. Oxford: Oxford University Press.

Lewis, David 1969: *Convention*. Oxford: Blackwell.

Lindblom, C. E. 1977: *Politics and Markets*. New York: Basic Books.

Lipsey, Richard G. and Lancaster, Kelvin 1956: The general theory of second best. *Review of Economic Studies* 24: 11–33.

Little, I. M. D. and Mirrlees, J. A. 1974: *Project Appraisal and Planning for Developing Countries*. London: Heinemann.

Lovelock, J. E. 1987: *Gaia: A New Look at Life on Earth*. Oxford: Oxford University Press.

—— 1989: *The Ages of Gaia: A Biography of our Living Earth*. Oxford: Oxford University Press.

Lovins, Amory B. 1976: Energy strategy: the road not taken? *Foreign Affairs* 55: 119–32.

—— 1977: *Soft Energy Paths: Toward a Durable Peace*. Harmondsworth, Mddx: Penguin.

Lovins, Amory B. and Lovins, Hunter 1987: Building real security. In Tom Woodhouse (ed.), *People and Planet*, Bideford, Devon: Green Books, 10–21.

Lowe, Philip D. and Rüdig, Wolfgang 1986: Review article: political ecology and the social sciences. *British Journal of Political Science* 16: 513–50.

Luce, R. Duncan and Raiffa, Howard 1957: *Games and Decisions*. New York: Wiley.

Luke, Tim 1988: The dreams of deep ecology. *Telos*, no. 76: 65–92.

MacCallum, Gerald 1967: Negative and positive freedom. *Philosophical Review* 76: 312–45.

McCormick, John 1989: *Reclaiming Paradise: The Global Environmental Movement*. Bloomington, Ind.: Indiana University Press.

McKibben, Bill 1988: Is the world getting hotter? *New York Review of Books* 35. 19: 7–11.

—— 1989: *The End of Nature*. New York: Random House.

MacLean, Douglas and Brown, Peter G. (eds) 1983: *Energy and the Future*. Totowa, N.J.: Rowman and Littlefield.

Macpherson, C. B. 1977a: Human rights as property rights. *Dissent* 24: 72–7.

—— 1977b: *The Life and Times of Liberal Democracy*. Oxford: Oxford University Press.

Madison, James 1787: The Federalist, no. 10. In Jacob E. Cooke (ed.), *The Federalist*. Middletown, Conn.: Wesleyan University Press, 1961, 56–65.

Malthus, T. H. 1798: *Essay on the Principles of Population*, 6th edn. London: J. Murray, 1826.

Manes, Christopher 1990: *Green Rage*. Boston: Little, Brown.

Manion, M.M. 1991: The humanities and the Australian environment. In D. J. Mulvaney (ed.), *The Humanities and the Australian Environment*, Canberra: Australian Academy of the Humanities, 49–60.

Mannison, Don, McRobbie, Michael and Routley, Richard (eds) 1980: *Environmental Philosophy*. Monograph series 2. Canberra: Department of Philosophy, RSSS, Australian National University.

Mansbridge, Jane J. 1980. *Beyond Adversary Democracy*. New York: Basic Books.

Marglin, Stephen A. 1962: Economic factors affecting system design. In Arthur Maass et al., *Design of Water Resource Systems*, Cambridge, Mass.: Harvard University Press, 159–225.

—— 1963: The social rate of discount and the optimal rate of investment. *Quarterly Journal of Economics* 77: 95–111.

—— 1967: *Public Investment Criteria*. London: Allen and Unwin.

Marris, Robin 1964: *The Economic Theory of Managerial Capitalism*. London: Macmillan.

Marris, Robin and Mueller, Dennis C. 1980: The corporation, competition and the invisible hand. *Journal of Economic Literature* 18: 32–63.

Martin, John N. 1979: The concept of the irreplaceable. *Environmental Ethics* 1: 3–48.

Maslow, Abraham H. 1954: *Motivation and Personality*. New York: Harper.

Mathews, Jessica Tuchman 1989: Redefining security. *Foreign Affairs* 68: 162–77.

Matthews, Donald R. 1959: The folkways of the United States Senate. *American Political Science Review* 53: 1064–89.

Meade, James E. 1952: External economies and diseconomies in a competitive situation. *Economic Journal* 62:54–67.

Meadows, Donella H. 1991: Four not-so-easy things you can do to save the planet. *Utne Reader* 44 (March/April): 113.

Meadows, Donella H., Meadows, Dennis L. Randers, Jørgen and Behrens, William W. III 1972: *The Limits to Growth*. London: Earth Island.

Merchant, Carolyn 1989: *Ecological Revolutions: Nature, Gender and Science in New England*. Chapel Hill: University of North Carolina Press.

Michels, Roberto 1915: *Political Parties*. Glencoe, Ill.: Free Press, 1949.

Mill, John Stuart 1874: Nature. In J. M. Robson (ed.), *Collected Works of John Stuart Mill*, vol. 10, Toronto: University of Toronto Press, 1969, 373–402.

Mishan, E. J. 1967: *The Costs of Economic Growth*. Harmondsworth: Penguin, 1969.

Montreal Protocol 1987: Protocol on Substances that Deplete the Ozone Layer. *International Legal Materials* 26: 1550–61.

Morgenstern, Oskar 1963: *On the Accuracy of Economic Observations*, 2nd edn. Princeton, NJ: Princeton University Press.

Mukerji, Chandra 1990: Reading and writing with nature: social claims and the French formal garden. *Theory and Society* 19: 651–79.

Mulvaney, D. J. 1991: Visions of environment: an afterview. In D. J. Mulvaney (ed.), *The Humanities and the Australian Environment*, Canberra: Australian Academy of the Humanities, 111–22.

Myers, Norman 1989: Environment and security. *Foreign Policy* 74: 23–41.

Naess, Arne 1973: The shallow and the deep, long-range ecology movements. *Inquiry* 16: 95–100.

—— 1984: A defense of the deep ecology movement. *Environmental Ethics* 6: 265–70.

—— 1989: *Ecology, Community and Lifestyle*, trans. and ed. David Rothenberg. Cambridge: Cambridge University Press.

Nash, Roderick Frazier 1970: The American invention of national parks. *American Quarterly* 22: 726–35.

—— 1973: *Wilderness and the American Mind*, rev. edn. New Haven, Conn.: Yale University Press.

—— 1989: *The Rights of Nature: A History of Environmental Ethics*. Madison: University of Wisconsin Press.

New Hampshire and Vermont Greens n.d.: *Toward a New Politics: A Green Statement of Principles*. White River Junction, Vt: New Hampshire and Vermont Greens.

Nilsen, Richard (ed.) 1990: Environmental restoration: a special issue. *Whole Earth Review* 66: 2–160.

Nordhaus, William 1982: How fast should we graze the global commons? *American Economic Review (Papers and Proceedings)* 72: 242–6.

Norton, Bryan G. (ed.) 1986: *The Preservation of Species*. Princeton, NJ: Princeton University Press.

—— 1987: *Why Preserve Natural Variety?* Princeton, NJ: Princeton University Press.

Nozick, Robert 1974: *Anarchy, State and Utopia*. Oxford: Blackwell.

—— 1981: *Philosophical Explanations*. Cambridge, Mass.: Harvard University Press.

Offe, Claus 1983: 'Reaching for the brake': the Greens in Germany. *New Political Science*, no. 11: 45–52. Reprinted from *Die Zeit*, 20 August 1982; trans. B. Helfferich.

—— 1985: New social movements: challenging the boundaries of institutional politics. *Social Research* 52: 817–68.

—— 1990: Reflections on the institutional self-transformation of movement politics. In R. J. Dalton and M. Kuechler (eds.), *Challenging the Political Order*, Cambridge: Polity Press.

Olson, Mancur Jr 1965: *The Logic of Collective Action*. Cambridge, Mass.: Harvard University Press.

—— (ed.) 1973: Symposium: the no-growth society. *Daedalus*, 102, 4.

O'Neill, Onora 1986: *Faces of Hunger*. London: Allen and Unwin.

Ophuls, William 1977: *Ecology and the Politics of Scarcity: Prologue to a Political Theory of the Steady State*. San Francisco, Calif.: W. H. Freeman

O'Riordan, Timothy 1976: *Environmentalism*. London: Pion Press.

—— 1991: Stability and transformation in environmental government. *Political Quarterly* 62: 167–85.

Ostrom, Elinor 1991: *Governing the Commons*. Cambridge: Cambridge University Press.

Ostrom, Vincent, Tiebout, Charles M. and Warren, Robert 1961: The organization of government in metropolitan areas. *American Political Science Review* 55: 831–42.

Packard, Vance 1960: *The Waste Makers*. New York: David McKay.

Paehlke, Robert C. 1989: *Environmentalism and the Future of Progressive Politics*. New Haven, Conn.: Yale University Press.

Page, Talbot 1977: *Conservation and Economic Efficiency*. Baltimore, Md: Johns Hopkins University Press (for Resources for the Future).

Paley, William S., chair 1952: *Resources for Freedom*. Report of the President's Materials Policy Commission. Washington, DC: Government Printing Office.

Papadakis, Elim 1988: Social movements, self-limiting radicalism and the Green Party in West Germany. *Sociology* 22: 433–54.

—— 1989: Green issues and other parties: *Themenklau* or new flexibility? In Eva Kolinsky (ed.), *The Greens in West Germany*, Oxford: Berg, 61–85.

Parfit, Derek 1983: Energy policy and the further future: the social discount rate. In Douglas MacLean and Peter G. Brown (eds.), *Energy and the Future*, Totowa, NJ: Rowman and Littlefield, 31–8. Reprinted in Parfit 1984.

—— 1984: *Reasons and Persons*. Oxford: Clarendon Press.

Parkin, Sara 1988: Green strategy. In Felix Dodds (ed.), *Into the 21st Century: An Agenda for Political Realignment*, Basingstoke, Hants: Green Print, 163–80.

Partridge, Ernest (ed.) 1981: *Responsibilities to Future Generations*. Buffalo, NY: Prometheus.

Passmore, John 1975: Attitudes to nature. In R. S. Peters (ed.), *Nature and Conduct*. Royal Institute of Philosophy Lectures, vol. 8, London: Macmillan, 251–64. Reprinted in Passmore 1980.

—— 1980: *Man's Responsibility for Nature*, 2nd edn. London: Duckworth.

Pateman, Carole 1970: *Participation and Democratic Theory*. Cambridge: Cambridge University Press.

—— 1971: Political culture, political structure and political change. *British Journal of Political Science* 1: 291–305.

—— 1974: To them that hath, shall be given. *Politics* 9: 139–45.

Patten, B.C. and Odum, E.P. 1981: The cybernetic nature of ecosystems. *American Naturalist* 118: 886–95.

Paul, Joel E. 1991: Comity in international law. *Harvard International Law Journal* 32: 1–80.

Pearce, David 1973: Is ecology elitist? *The Ecologist* 3 (Feb.): 61–3.

—— (ed.) 1991: *Blueprint 2: Greening the World Economy*. London: Earthscan.

Pearce, David, Markandya, Anil and Barbier, Edward B. 1989: *Blueprint for a Green Economy*. A report for the UK Department of the Environment. London: Earthscan.

Pigou, A. C. 1932: *The Economics of Welfare*, 4th edn. London: Macmillan.

Plamenatz, John 1973: *Democracy and Illusion*. London: Longman.

Plumwood, Val 1986: Ecofeminism: an overview and discussion of positions and arguments. *Australasian Journal of Philosophy* 64 (supplement): 120–38.

Poguntke, Thomas 1987: The organization of a participatory party – the German Greens. *European Journal of Political Research* 15: 609–33.

Porritt, Jonathon 1984: *Seeing Green*. Oxford: Blackwell.

—— (ed.) 1987: *Friends of the Earth Handbook*. London: Optima Books.

—— 1988: Re-aligning the vision In Felix Dodds (ed.), *Into the 21st Century: An Agenda for Political Realignment*, Basingstoke, Hants: Green Print, 195–203.

Porritt, Jonathon and Winner, David 1988: *The Coming of the Greens*. London: Fontana.

Quine, Willard van Orman 1961: *From a Logical Point of View*, 2nd edn. Cambridge, Mass.: Harvard University Press.

Radford, Colin 1978: Fakes. *Mind* 87: 66–76.

Ramsey, F. P. 1928: A mathematical theory of savings. *Economic Journal* 38: 543–59.

Rawls, John 1971: *A Theory of Justice*. Cambridge, Mass.: Harvard University Press.

—— 1982: Social unity and primary goods. In Amartya Sen and Bernard Williams (eds.), *Utilitarianism and Beyond*, Cambridge: Cambridge University Press, 159–86.

Redclift, Michael 1987: *Sustainable Development: Exploring the Contradictions*. London: Methuen.

Reeve, Andrew 1986: *Property*. London: Macmillan.

Regan, Donald H. 1980: *Utilitarianism and Co-operation*. Oxford: Clarendon Press.

—— 1986: Duties of preservation. In Bryan G. Norton (ed.), *The Preservation of Species*, Princeton, NJ: Princeton University Press, 195–220.

Reich, Charles A. 1970: *The Greening of America*. New York: Random House.

Reisner, Marc 1986: *Cadillac Desert: The American West and its Disappearing Water*. New York: Viking Penguin.

Rieselbach, Leroy N. 1986: *Congressional Reform*. Washington, DC: Congressional Quarterly Press.

Robbins, Lionel 1932: *An Essay on the Nature and Significance of Economic Science*. London: Macmillan.

Roberts, Adam, (ed.) 1967: *The Strategy of Civilian Defence: Non-violent Resistance to Aggression*. London: Faber.

Rodgers, William H. Jr 1982: Bringing people back in: toward a comprehensive theory of taking in natural resources law. *Ecology Law Quarterly* 10: 205–52.

Rohrschneider, R. 1988: Citizens' attitudes toward environmental issues: selfish or selfless? *Comparative Political Studies* 21: 347–67.

Rolston, Holmes, III 1981. Values in nature. *Environmental Ethics* 3:113–28.

—— 1985: Valuing wildlands. *Environmental Ethics* 7: 23–48.

—— 1988: *Environmental Ethics*. Philadelphia, Pa.: Temple University Press.

Rose, Richard (ed.) 1989: Whatever happened to social indicators? a symposium. *Journal of Public Policy* 9:399–450.

Ross, W: D. 1930: *The Right and the Good*. Oxford: Clarendon Press.

Roszak, Theodore 1972: *Where the Wasteland Ends*. Garden City, NY: Doubleday.

—— 1978: *Person/Planet*. Garden City, NY: Doubleday.

Rousseau, Jean-Jacques 1750: A discourse on the arts and sciences. In

The Social Contract and Discourses, trans. G. D. H. Cole, London: Everyman/Dent, 1973, 1–26.

—— 1755: A discourse on the origin of inequality. In *The Social Contract and Discourses*, trans. G. D. H. Cole, London: Everyman/ Dent, 1973, 27–114.

—— 1762: The social contract In *The Social Contract and Discourses*, trans. G. D. H. Cole, London: Everyman/Dent, 1973, 164–278.

Routley, Richard 1984: On the alleged inconsistency, moral insensitivity and fanaticism of pacifism. *Inquiry* 27: 117–28.

Routley, Richard and Routley, Val 1978. Nuclear energy and obligations to the future. *Inquiry* 21: 133–79.

—— 1979. Against the inevitability of human chauvinism. In K. E. Goodpaster and K. M. Sayre (eds.), *Ethics and Problems of the 21st Century*, Notre Dame, Ind.: University of Notre Dame Press, 36–59.

—— 1980: Human chauvinism and environmental ethics. In Don Mannison, Michael McRobbie and Richard Routley (eds), *Environmental Philosophy*, Canberra: Department of Philosophy, RSSS, Australian National University, 96–189.

Sagoff, Mark 1974: On preserving the natural environment. *Yale Law Journal* 84: 205–67.

—— 1976: The aesthetic status of forgeries. *Journal of Aesthetics and Art Criticism* 35: 169–80. Reprinted in Dutton 1983

—— 1978: On restoring and reproducing art. *Journal of Philosophy* 75: 453–70.

—— 1988: *The Economy of the Earth*. Cambridge: Cambridge University Press.

Sale, Kirkpatrick 1980: *Human Scale*. New York: Coward, Cann and Geoghegan.

—— 1984: Bioregionalism – a new way to treat the land. *The Ecologist* 14: 167–73.

—— 1985: *Dwellers in the Land: The Bioregional Vision*. San Francisco: Sierra Club Books.

—— 1990: The environmental crisis is not our fault. *Utne Reader* 40 (July/Aug.): 53–4.

Salleh, Ariel 1991: Eco-socialism/eco-feminism. *Capitalism, Nature, Socialism* 2: 129–34

Saward, Michael 1991: Green democracy. Paper presented to the Workshop on Green Political Theory, ECPR Joint Sessions, Colchester UK, March.

Scarrow, Howard A. 1972: The impact of British domestic air pollution legislation. *British Journal of Political Science* 2: 261–82.

Schell, Jonathan 1982: *The Fate of the Earth*. New York: Knopf.

Schelling, Thomas C. 1971: On the ecology of micromotives. *Public Interest* 25: 61–98.

Scherer, Donald and Attig, Thomas (eds) 1983: *Ethics and the Environment*. Englewood Cliffs, NJ: Prentice-Hall.

Schmidt, Alfred 1971: *The Concept of Nature in Marx*, trans. Ben Fowkes. London: New Left Books.

Schneider, Stephan H. 1989: The greenhouse effect: science and policy. *Science* 243: 771–81.

Schumacher, E. F. 1973: *Small is Beautiful: Economics as if People Mattered*. London: Blond and Briggs.

Schumpeter, Joseph A. 1950: *Capitalism, Socialism and Democracy*, 3rd edn. New York: Harper and Row.

Scitovsky, Tibor 1954: Two concepts of external economies. *Journal of Political Economy* 62: 143–51.

Sen, Amartya 1957: A note on Tinbergen on the optimum rate of saving. *Economic Journal* 67: 745–48.

—— 1961: On optimising the rate of savings. *Economic Journal* 71: 479–96.

—— 1966: Labour allocation in a cooperative enterprise. *Review of Economic Studies* 33: 361–71.

—— 1967: Isolation, assurance and the social rate of discount. *Quarterly Journal of Economics* 81: 112–24.

—— 1977: Rational fools. *Philosophy and Public Affairs* 6: 317–44.

—— 1980–1: Plural utility. *Proceedings of the Aristotelian Society* 81: 183–215.

—— 1985: *Commodities and Capabilities*. Amsterdam: North-Holland.

Sharp, Gene 1973: *The Politics of Nonviolent Action*. Boston: P. Sargent.

—— 1990: *Civilian-based Defense: A Post-military Weapons System*. Princeton, NJ: Princeton University Press.

Shoard, Marion 1987: *This Land is our Land: The Struggle for Britain's Countryside*. London: Paladin.

Sikora, R. I. and Barry, Brian (eds) 1978: *Obligations to Future Generations*. Philadelphia, Pa.: Temple University Press.

Simon, Julian L. 1981: Global confusion, 1980: a hard look at the Global 2000 report. *Public Interest* 62: 3–20.

Simon, Julian L. and Kahn, Herman (eds) 1984: *The Resourceful Earth: A Response to Global 2000*. Oxford: Blackwell.

Singer, Peter 1976: *Animal Liberation*. New York: Jonathan Cape.

—— 1979: *Practical Ethics*. Cambridge: Cambridge University Press.

Skolimonski, Henryk 1981: *Eco-philosophy*. Boston: Marion Boyars.

Smith, Joel B. and Tirpak, Dennis A. (eds) 1989: *The Potential Effects of Global Climate Change on the United States: A Draft Report to Congress*. United States Environmental Protection Agency. Washington, DC: Government Printing Office.

Snare, Frank 1972: The concept of property. *American Philosophical Quarterly* 9: 200–6.

Snidal, Duncan 1985: Coordination versus Prisoners' Dilemma: implications for international cooperation and regimes. *American Political Science Review* 79: 923–42.

Sober, Elliott 1986: Philosophical problems for environmentalism. In Bryan G. Norton (ed.), *The Preservation of Species*, Princeton, NJ: Princeton University Press, 173–94.

Sohn, Louis B. 1973: The Stockholm Declaration on the Human Environment. *Harvard International Law Journal* 14: 423–515.

Sorauf, Frank J. 1968: Party Politics in America. Boston: Little, Brown.

Spretnak, Charlene 1986: *The Spiritual Dimension of Green Politics*. Santa Fe, NM: Bear.

Spretnak, Charlene and Capra, Fritjof 1986: *Green Politics: The Global Promise*. Santa Fe, NM: Bear.

Stewart, Alexander P. and Jenkins, Edward 1867: *The Medical and Legal Aspects of Sanitary Reform*, 2 edn., ed. M. W. Flinn. New York: Humanities Press, 1969.

Stockholm Declaration 1972: Declaration on the human environment of the United Nations Conference on the Human Environment. *International Legal Materials* 11: 1416–21.

Stokey, Edith and Zeckhauser, Richard 1978: *A Primer for Policy Analysis*. New York: Norton.

Stone, Christopher D. 1972: Should trees have standing? Toward legal rights for natural objects. *Southern California Law Review* 45: 450–501. Reprinted in Stone 1988.

—— 1985: 'Should trees have standing?' revisited: how far will law and morals reach? A pluralist perspective. *Southern California Law Review* 59: 1–154.

—— 1987: *Earth and Other Ethics*. New York: Harper and Row.

—— 1988: *Should Trees Have Standing? Toward Legal Rights for Natural Objects*, 2nd edn. Palo Alto, Calif.: Tioga Publishing.

Stretton, Hugh 1976: *Capitalism, Socialism and the Environment* Cambridge: Cambridge University Press.

Sylvan, Richard 1985: A critique of deep ecology. *Radical Philosophy* 40: 2–12 and 41: 10–22.

Taylor, Charles 1985: *Human Agency and Language*. Cambridge: Cambridge University Press.

—— 1976: Responsibility for Self. In A. O. Rorty (ed.), *The Identities of Persons*, Berkeley: University of California Press, 281–300.

Taylor, Michael 1976: *Anarchy and Cooperation*. London: Wiley.

—— 1987: *The Possibility of Cooperation*. Cambridge: Cambridge University Press.

Taylor, Michael and Ward, Hugh 1982: Chickens, whales and lumpy public goods: alternative models of public-goods provision. *Political Studies* 30: 350–70.

Taylor, Serge 1984: *Making Bureaucracies Think: The Environmental Impact Statement Strategy of Administrative Reform*. Stanford, Calif.: Stanford University Press.

Thomas, Keith 1984: *Man and the Natural World: Changing Attitudes in England, 1500–1800*. Harmondsworth, Mddx: Penguin.

Tobey, James A. 1990: The effects of domestic environmental policies on patterns of world trade: an empirical test. *Kyklos* 43: 191–210.

Tokar, Brian 1987: *The Green Alternative*. San Pedro, Calif.: R. and E. Miles.

Tribe, Lawrence H. 1973: Technology assessment and the fourth discontinuity: the limits of instrumental rationality. *Southern California Law Review* 46: 617–60.

—— 1974: Ways not to think about plastic trees: new foundations for environmental law. *Yale Law Journal* 83: 1315–48.

—— 1975: From environmental foundations to constitutional law: learning from nature's future. *Yale Law Journal* 85: 545–56.

Tyler, Tom R. 1990: *Why People Obey the Law*. New Haven, Conn.: Yale University Press.

United Nations. Conference on the Human Environment 1972: Declaration on the human environment (Stockholm Declaration). *International Legal Materials* 11: 1416–21.

United States. Council on Environmental Quality (US CEQ) 1980: *The Global 2000 Report to the President: Entering the Twenty-first Century*. Washington, DC: CEQ.

—— 1981: *Global Future: Time to Act*. Washington, DC: CEQ.

United States. Department of Health, Education and Welfare (US DHEW) 1969: *Toward a Social Report*. Washington, DC: Government Printing Office.

United States. National Research Council (US NRC) 1989: *Ozone Depletion, Greenhouse Gases, and Climate Change*. Proceedings of a Joint Symposium. Washington, DC: National Academy Press.

Urmson, J. O. 1958: Saints and heroes. In A. I. Melden (ed.), *Essays in Moral Philosophy*, Seattle: University of Washington Press, 198–216.

Uslaner, Eric M. 1990: What sustains Congressional norms? Paper presented to the Annual Meetings of the American Political Science Association, San Francisco, Calif., 30 August.

van der Veen, Robert and Van Parijs, Philippe 1987: A capitalist road to communism. *Theory and Society* 15: 635–55.

Vanek, Jaroslav (ed.) 1975: *Self-management: Economic Liberation of Man*. Harmondsworth, Mddx: Penguin.

Van Parijs, Philippe 1990: The second marriage of justice and efficiency. *Journal of Social Policy* 19: 1–25.

—— 1991a: Why surfers should be fed: the liberal case for an unconditional basic income. *Philosophy and Public Affairs* 20: 101–31.

—— 1991b: *Arguing for Basic Income*. London: Verso.

Verba, Sidney, Nie, Norman H. and Kim, Jae-on 1978: *Participation and Political Equality*. Cambridge: Cambridge University Press.

Vianello, Fernando 1987: Labour theory of value. In John Eatwell, Murray Milgate, Peter K. Newman and R. H. I. Palgrave (eds), *The New Palgrave*, vol. 3, London: Macmillan, 107–13.

Vienna Convention 1985: Convention for the Protection of the Ozone Layer. *International Legal Materials* 26 (1987): 1529–40.

Wainwright, Hilary 1988: Reclaiming the politics of emancipation. In Felix Dodds (ed.), *Into the 21st Century: An Agenda for Political Realignment*, Basingstoke, Hants: Green Print, 93–106.

Walzer, Michael 1980: *Radical Principles*. New York: Basic Books.

Ward, Barbara 1966: *Spaceship Earth*. New York: Columbia University Press.

—— 1979: *Progress for a Small Planet*. London: Maurice Temple Smith.

Ward, Barbara and Dubois, René 1972: *Only One Earth*. Harmondsworth, Mddx: Penguin.

Ward, Hugh 1987: The risks of a reputation for toughness: strategy in public goods provision problems modelled by Chicken supergames. *British Journal of Political Science* 17: 23–52.

Ward, Hugh and Edwards, Geoffrey 1990: Chicken and technology: the politics of the EC's budget for research and development. *Review of International Studies* 16: 111–30.

Weimer, David L. 1990: An earmarked fossil fuels tax to save the rain forests. *Journal of Policy Analysis and Management* 9: 254–9.

Weinstein, M. C. and Stason, W. B. 1977: Foundations of cost-effectiveness for health and medical practices. *New England Journal of Medicine* 296: 716–21.

Weiss, Janet A. and Gruber, Judith 1984: Using knowledge for control in fragmented policy arenas. *Journal of Policy Analysis and Management* 3: 225–47.

Weulersse, G. 1935: Economics: History of economic thought: the physiocrats. In E. R. A. Seligman (ed.), *Encyclopedia of the Social Sciences*, vol. 5, New York: Macmillan, 348–51.

White, Alan R. (ed.) 1968: *The Philosophy of Action*. London: Oxford University Press.

Wildavsky, Aaron 1988: *Searching for Safety*. New Brunswick, NJ: Transaction.

Williams, Bernard 1973: A critique of utilitarianism. In J. J. C. Smart and Bernard Williams, *Utilitarianism, For and Against*, Cambridge: Cambridge University Press, 75–150.

—— 1981: *Moral Luck*. Cambridge: Cambridge University Press.

Williams, Mary B. 1978: Discounting versus maximum sustainable yield. In R. I. Sikora and Brian Barry (eds), *Obligations to Future Generations*, Philadelphia, Pa.: Temple University Press, 169–79.

Wilson, Carroll L., chair 1970: *Man's Impact on the Global Environment: Assessment and Recommendations for Action*. Report of the Study of Critical Environmental Problems Group, Massachusetts Institute of Technology. Cambridge, Mass.: MIT Press.

—— 1971: *Inadvertent Climate Modification*. Report of conference on Man's Impact on Climate, hosted by Royal Swedish Academy of Sciences and Royal Swedish Academy of Engineering Sciences. Cambridge, Mass.: MIT Press.

Winner, Langdon 1978: *Autonomous Technology*. Cambridge, Mass.: MIT Press.

—— 1986: *The Whale and the Reactor*. Chicago: University of Chicago Press.

Wirth, David A. 1989: Climate chaos. *Foreign Policy* 74: 3–22.

Wolff, Robert Paul 1970: *In Defense of Anarchism*. New York: Harper and Row.

Wollheim, Richard 1984: *The Thread of Life*. Cambridge: Cambridge University Press.

Woodcock, George 1974: Anarchism and ecology. *The Ecologist* 4: 84–8.

World Bank 1984: *Toward Sustained Development in Sub-Saharan Africa*. Washington, DC: World Bank.

World Commission on Environment and Development (WCED), Gro Harlem Brundtland, chair 1987: *Our Common Future*. Oxford: Oxford University Press.

Xenos, Nicholas 1989: *Scarcity and Modernity*. London: Routledge.

Young, Oran R. 1989: *International Cooperation: Building Regimes for Natural Resources and the Environment*. Ithaca, NY: Cornell University Press.

Zeckhauser, Richard 1975: Procedures for valuing lives. *Public Policy* 23: 419–64.

Zile, Zigurds L. 1982: Glimpses of the scientific revolution in Soviet environmental law. In Peter B. Maggs, Gordon B. Smith and George Ginsburg (eds), *Law and Economic Development in the Soviet Union*, Boulder, Colo.: Westview Press, 187–216.

Name Index

Subject Index

Indexes compiled by Ann Barham